Philosophy as Higher Enlightenment

American University Studies

Series V
Philosophy
Vol. 160

PETER LANG
New York • Washington, D.C./Baltimore • San Francisco
Bern • Frankfurt am Main • Berlin • Vienna • Paris

Ash Gobár

Philosophy as Higher Enlightenment

Paradigms toward a New Worldview from
the Perspective of Dialectical Realism

PETER LANG
New York • Washington, D.C. • Baltimore • San Francisco
Bern • Frankfurt am Main • Berlin • Vienna • Paris

Library of Congress Cataloging-in-Publication Data

Gobár, Ash.
 Philosophy as higher enlightenment: paradigms toward a new worldview
from the perspective of dialectical realism / Ash Gobár.
  p. cm. — (American university studies. Series V, Philosophy;
vol. 160)
 Includes bibliographical references and index.
 1. Philosophy. 2. Realism. 3. Dialectic. I. Title. II. Title: Higher
enlightenment. III. Title: Worldview from the perspective of a dialectical
realism. IV. Series.
B945.G683P48   1994   149'.2—dc20   93-34536
ISBN 0-8204-2392-0   CIP
ISSN 0739-6392

Die Deutsche Bibliothek-CIP-Einheitsaufnahme

Gobár, Ash:
Philosophy as higher enlightenment: paradigms toward a new worldview from
the perspective of dialectical realism / Ash Gobár. - New York;
San Francisco; Bern; Baltimore; Frankfurt am Main; Berlin; Wien; Paris:
Lang, 1994
 (American university studies: Ser. 5, Philosophy; Vol. 160)
 ISBN 0-8204-2392-0
NE: American university studies / 05

Motto

*A philosophical thinker is one who has a
certain store of articulate paradigms
and argument patterns which he has acquired
in trying to answer philosophical questions.*

— *Gustav Bergmann*

ACKNOWLEDGMENT

In my philosophical journey I have walked with Plato and Aristotle and Kant — and have dwelled with William James, Franz Brentano, Nicolai Hartmann, Ludwig Wittgenstein, and Martin Heidegger — and survived as a thinker.

I have benefited from personal and/or literary association with these contemporary philosophers especially: Robert Audi (APA), Sergi Avaliani (Akademia/Tbilisi), Kurt Baier (Pittsburgh), Augustin Basave (Monterrey), John Beloff (Edinburgh), Gustav Bergmann (Vienna & Iowa), Mario Bunge (Buenos Aires & Montréal), Guido Calogero (Roma), Henri Dumont (Institut de Culture/Québec), J.N. Findlay (Boston), Leo Gabriel (Vienna), Jeanne Hersch (Genève), Herbert Hörz (Berlin), Ervin Laszlo (Vienna Academy for Study of Future), Hans Lenk (Karlsruhe), Alasdair MacIntyre (Notre Dame), Nelli Motrošilova (Moscow), Igor Narskii (Moscow), David L. Norton (Delaware), H.H. Price (Oxford), D.R.C. Reed (Wittenberg), Josef Seifert (Internationale Akademie für Philosophie), Wolfgang Stegmüller (München), Erik Stenius (Abo Academy), Anfinn Stigen (Oslo), Guram Tevzadze (Tbilisi), Hermann Wein (Göttingen), Johannes Witt-Hansen (Copenhagen), G.H. Von Wright (Helsinki), and Walther Ch. Zimmerli (Bamberg).

Recognition is due to the philosophical journals and symposia, wherein my previous essays have appeared, on some of which I have drawn in the present work: *Akten des Internationalen Kongresses für Philosophie* (1968), *Critica* (1985), *International Philosophical Quarterly* (1987), *Journal of Philosophical Research* (1989), *Philosophical Inquiry* (1982), *Philosophie et Culture* (Congrès Mondial de Philosophie/1983), *Philosophy Today* (1976/1981/1982), *Proceedings of the American Philosophical Society* (1970), and *Zeitschrift für Philosophische Forschung* (1991), especially. I thank their editors for permission to make appropriate use of these materials here.

I thank Karen Berry for typing my handwritten manuscript, Marian Mollé for proof-reading, Mary Helen Flanagan for typographic design, and Nona Reuter of Peter Lang Publishing, Inc.; Transylvania University for its research grant; and the Library of Transylvania University for its good services.

My old friend, William Morrison, awaited long for the "philosophy of life" which this book promised; but the tides of life drowned him ere its composition.

I remain grateful for the abiding support of Anne Gobar, my companion in life's journey, throughout the writing of this my most important work.

A.G.

CONTENTS

FOREWORD

This book presents one philosopher's re-vision of modern philosophy: *that philosophy is to be conceived as higher enlightenment.* In the light of this ideal, the theoretical interest and the existential interest of philosophy may be reconciled; and hence the two disparate dimensions of philosophical inquiry — as "metascience" and as "worldview" — may be interrelated. Accordingly this work contributes some paradigms toward a reconstruction in philosophy —and toward a new worldview—from the perspective of 'dialectical realism'. I have dared then, in this age of hyperspecialization, to seek an integrative picture.

As I sketch my reconstruction against the background of contemporary philosophical scene, I feel keenly the diversity of philosophical trends (and indeed the ideological jungle which they have spawned): ranging from scholasticism and empiricism to neopositivism and existentialism, from naive realism and nominalism to skepticism and nihilism, and lately the ideology of postmodernity. Against this scene I propose my 'reconstruction' — as a dialectical answer to the varieties of 'deconstruction'. I am well aware that, in doing so, I go against some prevailing currents of the times. But, then, a philosophical reconstruction is also a philosophical critique.

In a wider sense, this book presents a contribution to the theme of utopia and praxis philosophy. For, as a consequence of presenting the theme of philosophy as "higher enlightenment", it also articulates the role of philosophy as a "cultural healer". Thus, while it handles the questions of truth, consciousness, and existence, it also explores the questions of value, higher humanism, and quality of life at a dialectical plane of discourse. I hope that I have been able to demonstrate anew the import of *Weltanschauung* in our time.

There are elegant constructions, cathedrals of meaning, enshrouded in academic philosophy; and this work opens a new window onto them. Therefore this book is intended for scholars as well as the general reader with some background in the arts, sciences, or humanistic studies. Nevertheless, a serious philosophical work of this kind would contain sections which only the professional students of philosophy might understand and appreciate.

If there be an affinity between philosophy and music, then my work might be compared with the compositions of Igor Stravinsky, in this way: that both blend the nostalgia of past themes with the innovation of future themes; and in both there is a striving to attain a dialectical resolution to the contradictory concerns of the composition.

The main idea which has motivated the writing of this work may be stated in this way: *That philosophy leads to a higher enlightenment (personally and societaly) — or it leads to nothing.*

CHAPTER I

Transfiguration of Philosophy

The "transfiguration of philosophy" of which I write represents — not any series of transformations in the various aspects of modern philosophy in the recent past which remain a proper task for the historians of philosophy to elucidate — but rather a re-vision and a critique, a renewed understanding as it were, by the author who has sought to rethink his way through the veritable jungle of thought which contemporary philosophy has become.

Nor was this re-vision of modern philosophy attained accidentally. It was occasioned by the author's having taken the 'conceptual turn' — to be explained later — as a radical response to paradoxes and dilemmas harbored in contemporary philosophy. The result was the conception of philosophy as *higher enlightenment:* under this ideal the hitherto disparate images of philosophy — as an objective *metascience* or as a subjective *worldview* — would find their integration. The import of philosophy for art, science, and life would then be articulated anew. And we would be able to speak of philosophy as *ars combinatoria* once again.

What, then, is the character and meaning of philosophy as 'higher enlightenment'? How are its questions (and propositions) to be distinguished from other non-philosophical questions (and propositions)? What is the import of philosophy for the "big questions", which underlie the arts and sciences, or the life of the human psyche, or arise at the horizon of culture and civilization? These issues, foremost among others, will be handled, in the course of this work, from the perspective of dialectical realism.

§ 1

What is Philosophical Enlightenment?

I envision 'philosophy' as a conceptual inquiry — into the deeper questions which lie at the foundation or at the horizon of our thinking — leading to a higher level of enlightenment.

What does this assertion mean precisely?

It means that philosophical inquiry draws out the underlying issues, from the unexamined regions of their dark origins, into the light of critical elucidation and interpretation. It means that philosophical thinking unveils hidden assumptions and discloses unforeseen consequences of our belief systems. It means — to use the expression of the ancient Greek thinkers — *légein tà legómena*, i.e., to lay out, in the light of reason, the essence and the meaning of our picture of the world.

For philosophical thinking has the potential power to handle the "big questions" underlying the arts, the sciences, and life. It has the power of descending ever deeper into the strata of human consciousness, exposing our most fundamental assumptions, and suggesting their critical reconstruction in the light of reason. Whether philosophical inquiry be elucidatory or creative, analytical or dialectical, it will necessarily lead to enlightenment.

An analogy from Plato will serve to illustrate my conception of 'philosophy as enlightenment':

In every case of vision — he observes in the *Republic* (VI:507) — there are three things involved: the object to be seen, the eye of the seer, and (what one is not conscious of in the act of seeing but takes for granted) the light of the sun providing the context of possible vision. Analogously, I say that the object of seeing corresponds to the world, the eye of the observer to the arts and sciences, and the light of the sun to philosophy. For philosophy provides the context of intelligibility for our experience of the world; and, without it, our arts and sciences and other belief systems would remain eclipsed at their foundations and shrouded by darkness at their horizons.

Philosophy emerges as the illuminator of the deeper questions (and deeper truths) which lie buried in the context of our understanding.

Philosophy asks only ground-questions or horizon-questions.

This shows that philosophy has a Janus-face: it looks *backward* into the deepest assumptions of our thinking, and it looks *forward* into the farthest consequences of our thinking. When it looks backward, philosophy emerges as *'metascience'*; and when it looks forward, philosophy emerges as *'worldview'*. In either case, philosophy operates by means of conceptual elucidation and dialectical argumentation; and it results in the reconstruction of paradigms for our thinking.[1] The hitherto conflicting approaches to philosophy, i.e. the objective and the subjective, represent complementary aspects of 'philosophical enlightenment'.

"But can philosophy be defined exactly?"—the discerning reader will inquire.

I see 'philosophy', from the perspective of dialectical realism, as an inquiry leading to 'higher enlightenment':

Philosophy is a conceptual inquiry into the deeper questions (and deeper truths) which lie at the foundations of thinking or lie at the horizon of thinking, resulting in the construction of paradigms, which have significance for art, science, and life.

This transcendental image of 'philosophy' is given symbolic expression by an incidental observation of Wittgenstein: "The word 'philosophy' must mean something which stands above or below, but not beside, the natural sciences"[2] — *above* or *below* — but in a more radical sense than that which Wittgenstein (and, indeed, the Vienna Circle entire) assigned to it.

For philosophical discourse concerns, as one says, the 'logic of' or the 'dialectic of' issues. The unique mark of philosophical questions (and propositions) consists in that: *firstly*, they are conceptual in character, rather than being factual or linguistic in character; and, *secondly*, they are radical or transcendental in character. These two characteristics, taken together, distinguish philosophical from non-philosophical questions (and propositions).

Hence a 'philosopher' is a thinker who represents a certain level of 'higher consciousness': a thinker who, in response to some philosophical questions, develops some conceptual paradigms and some argument patterns; a thinker who sees the dialectical relations between systems of relations; a thinker who draws the import of philosophical inquiry for the meaning and quality of human life: a thinker who strives toward forming an intelligible picture of the world.

In speaking of philosophy as "higher enlightenment", I am giving a new meaning to an old expression, thereby breathing a new life into it as it were. For philosophical enlightenment is to be distinguished from other special forms of enlightenment: artistic enlightenment and scientific enlightenment which have contributed their own shares to modern life. Too, I set *philosophical enlightenment* in stark relief against *historical enlightenment*. The latter — deriving from the *Aufklärung* of the early modern era[3] — has resulted in the modern age.

Philosophical enlightenment, as I see it, presents a context of understanding and/or critique for the special forms of enlightenment provided by the arts and the sciences and by our historical heritage. How deep or superficial this understanding/critique may be is determined by the philosopher's perspective. The perspective which this author represents is that of *dialectical realism* as an approach to philosophical issues.[4] We shall have more to say on this issue later.

§ 2

Philosophy as Metascience

Let X = Reality. Assume that X represents an unknown, but knowable, order; and assume, further, that X displays a complex crystalline structure. How do we acquire the knowledge of X?

The several aspects of X would be perceivable to various observers from their various perspectives. This would present a series of phenomenological pictures of reality: the pictures of the world in everyday experience — and, at a refined level, the aesthetic pictures of the world as in art and literature. I call this a *first-order* inquiry into reality.

Now assume that we have acquired a set of objective methods, by which we can describe the various aspects of X, and explain the phenomena in the contexts of the several dimensions. The result would be the intersubjective pictures of the world, as it were, underlying the subjective pictures of everyday experience. To give one example: the depiction of the phenomena of color in everyday experience as the interaction of light waves and material surfaces in modern science. I call this a *second-order* inquiry into reality.

Where does philosophy enter the scene?

Philosophy enters the scene as a *third-order* inquiry, as it were, from below and from above.

Scientific pictures of reality rest on a set of assumptions and contain a set of invariant concepts. The truth of these assumptions and the meanings of these concepts are presupposed in their discourses. Examples of philosophical assumptions are: The postulates of causality, of conservation, and of the irreversibility of time; etc. And examples of invariant concepts are: truth, meaning, intentionality, potentiality, relation, property, existence, etc. Philosophy enters the scene, from below, through the examination and elucidation of the ground and meaning of these metascientific ideas.

Further, scientific theories and technological discoveries entail consequences for the quality of human life on earth. The qualitative assessment of these implications and consequences presupposes a philosophical conception of "good life" as well as the criteria for "progress". Philosophy enters the scene then, from above as it were, by providing a critique of our value hierarchy in the light of which the import of scientific and technological discoveries for the quality of life may be assessed.

Philosophy as *metascience*, then, represents a third-order inquiry as it were: an inquiry into the epistemological framework and the ontological foundations of the sciences; and an inquiry into the implications and consequences of the discoveries of science and technology for the quality of life on earth. The methodologies of the special sciences are not designed to handle these metascientific issues. We need the resources of philosophy, with its dialectical methodology, to serve as a metascience whose function is a higher order critique of science. Hence the complementarity of science and philosophy.

The above remarks explain the two important meanings of the expression *"the philosophy of"*, as *the logic of or the dialectic of*, the arts and the sciences.

The epistemological relation between science and philosophy rests upon the distinction—delineated by Kant originally—between "empirical concepts" and the "pure concepts" of understanding. The beauty of the distinction lies in that it represents the levels of the epistemological dimension: i.e. the relation between a set of "truths" and the corresponding set of "deeper truths". This, too, is what we mean when we speak of the philosophical dimension of arts and sciences.

However, when an art or science remains oblivious to its own philosophical dimension, it becomes something less than an authentic art or science. It becomes an intellectual toy for "bourgeois professionalism"—serving only the dictates of its profession and the utilitarian demands of the marketplace. Too, there are such phenomena as the "diseases of science", and the "sickness of art", of which we shall speak later.

"Metascience"—the very designation emits an aura of ineffability — an expression which represents the abstract aspect of the Janus-faced goddess of philosophy. Nor has it anything to do with "metagrammar", its counterfeit icon, as circulated in some circles. It is — seen with a critical and unpresumptive eye — an inquiry into the philosophical truths which render the articulation of the truths of science intelligible. Perhaps this book — in chapters IV, V, VI especially — will open some windows (from the perspective of dialectical realism) onto this crystalline world.

(I speak of 'metascience', rather than of 'metaphysics', in order to avoid the usual anti-scientific connotation of the latter designation and yet allow for the transcendental function of philosophy.)

§ 3

Philosophy as Worldview

Every reflective person forms a picture of the world. This picture represents a given order (and disorder) of how things hang-together in the world. But behind every ordinary world-picture lies the philosophical question: How true is this naive picture of the world; and, however true or false, what meaning does it harbor for one's life?

Philosophy as *worldview* (for which stands the beautifully expressive word, *Weltanschauung*, in the German language) inquires into the horizon of our understanding. It explores the ways in which we may integrate our ideas concerning the world, the psyche, and life. It is the attempt to understand(dialectically) how things hang-together in the cosmos. It is the tapestry of "reality" handwoven by the psyche for the purposes of its life as it were.

For man is a reflective being — perhaps the only reflective being —who asks philosophical questions about the world. Consider the three questions (asked by Kant as a spokesman for humanity): "What can I know? What should I do? What may I hope?"[5] These simple and deep questions lead to the threshold of higher consciousness; and the answers to them would enlighten our earthly existence.

These, too, were the very questions that originally drove the early Greek thinkers to embark on the perilous path of philosophical inquiry, in defiance of their cultural inertia, and despite the consolations of their mythological religion. Inevitably Plato came to regard 'philosophy'(φιλοσοφία) as the veritable 'art of life'[6] — and hence "the greatest of the arts" as he called it — and warned the youth against the danger of losing their nascent philosophical dream in life under the corrupting tides of culture in society. And this vision of 'philosophy', as a higher art, was to be recaptured by Nietzsche, nearly 2000 years later, a thinker who had drunk deeply from the well of Greek thought. For Nietzsche proposed to resolve the dilemma of modern philosophy — i.e. whether philosophy is an art or a science — unequivocally in favor of art: "Both in its purpose and its result it is an art," he wrote, and yet admitting, as a corrective, that philosophy has a methodological affinity with science, since it uses "the same means as science"[7], i.e. reason. A prolonged, and broken, discourse concerning philosophy as the 'art of life' — continuing to our day — and finding its most recent articulation in the work of Martin Heidegger which recasts the debate on the niveau of phenomenology.[8]

However, with due appreciation for the contribution of phenomenology, it should be noted that: the issue of the formation of a "philosophical worldview' and of a "philosophy of life" requires, beyond phenomenological description, a dialectical interpretation.

On the issue of the transcendental character of philosophical thinking — and its connection with higher enlightenment — the views of three contemporary philosophers converge with that of the author:

Hermann Wein, in depicting philosophy as the "theory of experience" (*Erfahrungswissenschaft*), distinguishes the experience *of* the world from reflection *upon* the world of experience — as the dialectical process of higher consciousness in human life.[9] Anfinn Stigen depicts 'philosophy as worldview' to be a conceptual system "within which we think and with the aid of which we arrange all things"; and defines the "philosophical character" of a question in terms of its being "crucial to our conception of man's place in the universe"[10] — rather than in terms of a linguistic game. And J.N. Findlay writes: "Philosophy may be said to be in part merely the changeover from a confused combination of many ill-developed ways of regarding the cave (i.e. the world) and its contents, to a single clearly focused and pregnant way, or to a sequence of such clearly focused ways, which may in their turn bring on a new deliberately blurred kind of vision, and so on . . . Philosophy may in fact be essentially revisionary and creative, though it builds, and must build, on the notions and usages embedded in ordinary thought and speech . . . (in order to) see factors hanging together in bonds of mutual requirement."[11]

While the convergence of views does not mean an indication of truth—yet it is significant that three thinkers with markedly different perspectives should arrive at a similar recognition — I have cited these texts only to illustrate my main proposition: that philosophical thinking concerning the world (and the meaning of life) involves a measure of 'higher consciousness' without which 'philosophy', as a transcendental inquiry, would be impossible.

Already, more than a decade ago, Ervin Laszlo boldly attempted to outline a new paradigm for modern thought, on the basis of a reconstruction of "systems-philosophy". He explained his concern: "The demand for 'seeing things whole' and seeing the world as an interconnected, interdependent, field or continuum, is in itself a healthy reaction to the loss of meaning entailed by our over-compartmentalized research and piecemeal analysis . . .failing in relevance to anything of human concern."[12] That is our concern too. For man cannot live a meaningful and successful life without ideals and without a dream. And the highest dream of man can be none other than his "philosophy of life".

"But," the skeptical reader will ask, "may we not live quite well without philosophy and without philosophical inquiry — provided that we are masters of our applied arts and sciences?"

We may — we answer — provided also that our applied arts and sciences, pursued without philosophy, not generate pragmatically self-defeating consequences. But, in the absence of a philosophically grounded system of value hierarchy, inevitably particular values would compete, and destroy each other in the process. That is what is happening in various areas of our civilization today. And, lest we forget, it was *because* the culture of the early 20th Century (during the period between the two world wars) attempted to live *without* a "philosophy of life", or a warped one, that the civilization of the late 20th Century began reaping the ugly harvests of environmental pollution, disease epidemics, and social decadence — bringing us to the very eve of earthly disaster . . .

For one's "philosophical worldview" determines one's system of values— which, in turn, determines one's quality of life. And the transformation of one's philosophy of life entails a reordering of one's value hierarchy: it engenders or eliminates *a priori* a swarm of problems in the horizon of one's life. Thus one's philosophical worldview serves as the only reliable guide in the perilous journey we call life. In the absence of a philosophical worldview — and a "philosophy of life" consequently — the life of man would remain beset by fragmentation. It would remain shrouded by existential vacuum. And — as existential psychiatrists have observed already[13] — it is understandable why *Angst*, and psychological disorders, prevail in our time. Wither would modern man turn, then, to seek a cure for his ailing psyche? An intriguing, and disquieting, question — in view of the possibilities in its wake. For the occult-religionists and the soul-magicians — who are just waiting at the gates — would be ready to enter the scene, with their baggage of bad literature, and present their irrational and bizarre views of the world and life, as proper remedies for the spiritual ailments of modern man, and as proper substitutes for our reason and our philosophical heritage.

POSTSCRIPT:

A Note on the Author's Motive for Taking the Conceptual Turn

What were the original motives which led the author to seek the 'conceptual turn', against the prevailing philosophical currents of the time, overcoming critical problems and redefining the image of philosophy as 'higher enlightenment'?

When I entered the field of philosophy as a young thinker — (from a background of the history of ideas) — I assumed naturally that in this field the logic of discovery would be evident and the line of progress would be determinable. But I found, on the contrary, that it was nigh impossible to form a clear image of 'philosophy' — much less a *Weltanschauung* — not to mention comprehending its line of progress. What I encountered in the philosophical world was a perplexing and baffling scene: an unmanageable array of conflicting, and seemingly irreconcilable, approaches and viewpoints — each with its own "programme" and its own "language" — (and the retort, "I don't speak your language!", would be hurled by speakers and commentators at each other, in congresses, at the slightest indication of a dialectical challenge, thus foreclosing the possibility of any real dialogue) — shattering the prospect of forming any clear 'understanding' in philosophy. For contemporary philosophy is beset by the strife of "schools", bypassing each other when not actually clashing, and providing grist for the mill of "marginal philosophers". My immediate impression upon entering the philosophical scene was that of having entered an intellectual jungle: where, amidst a primeval thicket and mist, roamed all kinds of beings, both benign and fiendish, following their half-visible pathways and byways. My immediate impulse was to withdraw from the scene altogether — but, as "wonder" is the spring of philosophical inquiry, I remained. The philosophical scene engendered in me, instead of the usual despair, a nascent taste for the dialectical character of truth and reality. So I embarked on the perilous journey of a career in philosophy.

I then encountered a series of paradoxes (and a series of alarming dilemmas arising out of them) — revealing unresolved ground-problems — and indicating a hidden crisis in contemporary philosophy:

Paradox I
Philosophical propositions,
having no denotative function,
are "vacuous" and senseless.
and yet
Philosophical propositions
result in some kind of
"knowledge" and "understanding".

Paradox II
There are no "philosophical"
truths" and it is impossible
to claim any knowledge of them.
and yet
The continuation of
philosophical inquiry and
dialogue is enlightening and
desirable nevertheless.

Paradox III
The reliability of "reason" and
"rationality" in philosophical
inquiry is questionable.
and yet
Argumentative reasoning is
unquestionably a reliable means
in questioning the reliability
of "reason" and "rationality".

Paradox IV
There is no such a thing as
'philosophy'—for philosophy
cannot integrate its own
'philosophies'.
and yet
'Philosophy', in some sense, is
and must be the interpreter and
integrator of human knowledge.

Such are the paradoxes underlying many current movements in contemporary philosophy — as I see them[14] — and the dialectic of these paradoxes is as striking as it is disquieting:

How could philosophy, which takes the clarification of the meanings of concepts and propositions to be one of its proper functions, itself remain unclear as to the character of its own concepts and propositions? Or, how could we, after having denied the possibility of articulating 'philosophical truths', affirm the value, or even the meaningfulness, of continuing our hollow dialogues in philosophy? Or, how could philosophical inquiry, which derives its very intelligibility from 'reason', abandon 'reason' as being unreliable, without thereby rendering its own intelligibility impossible? Or, lastly, how could philosophy, whose primary aim is to serve as the interpreter and the integrator of knowledge, itself remain disintegrated and unreconstructed — with an unbridgeable gap between its objective conception as 'metascience' and its subjective conception as 'worldview'?

These paradoxes (and the dilemmas arising from them), in the opinion of this writer, constitute the "latent content" of the "manifest content" of the uncertainty and anxiety prevailing in many philosophical circles. Incidences of overly rhetorical argumentation in contemporary literature; of open attacks upon 'philosophical inquiry' as a rational process by professional philosophers themselves; and of hollow-sounding talk about the presumed "end of philosophy" in other circles; all these represent (I believe) but compensatory measures for the underlying anxiety and uncertainty of the philosophical Zeitgeist. Meanwhile, the deeper questions and the deeper truths — except in isolated cases in the works of singular philosophers — are brushed aside through their dissolution and trivialization. These early perceptions and impressions of the field I entered, gnawed at my reflective conscience, all the more since I took 'philosophical inquiry' seriously as a young thinker.

The feelings of despair that were evoked in me were akin to those of Kant, in his own troubled time, as expressed in a letter (written to Herr J.H. Lambert of the Academy of Sciences in Berlin in 1765): "For a number of years I have carried on my philosophical reflections on every earthly subject . . . I have always looked for the source of my error or tried to get some insight into the nature of my blunder . . ." he confessed, but deplored "the devastating disunity among supposed philosophers", and earnestly wished for "the euthanasia of (all) false philosophy."[15] We know the response that this philosophical challenge evoked from Kant — the Three Critiques — and the gifts that these brought us.

But we can derive little consolation from the fact that intellectual chaos always cluttered the atmosphere. For we are living under the umbrella of a more complex and a more difficult Zeitgeist. And today the plight of the young thinker is more exigent than ever before: One is greeted by the multiplicity of "languages" in one's own chosen field. One is challenged by the paradoxes and dilemmas of the various "schools", by the interminable rhetoric of innumerable publications and congresses, and by more than a hundred philosophical journals in the English language alone. It is less a question — so it would seem — of "saving" philosophy than of "saving" one's own sense of identity as a thinker.

The young Karl Jaspers confesses for all of us who, in our youth, have experienced a dismay after our initial encounter with professional philosophy: "I was discontent with myself and with the state of society, with the false beliefs prevalent in public life. My fundamental reaction was: something is radically wrong, not merely with humanity, but also with myself. . . Philosophy appeared to me as the highest and the unique concern of mankind. . . [Yet] philosophy courses in the university I soon dropped: Against philosophy professors I had an antipathy because they did not treat what really mattered most to me."[16] When philosophy ceases to enlighten those who grope in the darker regions of understanding — whatever its methodological pretexts may be — it fails in its promise of relevance to human life.

The question remains: Is it possible to gather and reconcile meaningfully these multifarious contemporary movements under one designation: "philosophy"?

No — (and, on this point, I agree with Professor Wolfgang Stegmüller)— for modern philosophy has passed forever the point of 'unification'." The ambiguity of the word 'philosophy' could only be reduced if entire philosophical currents were to 'die out' altogether . . ." observes Professor Stegmüller, "or if one should decide, no longer to call 'philosophy' all these assorted heterogeneous things, but to reserve that word for a somewhat sharply defined activity."[17] It is the latter alternative (I believe) that holds the prospect of progress in philosophy.

I struggled, for a decade, to redefine (for myself) the image of my art: 'philosophy'. But this was impossible to do—without descending into its very roots and confronting its ground-question. And the ground-question of modern philosophy (which seemed to have been obscured in contemporary debates) was: *What is the character of philosophical questions/propositions which distinguishes them from nonphilosophical questions/propositions?* This I took to be the metaquestion of modern philosophy in its simplest and unadorned formulation. And I believed that, unless this ground-question were handled properly, the entire "tree of philosophy" would eventually wither and die — and there were signs, even then, that some of its branches were dying or had died already. For the metaquestion of philosophy underlay, as it were, all the other philosophical problems. Yet this ground-question could not be handled adequately at the ordinary levels of discourse—i.e. the linguistic, the pragmatic, or the existential — owing to its transcendental character.

Then, in the year 1975, a ray of light shone upon my path. The problem, I came to see, could be handled only by assuming a conceptual approach. And this approach required that all empirical, linguistic, and existential issues be set aside as extraneous and irrelevant. Then I was able to formulate my fundamental thesis as follows:

That the character of philosophical questions (and propositions) lies in that they pertain essentially to the meanings/relations of concepts; and that, consequently, the proper methods of philosophical inquiry consist of conceptual elucidation and dialectical reasoning — leading to the reconstruction of philosophical paradigms.

By articulating an answer to the metaquestion of philosophy in purely conceptual terms, I had taken the 'conceptual turn'. And while it was evident that the 'unification' of philosophy was no longer possible, a 'reconstruction' in philosophy was still possible. My path — owing to the diversity of currents and cross-currents in the philosophical scene — was arduous and obstacle-laden. When, however, I had overcome the obstacles and taken the turn, I was able to envision the 'transfiguration of philosophy'.

And what does taking the 'conceptual turn' mean?

It means: (a) that philosophical questions (and propositions) are neither empirical nor linguistic, but are essentially conceptual in nature: i.e. they concern, as one says, the 'logic of' and the 'dialectic of' problems—(the issue of the "use of language" is no more relevant in philosophy than it is in the natural sciences); and (b) that the methods of philosophical inquiry consist of conceptual analysis, dialectical reasoning, and the construction of paradigms (which are applicable to art, science, and life).

By implication—the 'conceptual turn' means: That philosophical propositions have as their objects 'concepts' and 'hypotheses' (not "words" and "sentences"!); that there is a class of propositions representing *'philosophical truths'* concerning logical/ dialectical forms; and that reason, and reason alone, defines the limits of intelligibility in philosophical discourse.

In the *Tractatus* of Wittgenstein a significant thought is expressed which seems to have been subsequently forgotten by its author: i.e. "The aim of philosophy is the logical clarification of thoughts" (prop. 4112).But the philosophers who have taken the 'conceptual turn' have given this important thought a new life. Thus Anfinn Stigen writes: "It must be made quite clear that it is not the *use of language* that interests us most, but the *relationships between concepts* — even if it is language that puts us on the track of conceptual distinctions."[18] And conceptual relations can be elucidated — not by means of the "ordinary language" which is beset by ambiguities—but by means of an "ideal language" (to use Bergmann's designation[19]), i.e., a reconstructed language.

As I continued my path upward, along the rugged ranges of philosophical inquiry, it occasionally criss-crossed those of some other philosophers. I saw, in their writings, the recurrence of familiar expressions: "conceptual elucidation", "moulding of concepts", and "conceptual paradigms". And I recognized some points of convergence at the horizons of our perspectives. These moments of intersubjective understanding — rare as they were in the absence of a real "philosophical community" in our time[20] — were deeply gratifying. They indicated that I was not traveling alone in those high and desolate ranges of thought; that the 'transfiguration of philosophy', which I had envisioned, was also seen (variously) by some philosophers who had traveled their own independent paths; and that, perhaps, progress in philosophy was after all possible. But, conversely, I found that I differed in principle from, and parted ways with, many philosophers who had come to be in vogue.

Philosophical reconstruction is also philosophical critique.

CHAPTER II

Methodological Excursus

What are the methods requisite for a philosophy of dialectical realism? Three ways of philosophical inquiry interest us especially: conceptual elucidation, dialectical reasoning, and the use of paradigms. These I believe to be the most useful and the most creative methods in handling philosophical problems.

However, having laid out our methodological repertoire in this explicit manner, a critical question confronts us: Are we not assuming, in practicing these methods of inquiry, the existence of a transcendental matrix of rationality? For it must be admitted that a transcendental matrix of rationality alone would provide the necessary context for the possibility of meaningful inquiry and the intelligibility of philosophical discourse — including philosophical dialogue.

But how could dialogue be possible between thinkers whose conceptual worlds are *radically* different from each other?

I argue that dialogue between thinkers with different worldviews is possible only because (and insofar as) their discourses occur within the framework of understanding. For the object of genuine dialogue is, not the transference of *information* merely, but the *understanding* of a given viewpoint. And any understanding, between two dialogues, presupposes a matrix of rationality.

The possibility that dialogue (not to mention monologue) may have radically different contents in different contexts of discourse renders it contingent. Yet, in order for dialogue to remain intelligible, despite its contingency and its varied contents, it must occur within the framework of *rationality*. For in dialogue, each thinker brings something, which requires something else to be brought in its justification. And here, precisely, lies the genesis of the momentous question: "Why?" — a question which can only be satisfied by being given a *reason* as an answer. Otherwise, the question which seeks to *understand* "why" (i.e. "for what reason?") a given assertion is being made, would remain unsatisfied — and dialogue would die momentarily. Nor would the question "Why?" be satisfied with every reason as being equally good; rather it would seek, amongst the myriad of reasons, the "best reason" as the adequate explanation/justification for the given belief or action. Thus the dilemma — to answer the question "Why?" rationally or not to answer — becomes the dilemma: whether to continue the dialogue or to lapse into monologue (or, perhaps, silence).

Even if the skeptic were to question the questioner—for example: "Why, might I ask, must you ask 'Why?'?" — it would not absolve the skeptic of assuming the "burden" of rationality. The supererogatory question would not cancel the original question but, on the contrary, underscore it. It would demonstrate that the appeal to the transcendental matrix of rationality, as a necessary condition of understanding (and dialogue), remains a *sine qua non* even for the critique of rationality.

The skeptic has the privilege to say: It is not my moral obligation to be responsible for what I say — whether I make a dogmatic assertion or utter an ambiguous proposition or advocate a self-contradictory viewpoint — for I renounce beforehand the prospect of "dialogue" in favor of "monologue". But, in that case, it is questionable that the "monologue" of the skeptic would be really intelligible to himself *anymore than* his "dialogue" with others. What holds true of dialogue holds true of monologue: for monologue is (as Socrates noted) the dialogue of the psyche with itself. One must make sense to oneself before one can make sense to others. All philosophy begins in soliloquy.

Evidently, those who question the requirement of a transcendental matrix of rationality for meaningful philosophical inquiry and discourse retain a limited conception of "rationality". They confuse "logicality" with "rationality": they question that there is only "one logic" and, therefore, they question that there must be a shared framework of reason and rationality. But, as we shall see, *dialectical reason* has a wider range than *logic* proper. Our methodological repertoire, then, assumes the *transcendental matrix of rationality.* Without such an assumption, and without a methodological repertoire, philosophical discourse would degenerate — (as it has in some circles already) — into a rhetorical language-game.

§ 4

Conceptual Analysis

The aim of philosophical analysis is to clarify the meanings of, and the relations between, concepts. Of the several genres of analysis, practiced by modern philosophers, two are of special interest to us: *elucidatory analysis* and *transcendental analysis*. These we shall consider.

Elucidatory Analysis

The elucidation of a concept consists of the depiction of its logical form (and hence its meaning) by the techniques of deconstruction and reconstruction.

An elucidation results in a *definition*, i.e., a linguistic depiction in the ideal language. Since a definition remains vulnerable to the counter-example as Socrates, the master of the art of definition, demonstrated it may call for a redefinition. The constancy of the logical form of the concept is to be assumed — the assumption of conceptual reality. It is on the basis of this assumption that some attractive versions of the realist theory of definition have been formulated recently.[1]

The realist conception of the definition implies some variant of the "picture theory" of language (such as proposed by Wittgenstein[2]): that language depicts reality directly or obliquely. Its rival alternative is the nominalist theory of 'definition' (suggested by Quine and others). Quine's felicitous expression, "a convention of notational abbreviation"[3], symbolizes the nominalist idea, with its appeal to "traditional usage", and its implied programme for the nominalist interpretation of the language of science and philosophy entire. However sophisticated in its construction, the nominalist theory suffers from what I shall call the "Humpty Dumpty Fallacy" ("When I use a word," said Humpty Dumpty, "it means just what I choose it to mean!") the fallacy of assuming that our choice of definitions is an arbitrary matter. But without the constancy of meanings, given in concepts, the intersubjective understanding of concepts would be impossible.

For a 'concept' is a representation in thought of the logical form of a phenomenon. The 'logical form' of the concept is the *intension* of the concept; and the class of objects which fall under its range constitutes the *extension* of the concept. The 'intension' of the concept has been depicted variously by modern logicians: as "semantic object" (Bunge), as "formal image" (Klaus), etc.[4] The fact remains that, to understand the intension of a concept is to understand its extension, i.e., what must and must not fall under its range.

Concepts (and their intensions) are abstract objects in the realm of the possible; while, in the realm of the actual, concrete objects exemplify them. The nexus *exemplification* is but the recurrence of logical form. The issue is epistemological here; and I postpone the underlying ontological issue. That the intension and extension of concepts are not identical contrary to the view of empiricism is shown by the fact that there are concepts corresponding to classes which have no members, e.g., the mathematical zero. Also it is possible to show that two concepts, with different intensions, can have the same extension: e.g. the concept of "animal with lung" and the concept of "animal with liver" share a common extension in the same animal which exemplifies a complex concept as it were.

Since concepts are entities in logical space, and since logical space is multidimensional, do concepts then have multidimensional meanings?

An inquiry into the meaning of 'meaning' would show that this is indeed the case. Modern semantics has demonstrated — as may be seen in the elegant work of Mikhail Markovič concerning concepts and their meanings[5] — not only that there are dimensions of meaning but also that these are interrelated: that the 'sense' of a symbol is affected by its 'reference' as it were; that the 'connotations' of a symbol are parasitic upon both; and that the 'pragmatic meaning' of a symbol is uniquely determined by any or all of these taken together. An adequate representation of the meaning of a symbol (concept), then, must exhibit its dimensions as well as the dialectical interrelations involved.

Schematically:

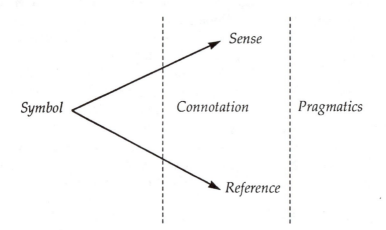

To see the distinction between 'sense' and 'reference' consider the expressions 'Morning Star' and 'Evening Star', which have different *senses*, yet the same *reference* (the planet Venus). And to understand the third kind of meaning, *connotation*, consider the pair of propositions:
(a) I see dark clouds in the sky.
(b) I see dark clouds in the horizon of my life.

While the expression "dark clouds" in (a) has an objective meaning, referring to an event in the external world, in (b) it harbors a subjective meaning to the speaker alone. Connotations play an important role in literary language, but they are not restricted thereto. Symbols and symbolic expressions in the arts also have a wide and complex range of connotations. For example, the hues of color in a painting may connote warmth or melancholy; and something similar may be said of notes in a musical composition. All these kinds of meaning are epistemologically prior to the 'pragmatic meanings', as the *essentia* of the *existentia*, for the latter derive their import from the former.

(The linguistic philosopher, J.L. Austin, says: While it makes "sense" to ask "What-is-the-meaning-of (the word) X?", it is "nonsense" to ask "What-is-the-meaning-of a word in general?" (i.e. to ask the meaning of 'meaning' generally).[6] But, epistemologically speaking, the possibility of asking the former question presupposes the possibility of asking the latter question: unless we understand the meaning-of-meaning in general it does not makes sense to speak of the meaning of anything in particular.)

Transcendental Analysis

Transcendental analysis perhaps the most profound form of philosophical analysis concerns the elucidation of the presuppositions of belief, by proceeding from the conditioned to its conditions, in order to render the former intelligible in the light of the latter.

As an example of transcendental analysis consider the following argument:

P1 Empirical language contains color propositions.

P2 Some of the color words are definable in terms of others, but not all are definable at the language level.

P3 It is impossible to use empirical language meaningfully, in which not all words are definable, *unless* some of its words denote properties of perceptual objects in the external world.

P4 The perception of colored objects is a precondition of the meaningfulness of empirical language.

The existence of a 'world', as the matrix of the existence of colored objects, is a precondition of the intelligibility of empirical language.

A second transcendental argument, then, can be evoked to explain the necessary preconditions of the intelligibility of the perception of objects which is a precondition of the intelligibility of empirical language in terms of the categorical forms of the 'external world'. Thus there are levels of transcendental analysis wherein we descend from the surface truths to intermediate truths and thence to deeper truths.

A purified schema for transcendental analysis is the following:

Existential Hypotheses
(I know/believe that X)
↓   ↑
Categorial Presuppositions
(including an independent reality)
↓   ↑
A Priori Schemata
(logical/dialectical form of reality)

Here the downward arrows designate the *linear regression* from the contingency of existential hypotheses to their presuppositions; and the upward arrows designate the *linear progression* from the *a priori* presuppositions to the necessity of the given hypotheses. Thus transcendental analysis reconstructs the conceptual framework for the intelligibility of our thoughts concerning the experience of the external world. The result of transcendental analysis is the elucidation of basic categories and *a priori* schemata.

The method of transcendental analysis has received criticism (in neopositivist circles) on empirical grounds.[7] The objection seems to be that a transcendental schema, even if susceptible of articulation, does not fit (being empirically unverifiable) in the matrix of empirical knowledge which we call "science". But, if the transcendental schema constitutes the framework *of* empirical knowledge, then it is to be expected that it would not fit *in* the matrix of empirical knowledge. For transcendental analysis discloses the rules of 'compossibility' and 'interdependence' implicit in the logic of empirical discourse. And the conclusions which transcendental analysis seeks to establish are none other than the very assumptions which lie at the ground of (and therefore beyond the scope of) scientific explanation. The blindspot of the critics of the transcendental method lies in that what they overtly repudiate they covertly assume.

§ 5

Dialectical Thinking

The most beautiful axiom of formal logic is perhaps the *axiom of truth*. It states that (for any given argument) if the premises be true, and if the form of inference be valid, then the conclusion will always be necessarily true. It may be said, without exaggeration, that this axiom enables us to *derive* "new truths" from "old truths". And, without this axiom, the entire structure of the sciences, as theoretical constructions, would collapse.

Yet, one might ask: What if the premises of a given argument be, neither unequivocally true nor false, but merely partially true (or partially false). Then the classical axiom of truth would no longer apply. And it is here that we need to go beyond formal logic: it is precisely here that dialectical logic enters the scene.

For dialectical logic seeks to *build* "new truths" on the basis of "partial truths". Here the *dialectical axiom of truth* replaces the older axiom. It may be stated as follows: Given a set of propositions, representing partial (and even conflicting) truths, then it is possible to draw a conclusion which represents a "higher degree" of truth. It requires no small degree of ingenuity to supersede the restricted domain of formal logic — and credit is due to Hegel who pioneered this line of inquiry — in order to be able to handle partially- true propositions and incompatible premises constructively. Thus dialectical logic represents a special genre of creative thinking.

I shall review here the main principles of the dialectical thinking — as I have come to understand them and interpret them:

Principle of Perspective
It is possible to view a given object X from a plurality of perspectives each representing a different aspect of truth about reality.

Thus one may view the object X from the perspective of its inner/ outer being, or its actual/potential modality, or its past/future history; etc. Or, again, focussing on one of these dimensions alone, it is possible to view the "outer being" of the object X from a number of perspectives: the phenomenological, the empirical, the cosmological, etc. For example, one may view a body of water in a lake: from the phenomenological perspective, as an undulating and shimmering liquid which offers mobile resistance to the body; or from the empirical perspective as a substance (H_2O) which is capable of solidification (freezing-point) and evaporation (boiling-point); or from the cosmological perspective as a great substance, contributing to world-formation, and sustaining the realm of life-forms; etc. Each perspective renders a different aspect of reality accessible to us.

Principle of Degrees of Truth

There are antinomies where every viewpoint is countered by an opposite viewpoint therefore all viewpoints represent but partial truths.

Yet partial truths, insofar as they are true, are also evidently true. And, between evidently true propositions, genuine contradiction is possible. For the negation of an evidently true proposition would be evidently false; and conversely. Hence the negation of the negation of an evidently true proposition would be evidently true. This is the meaning of the "law of double negation" where: $\sim(\sim p) = p$. And, further, if a given hypothesis (p) implies a given consequence (q), and q is evidently false, then we must reject p also as being false. Thus the *reductio ad absurdum* too holds good in dialectical thinking.

However, to complete the dialectical scenario, we must introduce the issue of the truth/falsity of both the *assumption* and the *consequence* of a given hypothesis. Consider the case of the skeptic who asserts: "Objective truth does not exist." The very possibility of this assertion rests upon the implicit assumption that "There is at least one objective truth which the skeptic may articulate." Yet the assertion of the skeptic implies the consequence that "No objective truth can be articulated by anyone." Since the assumption of the skeptic's hypothesis and its consequence are clearly contradictory, therefore the hypothesis itself is false. The significance of this "Socratic checkmate" for dialectical thinking is clear: No proposition stands alone.

And this brings us to the third principle of dialectical method, namely:

Principle of Critical Synthesis

It is possible for thought to move from a set of partial truths even when these are contradictory to relatively whole truths.

But this movement of thought is as complex as it is creative. It involves, as its opening move, the cancellation of the given propositions as they stand; and, as its middle move, the revision of the given propositions as potential premises; and, as its final move, their critical integration into a newly inferred proposition which represents a higher degree of truth. Symbolically: $(A \degree B) \Rightarrow C$ (where A and B denote the revised premises, the symbol ' $\degree$ ' the critical integration, and ' $\Rightarrow$ ' the creative inference of the new hypothesis C). Thus it appears that 'contradiction' between propositions (ideas), which is rightly regarded to be an evil thing in formal logic, may serve in dialectical thinking as the occasion for the process of creative reconstruction.

It should be evident that the relations between ideas represent the dynamics of thinking. This is especially illustrated in the domain of empirical hypotheses which may be seen as a set of 'cognitive termini' in the matrix of time. The integration of these cognitive termini, within a more comprehensive cognitive matrix, involves more than a mere logical conjunction: it involves bringing them under a higher conception, wherein their contradictions dissolve, as it were.

However, dialectical synthesis does not apply to true propositions with mutually exclusive ranges, or to utterly false propositions, or to cases where one proposition is evidently true and the other evidently false.

Where should the dialectical line be drawn then?

In response to this question we must appeal to an epistemological model — suggested by Igor Narskii originally[8] — namely: that in our theory of knowledge we must recognize three levels of cognition at least. These are: the level of protocol truths; the level of antinomies arising in the context of discourse concerning the protocol truths; and the level of critical reflection wherein the antinomies are dissolved, through theoretical reconstructions.

The dialectical method itself has undergone an evolution from Socrates through Hegal to our time and has been susceptible of diverse interpretations. But its essential objective, beyond its techniques, has remained constant: "Logos is born for us through the weaving together of forms" as the Socratic Stranger says in the last pages of the *Sophist* (260a) which was among Plato's last writings. So we moderns, too, must "weave" conflicting ideas together, as the strands of partial truths, in the progressive effort to rebuild the image of a more whole truth.

§ 6

The Role of Paradigms

The word *paradigm* derived from the Greek *paradeigma* meaning "pattern"[9] is a classical gift to modern thinking. It may be conceived as an ideal model, a form of higher synthesis, which depicts and explains the relations between systems of relations.

What, then, is the 'higher synthesis' implicit in the paradigm? "By *synthesis* in its most general sense I understand the bringing together of different representations, and the comprehension of their diversity, under one conceptual cognition" wrote Kant, the master of the art of synthesis, on another occasion.[10] We, too, understand by 'synthesis' something similar.

Paradigms are higher-order modes of synthesis: they depict the logical form of lower-order models. A 'model' (whether in science or in philosophy) performs two functions: (a) it *simplifies* what it represents; and (b) it *idealizes* what it represents. Paradigms serve, then, as ideal "umbrellas" for collections of theories and hypotheses: they represent ideals for thinking, for explanation, and for praxis.

A contemporary philosopher says: "A paradigm serves to represent the world... while lying on the nether side of representation."[11] And I add: If a paradigm "represents" the world, then it can only be the dialectical form of the world that it represents.

Paradigms are formed through the creative generalization which goes beyond mere analogical thinking. A paradigm appears as a result of the crystallization of a thought-experiment into an ideal model. Consider, e.g., Einstein's ideal model of the "curved space" as a paradigm of modern physics: it was the product of a thought-experiment concerning the problems associated with mass, velocity, and gravitation. A paradigm, as such, represents a transcendental image in scientific thinking or in philosophical thinking.

A special application of the 'paradigm' in philosophical discourse is the 'paradigm case argument' (PCA). Its logical form is the following: A given case conforms to a given model (M), and a second case is analogous to the first case; therefore the second case must conform to the same model (M). Symbolically: (a εM)/ a::b/ (b εM). It is evident that the validity of the PCA rests upon the validity of its analogical inference. This shows that the PCA is essentially a conceptual argument and not (as some have held mistakenly) an empirical or a linguistic argument.

Indeed, the entire history of scientific and philosophical thinking may be viewed (and Wolfgang Stegmüller and T.S. Kuhn have elaborated the case for this viewpoint) as the history of the formation and transformation of paradigms, their confrontation by singular hypotheses arising from some critical experiment or observation, and their dialectical response to the challenge. The fate of the paradigm like the fate of the definition is to be determined by its response to the "counter-example".

It may be observed that our exposition of the character and role of 'paradigms' in philosophical inquiry derives from a *conceptual interpretation* which is at variance with the *linguistic interpretation*. In the one, the burden of discourse rests upon the meanings of concepts and the dialectical relations involved; in the other, the burden of discourse is placed upon the "proper usage" of ordinary language (or, in some cases, a language game). The contrast between the two interpretations could not be starker.[12] I need not restate again as I have stated earlier the case for the 'conceptual turn'. But its relevant methodological consequence must be noted here: In philosophy (no less than in natural science) nothing of substance can be demonstrated by an appeal to ordinary language.

CHAPTER III

Categorial Schema

The 'conceptual turn' in philosophy involves some epistemological and ontological assumptions. These, taken collectively, constitute a categorial schema. The designation 'dialectical realism' is my name for the viewpoint under which this categorial schema is accessed and reconstructed.

§7

Meaning of Dialectical Realism

Dialectical realism represents a movement of thought, in the sense that it consists of an approach in philosophical inquiry rather than a body of doctrines subscribed to by a particular group of thinkers. And yet it is true that a given approach bears some fruits distinct from those of other approaches. And those who take the conceptual turn, and therewith embrace some form of a critical realism, might arrive at different philosophical constructions.

What then is the meaning of 'dialectical realism', and, what are its main hypotheses?

Semantics of Realism

I use the word 'realism', philosophically, in three senses:

$Realism_1$ — that mental acts exist, or, have ontological status.

$Realism_2$ — that the external world exists (in some form) independently of our consciousness.

$Realism_3$ — that the symbolic expressions of scientific/ philosophical language have a denotative function.

And I use the word 'dialectical' (as the qualifier to my 'realism') to indicate: (a) *perspectivism*, i.e., the recognition of the multidimensional character of 'truth' (since a given object X can be seen from an n-number of perspectives); and (b) *dynamism*, i.e., that our paradigms of reality represent but 'degrees of truth' — corresponding to the levels of our cognitive integration.

The dialectical relations between the several senses of realism are noteworthy:

Being a realist in the sense of $Realism_1$ does not entail being a realist in the sense of $Realism_2$, and conversely. But being a realist in the sense of either Realism$_1$, or Realism$_2$, entails being a realist in the sense of Realism$_3$. This, then, is the common bond between these two forms of realism against nominalism. Some philosophers are realists of one kind (blending Realism$_1$ and Realism$_2$); or of another (blending Realism$_2$ and Realism$_3$). They are, strictly speaking, quasi-realists. There are also the naive-realists, who fail to distinguish Realism$_1$ and Realism$_2$. Thus, 'dialectical realism' stands in stark relief against the varieties of naive realism, common-sense realism, and other quasi-realisms.

Realism refers to beings in the world. What does it mean to *be* — to *exist*? Bergmann suggests[1]: to be is to be the referent of a sign in the context of a   significance pattern in the ideal language.   The 'significance pattern' is the   crucial factor: it assigns a place, an ontological status, to the object within our reconstructed picture of the world.

How one defines the 'ontological field' determines the range of entities one may admit into one's world.   Thus, for example, phenomenalists limit their field to include only what is presented to them as phenomena; empiricists include in their field anything that is verifiable or inferable experimentally within the space / time matrix; and pragmatists delimit their field to the functionally meaningful experiences only.   The price one pays for a definition of one's 'ontological field' is none other than the range of reality itself.

An interesting definition of the 'ontological field' is proposed by formalists: they define the range of existence to contain whatever happens to be the values of variables in their formal language. Thus Quine's formula — "To be is to be the value of a bound-variable" — is presumed to determine what he calls the "ontological commitment" of a philosopher. But the question arises: Does this formula mean that whenever the formalist chooses to redesign his language — i.e. adding or eliminating certain symbols in his linguistic repertoire — thereby he conjures into existence hitherto non-entities, or, annihilates existing entities from the ontological field, by a mere stroke of the pen as it were? It might well mean that. It was in this way, e.g., that Goodman elevated two phenomenological hues, among a thousand possible hues, to the status of ideal entities in his "world", by simply coining the words "grue" and "bleen". Formalism then, inevitably and inexorably, leads to nominalism — but of this issue we shall say more later.

'Existence' emerges then, not as a particular attribute, but rather (to use the expression of Reinhardt Grossmann[2]), as a 'substratum of attributes'. Nor to have defined 'existence' is to have disclosed the contents of the 'ontological field'. The presentation of the contents of the field is another issue: the issue is *existence* (which is one) and not *existents* (which are many).

What is presented to me, may be taken as an object *per se*, or it may be taken as 'evidence' for inferring the existence of another object which is not presented to me. Thus, e.g., seeing footprints in the sand, I infer that there must have been an animal that walked there; or, again, if it be evident to me that a person has a given set of symptoms, then I infer that he must have a particular disease. By contrast, in the realm of abstract objects, the inference from what is presented in intuition to what is not presented but is intelligible, is purely logical: Here, given x such that it logically implies y, one may infer that y too must be the case; or, conversely, given y such that it presupposes x for its intelligibility, one may infer that x too must be the case.

In all such cases of inference, an epistemological principle is to be evoked: namely, that if a certain evidence obtains, then (given a set of *a priori* schemata) one may infer (in the absence of counter-evidence) that something else also obtains. And this principle remains *neutral* as to the kind of evidence (or counter-evidence) involved. Thus, in the perspective of 'dialectical realism', *abstract objects* no less than *concrete objects*, may be granted ontological status, or if you please, existence.

Hypothesis of Epistemological Levels

Intentionality — the noetic relation of the mind to the world — appears at first sight to be a simple relation: the directedness of consciousness to an object. Phenomenologists (ever since Franz Brentano) are fond of stressing the primacy of this mental act above all others. And neopositivists (reared in the tradition of the Lockean "mirror theory" of perception) are equally fond of denying its reality. But dialectical realism represents another alternative: it notes the multidimensional character of intentionality.

Consider:

(a) consciousness directed to the phenomenon X

(b) consciousness directed to the concept of the phenomenon X

(c) consciousness directed to the transcendental matrix of the given concept S

Clearly, the objects of intentionality — but also the modes of intentionality (as the different objects *are accessible to* different modes) — are different in each of these cases.

We may, then, distinguish three levels of epistemological inquiry:

(a) phenomenological inquiry: where the phenomenon itself is taken as the object of inquiry;

(b) scientific inquiry: where conceptual constructions (which may explain the phenomena) constitute the object of inquiry;

(c) philosophical inquiry: where metaquestions concerning the conceptual framework of arts and sciences — i.e., their presuppositions and/or implications — are articulated.

(This analysis will recall the analysis of knowledge presented by Professor S. Avaliani who proposes a parallel schema—but with one critical difference: that where he speaks of "prescientific knowledge", or *donaučnoe poznánie*, I speak of "phenomenological knowledge" — in order to allow room for the aesthetic realms of art and literature.[3])

This demonstrates why 'philosophy' represents a third-order inquiry — as we have argued earlier.

Hypothesis of Ontological Strata

The phenomena of integrative wholes (*Gestalten*) recur at various levels of natural processes: they display some properties which their elements do not possess.

How may we explain these phenomena?

The doctrine of reductionism is the classic response to the question: it seeks to explain a given phenomenon ϕ, at a certain level of being, by the conceptual repertoire of a theory θ, corresponding to a lower level of discourse. Thus, e.g., a drop of water (H_2O) is to be defined, reductively, as a "complex gas" ($2H_2 + O_2$) despite its property of liquidity. But reductionism entails an ontological paradox: that two entities, A and B, which are not identical ($A \neq B$), are identical ($A = B$)

nevertheless.

The doctrine of reductionism focuses on the *continuity* of phenomena at the expense of their *discontinuity*. How to account for both aspects without eclipsing either? The *hypothesis of ontological strata* may be evoked as an answer.

This hypothesis — an earlier version of which was articulated by Nicolai Hartmann[4] — may be stated as follows:

(a) That the real world comprises strata such that every being belongs to one stratum at least;

(b) That the higher strata, having emerged from the lower strata, acquire their own special qualities and organizational laws;

(c) That the strata of reality are continuous *from below* but discontinuous *from above*: i.e. the lower strata are "represented" in the higher strata, but the latter are not "reducible" to the former.

This hypothesis explains the possibility (and reality) of the phenomena of emergence — i.e. *Gestaltqualitäten* — and avoids the error of ontological reductionism.

The various natural sciences, then, present pictures of the different levels of reality. One may not say, therefore, that the world-picture of one science is "more real" than that of another. For it would not be valid to argue that the world-picture of one science is "reducible" to that of another. To give but one example: the explanation of the phenomena of color by reference to the wavelengths of the light spectrum constitutes an epistemological correlation *but not* an ontological reduction; i.e. to the shorter waves correspond the blue colors and to the longer waves correspond the red colors, but colors are no "less real" than wavelengths for that reason.

The merit of the hypothesis of ontological strata lies in that it explains the entire range of natural phenomena: from material quanta to psychological gestalten. Its import for the human sciences is especially noteworthy: For, in this light, 'Man' is to be seen as a complex being, representing various levels of reality, a veritable microcosm whose life ranges from mere *existence* to reflective *eksistence*. The reductive (and distorted) images of Man — e.g., the materialist, the behaviorist, or the psychoanalytic images — are to be seen as diverse modes of ontological reductionism representing eclipsed perspectives. The dialectical perspective alone imbues the realm of the psyche — including the aesthetic and moral experiences of man — as the object of inquiry by the human sciences with renewed meaning. This approach will be illustrated in our discussion of the ideal of 'higher humanism', in our handling of the question of the 'meaning of life', and in our critique of modern culture.

§ 8

The Epistemological Triangle

The relations between the three things — World / Mind / Language — may be represented dialectically: the paradigm for this representation I shall call the *epistemological triangle*.

In this paradigm, it will be seen, the Mind plays the central role: on the one hand, the Mind receives from the World its representations; and on the other, it predetermines the character of these representations by a conceptual and interpretational matrix. Too, the Mind articulates its perceptions / thoughts by means of the symbolic system called 'Language', and uses the very same symbols to acquire access to the thoughts of other minds about the World. Thus the Mind neither passively "mirrors" the World (as objective materialism proposes), nor does it merely "dream" the World (as subjective idealism proposes), but rather the Mind forms its picture of the World by conceptual reconstruction.

The epistemological triangle, depicting the implicit relations between World / Mind / Language, may be illustrated as follows:

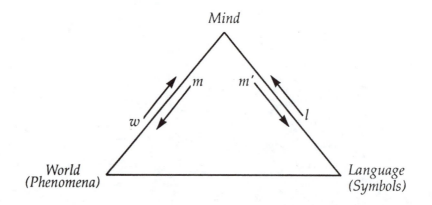

where:

m = conceptual and interpretational matrix

W = empirical content of actual experience: presentation of objects/events

m´ = symbolic expression of mental acts: including thoughts, intentions, concepts, propositions, imagery

l = symbolic presentation of mental/material denotata

Interpretation:

Firstly, the objective presentation of the world is determined by the *a priori* forms of understanding and experience (and we shall say more about this important relation in §11) as well as by an interpretational matrix.

Secondly, to be 'presented' to the mind means to become the object of intention (or a mental act). But, it must be noted, not everything is presented *in the same way*. Some objects are presented in 'perception' (i.e. the prehension of concrete objects in the matrix of space/time); other objects are presented in 'intuition' (i.e. the prehension of abstract objects in the matrix of logical space). One may speak then of the 'modes of presentation', and correspondingly, of the 'modalities of evidence'.

Thirdly, I use the word 'object' philosophically (and not in the ordinary language sense): I refer to 'concrete objects' in the space/time receptacle as well as to 'abstract objects' in logical space.[5]

Concrete objects have the following character: (a) that they represent congeries of qualia, (b) that they represent modalities which undergo change in time, and (c) that they formally belong to types, classes, levels — i.e. that they exemplify logical/dialectical forms. This last point *connects* concrete objects to abstract objects (which are conceptual gestalten).

(I observe, parenthetically, that Russell failed to eliminate the reference to abstract objects in his "theory of description": for the existential proposition of the form '($\exists x$) ϕx' entails the proposition of the form '($\exists \phi$)x $\varepsilon \phi$'; and the latter, asserting that there *is* a character which qualifies a particular, again shifts the reference *from* the existence of the concrete object to the existence of the abstract object.)

The epistemological triangle shows: that thought is epistemologically prior to language.

For *designation* — by which intentionality ties the *idea* to the *symbol* — is the most basic of all semantic relations. It is the original musical note which generates the symphony of language. Language speaks in "sentences", which express *propositions* (thoughts), and the two must not be confused. The same melody can be played by different instruments: in exactly the same manner the same proposition (thought) can be expressed by sentences in different languages.

The mediating role of the Mind, between the World and Language, is evident: it is to be expected, then, that contemporary "cognitive science" — despite its behavioristic underpinnings and despite its dogma of "thinking machines" — should evoke the concepts of "mental models" as explanatory entities.

Yet, Ludwig Wittgenstein writes (*Tractatus*: 5.6): "The limits of my language mean the limits of my world." But language *per se* — the Oxford philosophers notwithstanding — has no direct access to the world. The epistemological triangle demonstrates this by the absence of any arrow between the world and language. Therefore, I write (revising the above proposition radically): *The limits of my thought mean the limits of my world.* For, if language can give us a picture of the world, it is always *through* depicting some thought-picture, indirectly as it were.

The dialectical relations between the World, the Mind, and Language are complex and subtle. In some philosophical systems, one relation is overshadowed by another; in others, one relation is reduced to another. The outcome, in each case, is inevitably an eclipsed worldview.

The 'epistemological triangle' also makes it possible to compare the rival philosophical viewpoints dialectically: given the three categories of world *(W)*, mind *(M)*, and language *(L)*, and their relations *(m/w/m̂/l)*, a set of dialectical possibilities emerge. Then we see that, e.g., phenomenalism confuses M and W; that nominalism confuses L and M; that neopositivism draws a line where it could not be drawn (without the mediation of M) between L and W; *etcetera*. Three eclipsed worlds — representing, nevertheless, three possible worlds. We can reject them, each, on dialectical grounds alone. But it is possible to overcome them, again on dialectical grounds, by radically reconstructing them. The perspective of 'dialectical realism' represents such a reconstruction.

§ 9

"Picture Theory" Revisited

The epistemological triangle assumes some form of the "picture theory" of language. The picture theory, in its classical form, was introduced by Ludwig Wittgenstein. The question before us is: What is living and what is dead in the classical "picture theory"?

Though the "picture theory" was introduced by Wittgenstein in the *Tractatus*, it was abandoned in the *Investigations* subsequently, and replaced by a "game theory" by his epigones. Recently, however, some realist epistemologists have advanced a reconstruction of the "picture theory": I refer to the work of Mario Bunge in particular.[6] It is a version of such a reconstruction that we assume here.

What is *living* in the classical "picture theory" is its central insight: that language derives its meaning from its picturing function, or as we say, its designating function. "A symbol that does not stand for anything," said old Frege, "cometh of evil." And I must add: What a symbol stands for may be any object in the context of our reconstructed picture of the world.

What is *dead* in the classical "picture theory" is its twofold thesis that: (a) there is only *one level* of picturing; and, consequently, (b) that the *logical form* — which is assumed as a condition for the possibility of picturing (since the picture and the pictured must have *something in common* in order for the one to be a picture of the other) — can be *shown* but can never be *articulated*.

Let us recall the memorable passages in the *Tractatus* of Wittgenstein:

> A proposition is a picture of reality: for if I understand the proposition, I know the situation that it represents.
>
> At first sight a proposition — one set out on the printed page, for example — does not seem to be a picture of the reality with which it is concerned. But neither do written notes seem at first sight to be a picture of a piece of music, nor our phonetic notation (the alphabet) to be a picture of our speech.

And yet, these sign languages prove to be pictures, even in the ordinary sense, of what they represent.

A gramophone record, the musical idea, the written notes, and the sound-waves, all stand to one another in the same internal relation of depicting that holds between language and the world.

They are all constructed according to a common logical pattern.[7]

The explanation for these observations is given in the following passage:

There must be something identical in a picture and the pictured, in order that the one be a picture of the other generally . . . What any picture, of whatever form, must have in common with reality, in order to be able to depict it generally — correctly or incorrectly — is the logical form, i.e., the form of reality.[8]

And further:

Propositions cannot represent logical form: it is mirrored in them.

What finds its reflection in language, language cannot represent.

What expresses *itself* in language, *we* cannot express by means *of* language.

What *can* be shown, *cannot* be said.[9]

Yet Wittgenstein's conception of 'truth' requires the idea of 'logical form': "Only by being a picture of reality can a proposition be true or false" (*Tractatus*: prop. 406) — and a proposition can be a picture of reality *only* when it has a *logical form* in common with it. Wittgenstein, while recognizing the epistemological role of 'logical form', did not conceive the possibility of its articulation. The reason for this is clear in retrospect: in his system of logical atomism — wherein all propositions are of equal value — no distinction between *language* and *metalanguage* either could or would be made.

The basic ideas of the reconstructed 'picture theory' may be stated as follows then:

Firstly, that the essence of what is involved in 'picturing' is indicated by the word '*designation*'. Yet, while a symbolic expression derives its meaning from its designation, it is replaceable by another symbolic expression. And, further, the designata may be concrete objects or abstract objects — using the word 'object' philosophically.

Secondly, that the process of 'picturing' occurs at two epistemological levels: once at the level of thought (involving the mind/world relation) and again at the level of language (involving the mind/language relation). To speak/write is (as Wittgenstein would say) to depict pictures; but, insofar as we "make pictures for ourselves", thinking also involves picture making. Moreover, it is thinking which serves as the medium which connects the one picture with the other.

Thirdly, that the picture presents the object, not bare as it were, but in the context of an interpretational matrix.

What is a "picture" then? "A picture is an *interpreted* fact that represents..." writes Erik Stenius, the brilliant commentator on the *Tractatus*, "the *possibility* of their being combined in this way."[10] I, too, understand something like this by a "picture".

The 'picture theory' acquires — in the context of recent realist epistemology — a complex character: Here, by means of a priori schemata, a set of rigid designators, and modal operators of various kinds, a multidimensional system of semantics may be constructed to represent 'reality'.[11]

While *ordinary language* may not be capable of articulating the 'logical form' of the picture—but merely "show" it—the *metalanguage* may articulate the 'logical form'. The result is the recognition of "pictures within pictures", as it were, insofar as a family of concrete pictures may reflect the same abstract form. And the articulation of the 'logical form' results in the formation of 'philosophical pictures'.

The language thus reconstructed is, no longer an "ordinary language" but rather a 'conceptual language' — or (to use Bergmann's expression) an "ideal language". It is a language *about* abstract forms: about concepts/propositions, properties/relations, possibilities and modalities. It is a language in which all genuine philosophical questions and hypotheses can be articulated and examined.

My interest in the 'ideal language' need not preclude my interest in the 'things themselves': on the contrary, I appreciate the reality of the one only through the mode of representation of the other.

Consider a thought-experiment: Suppose I visit a distant island, and I discover an exotic plant there; and suppose a native artist presents me with an elegant watercolor of the same plant. I value the painting — but why? Is it for *what* it depicts, or is it for the *way* it depicts it. A nominalist would answer affirmatively to the second question; and an empiricist would answer affirmatively to the first question. But, dialectically speaking, to answer affirmatively to the second question does not preempt my answering affirmatively to the first question as well. A picture of the world can be philosophically true and yet aesthetically elegant at the same time.

Yvon Gauthier says: *"L'être du langage, c'est encore le langage de l'être"*[12] — yes, provided that we remember that the being of being is independent of the language of being, *even if* (as it may happen) our only access to the experience of being be through language, indirectly as it were. It is therefore, not the usage of language *per se*, but the *meanings* (thoughts) expressed by means of it, that primarily interest us in philosophical inquiry.

There is a convergence between the implications of the picture theory and the epistemological triangle: namely, that thought is *prior* to language. This involves the issue of the possibility of "private language" among other things. To this issue we shall return later.

CHAPTER IV

The Question of Being

Some philosophers build their worldview from the surface downwards — without ever reaching the bedrock of reality. Others seek to build their worldview from the base upwards — starting with the bedrock structures of reality wherein the deeper truths lie. The one group passes lightly over the question of 'being': these are the phenomenalists, the empiricists, and the nominalists. The other group engages the question of 'being' seriously: these are the realists and the essentialists of one kind or another. How does 'dialectical realism' encounter the question of being?

§ 10

Being qua Being

"The latent content of many recent debates in philosophy is ontological," Professor Gustav Bergmann remarked to me in one of the APA congresses, "but their manifest content is seemingly something else." This observation represents a penetrating insight into the "depth psychology" of contemporary philosophical inquiry. And I shall attempt to cast some light, from the perspective of dialectical realism, upon this dark region.

Our inquiry, then, is *ontological* and not *ontic* merely. The one involves the transcendental exposition of the object X (i.e. what must be the case for it to be the case); the other involves the phenomenological exposition of the object X (i.e. what is the case as it is given). Nor shall we mistake the "furniture of the world" (Russell's facile expression) for the 'form of the world'. And far be it from us to confuse (à la Sartre) the two issues: namely, the issue of the 'being of phenomena' and the issue of 'being qua being'.

The question of 'being qua being' was already posed by Aristotle, in the *Metaphysica*, where he depicted the multiple meanings of 'being' in the following passage:

> .. the unspecified term 'being' has many senses, one of which is being by accident, another is that which is true (and nonbeing is that which is false), and besides these senses there are the various categories (e.g., whatness, quality, quantity, whereness, whenness, and similarly any other meaning which the term may have), and in addition to these there is potential being and also actual being — since 'being', then, has many senses . . .1

We know that Aristotle ultimately identified the 'being' of a thing with the 'essence' of a thing. How this conception of 'being' is to be reconciled with the multiple senses of 'being' — therein lies the whole problem of Aristotelian ontology. We shall not discuss this issue here — nor comment on the passage quoted above — as these matters have been discussed by Franz Brentano and others.2 Our interest lies, rather, in the dialectical response to this approach to the question of 'being'.

The deep impression left on the young Heidegger, upon reading Brentano's commentary on Aristotle's doctrine of being, is known to everyone who is interested in these matters. And yet Heidegger's approach to the question of 'being' is markedly different from Aristotle's approach. For Heidegger is primarily concerned with 'being' *qua* being (and only secondarily qua essence): i.e. being as the *ground* of beings. Hence, Heidegger raises the question of being — *What is it, to be?* — anew: "Do we in our time have answer to the question of what we really mean by the word 'being'?" — he asks[3] — and accuses contemporary philosophy for having 'forgotten' this fundamental question.

The Heideggerian inquiry is twofold: (a) it questions the "a priori conditions" of the 'being of man' (*Dasein*) in the world; and (b) it questions the grounding of beings in 'Being' (*Sein*). It is thus an inquiry into the 'ground' (*Grund*), and not merely the 'origin' (*Ursprung*) of beings. Hence all categories, including space and time as the matrix of beings — topology and chronology of being as it were — become the components of the one meta-category of 'Being'.

But how can one have philosophical access to "Being"?

Heidegger answers: through the examination and interrogation of 'beings' which have *their being* in 'Being'. Specifically, through the interrogation (and self-interrogation) of *Dasein*, which represents the only being which harbors "the thought of" Being, and which can articulate the meaning of his 'being'. He is to be "questioned" as regards Being. "Thus to work out the question of Being adequately, we must make an entity — the inquirer — transparent in his own being..." writes Heidegger, "This entity which each of us is himself, and which includes inquiring as one of the possibilities of its Being, we shall denote by the term '*Dasein*'."[4] Thus Heidegger, in a circuitous way, approaches the central problem of ontology *through* phenomenology.

But is there no circularity in this approach, i.e., to interrogate a being (*Dasein*), as to the character of Being (*Sein*), while assuming beforehand its own being as a being? Indeed, the very question of being — "What is it, to be?" — could not even be asked without assuming that we already know the meaning of the '*is*' in its ontological sense. Yet Heidegger seems to believe that the epistemological circularity is negligible. The *Dasein*, which is to be interrogated as to the meaning of being, is already the harbinger of the "thought of Being", and can articulate his relation to Being. *Dasein* subsists in *Sein*: Man's living-world represents a philosophical index to Being. Hence the phenomenological program of the elucidation of the relation of *Dasein* to *Sein*, in the context of spatiality and temporality, and of the modes of his being — self-being (*Selbstsein*) and being-with (*Mitsein*), authentic existence and inauthentic existence — constitute the prolegomena to the question of Being.

Yet the interrogation of "Dasein" concerning the meaning of "Sein" results (in the work of Heidegger) more in the understanding of the *conditio humane* than in the understanding of *being qua being* — perhaps because he never really wrote the sequel to his magnum opus — though it provides an oblique approach to Being.

More recently, Augustin Basave has magnified the question of 'Being' as the great metaphysical question of our time: the question of *being qua being* purely. It has been resurrected, as it were, as the question concerning *arxé pánton* (origin of everything), which had haunted the early natural philosophers of Ancient Greece, and which haunts us still. But the meta-category which Basave evokes in answering this question is strikingly different from that of Heidegger. 'Habencia' — which echoes the *Apeiron* of Anaximander — appears at first sight to be analogous to 'Being'. But the range of 'Habencia' is presumably *wider* than the range of 'Being'.

What does 'Habencia' mean?

The neologism *'Habencia'* derives from the verb *haber* (whose irregular form *hay* refers to being as a generic term, *there-isness*, harboring complex connotations, yet itself remaining neutral, like the French *il y a*) whose meaning is to be distinguished from those of the related verbs, *ser* (to be in the existential sense: e.g. "He *is* a man") and *estar* (*to be* in a modal sense: e.g. "He *is* sad") in the Spanish language.

"Because *haber* is semantically so poor, I see the need to improvise the noun *habencia* — whose meaning approximates the Castelian expression *lo habido y por haber* (what there is and what there is to come) — to indicate *the totality of what there is...*" writes Basave, "And the *habencia* is not only the horizon but also the light by which we see the entities (beings) illuminated by the *hay* (there-isness)."[5]

Presumably, 'Habencia' represents the ontological matrix for the existence of beings in *all* possible worlds — including the being of beings that no longer are, but once were, or beings that are not yet, but might be at a future point of existence. Thus, within the range of 'Habencia' the boundaries between being and nonbeing seem to dissolve. Everything lies on the horizon of 'Habencia' — from zero to infinity (including both the class of entities and the class of non-entities) — for 'Habencia' represents the very "web of existence". And Basave takes pains to elucidate the regions, the dynamics, and the hermeneutics of 'Habencia' — bringing out its spiritual significance for human existence.

In this metaphysical system, "God" appears but as a tiny spider, perched on a specific point on the "web of existence", which he has wittingly woven. Somewhat perplexed by this philosophical vision, I asked Professor Basave (in a conversation during the XVIIth World Congress of Philosophy in Montreal 1983) as to his philosophical motive for proposing the category of 'Habencia' as a substitute for the category of 'Being'. He explained: "Since I could not derive the 'All' from 'Being', I sought to reverse the relation, and derived 'Being' from the 'All'". It is admirable how this metaphysics of existence reintroduces the ideal of pantheism implicit in the phenomenology of beings/nonbeings.

Yet the 'All' is problematic here. Evidently it does not signify the universal quantifier (∀) with its delimited range. Nor does it denote the range of phenomenological 'beings' whose ground 'Being' is, as that would render the inquiry *ontic* rather than *ontological*. Rather it signifies the web of existence entire: including both 'beings' and 'nonbeings'.

'Nonbeing' is, dialectically, the anti-category of 'Being'. If 'Being' represents the realm of the possible (and hence the actual as well), then 'Nonbeing' must represent the realm of the non-possible (and hence the non-actual as well). One may speak, then, of the 'nonbeing of the object X', *as the negation of the existence of* a particular being at a given point of the ontological field. But speaking of the nonbeing of a particular entity is *not* speaking of 'Nonbeing' *per se*. 'Negation' (and the negation of the negation) represents a dialectical relation between the modalities of the being and the nonbeing of an object.

An object may exist in one modality and not in another; and the 'negation' delineates the one from the other.

Even if we grant that the range of 'Existence' transcends that of 'Being', since it encompasses 'Nonbeing', the category of 'Being' still remains the basic ontological category. On this basic point the realist philosophers would agree. The disagreement arises over the relation between 'being' and 'being presented'. Some philosophers seek to eliminate the distinction — thereby hoping to eliminate the thorny problem of 'representation' — in order to acquire access to 'Being' directly.

Josef Seifert, in a remarkably original phenomenological study, argues for a return to "things in themselves" as an effort to attain access to being *qua* being.[6] The great merit of Seifert's inquiry lies in that he (unlike Husserl and others) rejects the prescinding of *existence* from *essence* and demonstrates their inseparability in the *being* of "things themselves". Thereby any absurd claim that the one might "precede" the other — (a claim that Sartre was to make and some existentialists still make) — is shown to be meaningless. Also the phenomenological crisis, occasioned by the debut of the *epoché* and its attendant modes of eidetic reduction, is overcome in the context of a critical methodology which involves both eidetic and conceptual analyses of the world of experience. This I take to be the starting point of the realist phenomenology.

Seifert then formulates the question of being as follows: "In our knowledge, do we also discover besides the appearances and constituted aspects of things, 'things in themselves', i.e., entities, essential structures and laws (*Wesenheiten und Wesengesetze*), and existents, which are in no way constituted by human consciousness?"[7]

Implicit already in this formulation of the question of being is a redefinition of *noumena* (things in themselves) as intelligible objects of human knowledge. It appears that, from the very start, Seifert departs radically from the Kantian conception of the *noumena as* objects of the unknowable realm of being. But does this radical departure really mean a negation of the unknowable noumenon (as Kant conceived it) or simply the introduction of a transphenomenal realm, as a middle realm between those of the phenomena and the noumena as it were, a realm which is conceptually accessible to human knowledge? I suspect it is the latter. And, if that were so, the apparent contradiction between the transcendental philosophy of Kant and the claims of realist phenomenology, over the question of being, would be reducible to a semantic issue.

The question remains however: Would not the knowledge of this middle realm (the transphenomenal realm) be still conditioned by our mental schemata?

Seifert writes: "The proper understanding of a given being 'in itself' is in all cases an indispensable, if not the most central, part of knowing a being."[8] And we note that the expression "in itself" is used here in a sense other than that intended by Kant. What are then these "things in themselves" which (for Seifert and his colleagues) constitute the objects of knowledge? They are: (a) the true essence of things, as they are, grasped by the intentional act without the intervention of opinion and/or language; and hence (b) the real objects which exist uncreated and unshaped by our consciousness. The realm of noemata is expanded, beyond the range of traditional phenomenology, by the addition of these objects.

This conception of 'real things', or "things in themselves" as it were, assumes the postulate of classical empiricism: namely, that the mind can "mirror" reality and that the light of consciousness, under which objects are apprehended, does not affect their character in the least degree. This assumption, however, is no longer acceptable from the perspective of dialectical realism. It is unacceptable because the primary epistemological question — the question which Kant formulated more boldly than anyone before or after — remains unanswered: i.e. Can we claim that we can have any knowledge of objects in the real world *without* the mediation of our consciousness and *without* their being conditioned by our modes of understanding? And the answer to this question —if we understand the epistemological problematik of 'being' and 'being presented' (a problematik which has been empirically substantiated by the discoveries of Gestalt Psychology recently) — is decidedly "No". Consequently, any philosophical theory which places the burden of "reality" entirely upon the object (as ordinary empiricism would) or entirely upon the subject (as subjective idealism would) would be, on dialectical grounds, unacceptable.

Granted that there are objects in the world which are not *constituted* by human consciousness; but I disagree that there are any known objects, actual or possible, which are not *conditioned* by human consciousness.

The phenomena/noumena dichotomy was Kant's ingenious way of handling the question of being. He evoked the noumena in order to explain (in the ontological sense) the being of phenomena, and assure their objectivity, while the being of noumena itself remained a dark mystery. Nevertheless, this grounding of "things" in "things in themselves" rendered them intelligible — providing an early answer to the Heideggerian question, "Why is there something rather than nothing?" And the noumena remained a bare intuition of Being. For the two senses of noumena (as distinguished by Kant himself in the *Kritik der reinen Vernunft*: B307), the negative sense (the Unknown) and the positive sense (the Ground), blended into one being. I have explained this central point in detail elsewhere.[9]

The concern of Professor Seifert — expressed in the aforementioned work and in his correspondence with this author[10] — may be expressed in this way: that the entire project of philosophy, as a rational understanding of reality in its objective and subjective aspects, requires the recognition of "things in themselves". The issue is *where* to place the "things in themselves". He places them *in medias res*, as it were, and even speaks of "phenomenology as noumenology". I place them (à la Kant) in the unknowable realm of noumena. And what he calls "things in themselves" I call "transphenomenal objects". For I see the "real thing" as a *doppelgänger* whose phenomenal structure is determined by its transphenomenal metastructure. The difference between us, in a word, is that whereas he recognizes only two realms of reality, I recognize three: the phenomena, the transphenomena, and the noumena. I retain the three realms for dialectical reasons. Nor do I abandon the belief in the limitation of human understanding: beyond which lies the realm of the Unknown and the unknowable —the very limit of philosophy — with all its aesthetic and spiritual significance for human life.

Even conceptual knowledge has its limitations. "What has not being cannot be categorized" — that is Grossmann's thesis[11] — against the Meinongian mixed world of 'beings and nonbeings'. And yet we must acknowledge the category of Nonbeing — as the negation of Being. Evidently Grossmann does not subscribe to the view that non-existing objects — e.g. Pegasus or Golden Mountain —

too can have properties which render them susceptible to philosophical handling. And this evokes the question, "What is a real thing?", to which we shall return presently.

Or, as Jeanne Hersch — in her penetrating commentary on the ontology of Karl Jaspers in the Congrès Mondial de Philosophie (Montréal) — stated: *"La pensée s'engage dans l'objectivité, mais elle doit l'evacuer au fur et à mesure afin de suggérer ce par quoi la réalité objective est."*[12] — the thought may engage itself in pursuit of objectivity, but it needs to disengage itself eventually in order to inquire what objective reality is.

The issue decidedly is 'is': What does it mean to 'be', to exist really, instead of being a phantom?

To be, we say, means to have ontological status, to occupy a locus in the ontological field as it were. And one's ontological field would be defined by one's ideal language. To be is to be the designatum of a symbol in the ideal language *in the context of* a significance pattern. (This Bergmannian version represents an improvement over the Quinean version). 'Existence', thus defined, retains an open range: including both actual/possible as well as concrete/abstract objects. The beauty of the open range is that it enables us to speak of the modalities of Being in dialectical terms.

§ 11

A Priori Forms of Experience

Some truths are deeper than other truths: they provide the rationale for other truths. Truths pertaining to *a priori* forms and categories are of this kind. However, to obtain access to them, we must take the transcendental turn.

Taking the 'transcendental turn' means transforming our knowledge of the world from a state of unreconstructed presuppositions to a state of reconstructed grounding. Here the basic epistemological question is: What *can* be given — instead of what *is* given merely? This question leads, inevitably, to ontology; and the central question of ontology is: What is the categorial structure of the real world? The answer to the epistemological question (concerning the *a priori* forms of experience) prepares the way for an answer to the ontological question. This is the dialectical connection between the two.

We are concerned here — besides the question of the *a priori forms* — with the very *intelligibility* of the world of experience. Ironically, empiricism — which calls itself the "philosophy of experience" — cannot explain, *on empirical grounds,* either the intelligibility of experience or the possibility of empirical knowledge. Let us see why this is the case — and why it could not be otherwise.

The only certain knowledge of an object — beyond the series of momentary impressions presented as the immediate data of consciousness — consists of the reconstructed *concept of the object.* If we grant that the experience of the phenomenon (φ) and the belief (S) concerning it are two distinct mental acts, then we must observe: that the former may *occasion* the latter, but it does not follow that the latter *mirrors* the former merely. One could imagine a species of thinking beings, from another planet, whose experiences of phenomena are like ours, but whose conceptual belief systems are at variance with ours; and yet they may claim an 'empirical knowledge' of *their* world as veridically as we claim an 'empirical knowledge' of *our* world. The epistemological problem, then, is: not to justify the experience of the phenomenon (φ), which is immediately presented in both cases, but to justify the belief system (S) concerning that experience.

Empiricism — as a belief-system about empirical beliefs — assumes that empirical knowledge presents a "true picture" of the world. This belief, in itself, represents a meta-empirical claim. And the dialectic of the case may be depicted in this way: Any set of beliefs about empirical beliefs has to be either empirical or non-empirical. If these meta-beliefs are empirical, then they themselves require an empirical grounding and justification; and that would amount to claiming that a given body of empirical beliefs is to be assigned the role of an unjustified justifier of knowledge. And if the meta-beliefs, concerning the adequacy of empirical knowledge, be non-empirical, then one must evoke transcendental arguments (and *a priori forms*), something which critical empiricists wish by all means to avoid.

The critical empiricist must then face the problem of the criterion of the adequacy of empirical knowledge again. Some respond by evoking the pragmatic argument. Thus, e.g., Van Fraassen writes: "To accept one theory rather than another one involves also a commitment to a research program . . ."; and this presumably explains "why, to some extent, adherents of a theory must talk *as if* they believed it to be true . . ."; for "commitment to a theory involves high stakes" (pragmatically speaking).[13] But a "commitment" does not represent an epistemological argument; it only represents an epistemological stance. And the question of the *explanation* of the adequacy of the given empirical stance remains. And Van Fraassen, in a desperate final move, questions the very meaning of the concept of 'explanation', proposing a convenient redefinition (à la Oxford): to ask for 'explanation', he suggests, is to ask for "more information" and nothing else. But such a superficial interpretation of 'explanation' results in the *mere* substitution of one set of empirical evidence for another. It leaves the problem of the adequacy of empirical knowledge, as a whole, unanswered.

More recently, Professor Bonjour has raised the question of the philosophical self-sufficiency of empiricism. Nor does Bonjour question the verifiability of empirical beliefs, *per se*, but rather their epistemological justifiability. He writes: " . . . the essential startingpoint for epistemological investigation is the *presumption* that the believer has a certain belief, the issue being whether or not the belief thus presumed to exist is justified, but the very existence of the belief being taken for granted in the context of the epistemological inquiry . . . "[14] Empiricism, he notes correctly, cannot rightfully evoke *a priori* grounds; and for it to evoke the immediate presentations would be to beg the question over again.

Left to its own devices, then, empiricism sinks deeper and deeper into the quagmire of its own *doxastic presumption* — the presumption that a first-order system of beliefs is self-sufficient as to its meaning and adequacy — until it is inevitably challenged by radical skepticism. And then, the dialectical demise of empiricism (and of its worldview) becomes inevitable: like a caterpillar, which begins and finishes by devouring the flat leaf upon which it rests, it is finally hurled into the abyss of uncertainty and epistemological nihilism. To this dialectic I attribute the recent epidemics of "irrationalism" in the literature of the philosophy of science. However, it would be a gross misunderstanding to take the failure of empiricism to mean the failure of natural science. For natural science may have a conceptual foundation far more certain and objective than any empirical philosophy could provide.

The dilemma of empiricism is evident: *either* it must remain without philosophical justification (since empirical knowledge cannot be justified on empirical grounds) or it must be possible to justify empirical knowledge on meta-empirical grounds. I argue that the latter is the case: for, although *a priori* forms remain inaccessible at the level of empirical discourse, they are accessible in the context of a meta-empirical discourse.

If the only possible justification of empirical knowledge rests in *a priori* forms, then the *a priori* forms may be said to constitute the theoretical scaffolding of our picture of the world. And if the *a priori* forms constitute the metastructure of our picture of the world, then the experience of phenomena would remain ultimately unintelligible without their transcendental matrix. 'Ontology' — as the metascience of 'being qua being' — must be able to demonstrate this basic truth and not merely assume it. And such a demonstration is possible only by taking the 'transcendental turn'.

I will present the basic argument for the 'transcendental turn' —

an argument which represents my reconstruction of the original Kantian argument — as follows:[15]

P1 Of all that is imaginable and conceivable to human understanding the *a priori forms* (i.e. the principles of pure understanding) must be valid.

P2 All experience of the world must be both imaginable and conceivable to human understanding. (i.e. No experience can be regarded as being meaningful unless it were imaginable and conceivable to human understanding.)

P3 Therefore, of all experience of the world the *a priori forms* must be valid.

The only restriction applicable to the claim of this argument is that the *a priori* forms (the principles of pure understanding) pertain to the world of phenomena (as given in our experience) and not to the world of things-in-themselves (apart from our experience).

When Kant took the 'transcendental turn' — after the initial trepidation and deep reflection in response to the skeptical challenge of Hume — he prepared the way for the critique of empirical knowledge. And when he asked the critical question — "How are synthetic propositions *a priori possible?*" (a question he took to be the main problem of the *Critique of Pure Reason*)[16] — he thereby opened a new realm of forms for investigation. I interpret Kant's question to mean: *How is the a priori knowledge of the form of the world possible?* And, since synthetic propositions *a priori* alone can depict the form of the world, their own possibility is also in question. Kant argues that they derive their possibility (and their truth), not from any strictly *logical necessity* (where their negation would involve contradiction), but from a deeper *transcendental necessity* (since their negation would involve an unintelligible and unimaginable state of affairs in the world). 'Unintelligible' and 'unimaginable' — that is, falling outside the objective framework of understanding and not merely outside the subjective understanding of any particular observer.

Consider three examples of synthetic *a priori* propositions:

(a) Every experience belongs to an observer.

(b) $(aRb) \cdot (bRc) \rightarrow (aRc)$

(c) Every phenomenon has a cause.

The ontological import of these propositions is evident: namely, that the world, as we experience it and as it can be the object of our possible experience, has and must have such a structure. The truth of (a) is presupposed by the possibility of any observer's knowledge-claim; the truth of (b) depicts a general condition for the relations between certain qualia; and the truth of (c) is assumed by the empirical knowledge of any interaction between phenomena, unless we are to confuse the succession of phenomena with phenomenon of succession. Whether one reads these propositions as representing "categorial truths" (as did Kant), or as representing "dimensional truths" (as Bergmann does), it is a semantic issue.[17] The point is that, to speak of a world without such an *a priori* structure, would be unintelligible and unimaginable.

Nor did Kant presume that the categorial truths expressed by this special class of propositions must reflect the form of the world *in-itself* but only the form of the world *as experienced* by us. He drew a stark line, between the *noumena* (the things in themselves) and the *phenomena*. Is the noumenon, then, anything but 'being qua being'? We must remember that there are two senses of the concept 'noumenon' in Kantian philosophy: the noumenon as a "transcendental object" of our thought (a positive sense), and the noumenon as a "bare object" of non-sensible intuition (a negative sense).[18] But even though an object may be "bare", from the standpoint of our *understanding,* it may still not be empty from the standpoint of *being*. Accordingly (and on this point I disagree with some commentators) the positive and the negative sense of the 'noumenon' appear to be complementary.

Since the *a priori* forms and the categories depict the metastructure of the world of experience, they represent the 'modes of being' accessible to our understanding. Hence, to inquire into the categories of being, and to elucidate the principles of categorial order, would be to describe the *a priori* 'structure of the world'. Here, then, we make the transition from *epistemology* to *ontology* proper: and here, too, we leave Kant and turn to the contribution of Nicolai Hartmann to this issue.

Nicolai Hartmann has constructed a "Table of Categories" (whose repertoire includes the four main Kantian categories) comprising twelve pairs of categories laid out in dialectical arrangement as following:[19]

Principle — Concretum	Unity — Multiplicity
Structure — Mode	Concord — Conflict
Form — Matter	Antinomy — Dimension
Inner — Outer	Discreteness — Continuity
Determination — Dependence	Structure—Relation
Quality — Quantity	Element — System

Such a table of categories is to be taken (as indeed Hartmann himself took it), not as a dogmatic doctrine, but as a preliminary "rhapsody of being". It presents a working schema, as it were, laying out the bare bones of the "categorial structure" of the world. For one must inquire, beyond this, into the dynamics of the "categorial order". And, on this point, Hartmann goes beyond Aristotle and Kant, elucidating some general principles concerning the *relations* between the categorial strata of being:[20]

(a) the *principle of import:* categories are, what they are, only as principles of something; they are not without their concreta, as the latter are not intelligible without the former.

(b) the *principles of coherence:* categories do not stand alone by themselves, but only in the assemblage of categorial strata; they are therewith interrelated and mutually defined.

(c) the *principle of stratification:* the categories of the lower strata recur in the higher strata, but not conversely.

(d) the *principle of dependency:* dependence is only unilateral, as that of the higher categories upon the lower; but it is a purely partial dependence, it allows the relatively autonomous higher categories a wide latitude.

The relations between the categories of being are as important as the categories themselves. For the categories do not stand as isolated entities, but interweave in the complex structure of reality. We think of lines, representing different dimensions, criss-crossing on the curved surface of a sphere: then numerous points of intersection are created. And that is how the "modalities of being" are generated. Dialectically speaking: No real mode is neutral with respect to any other.

The real world, as seen from the perspective of its dialectical structure, displays a double aspect: It represents a realm of distinct *strata* and *regions* of being; and it represents a sphere of *pervasive interdependence.* Nor are these categories "reducible" to each other.

'Reductionism' is the theory which projects the arbitrary contraction of the range of some categories and the expansion of others — i.e. an infringement of categorial boundaries for the sake of epistemological simplicity — resulting in a distorted ontology.

There is, however, another kind of reduction — which is far more problematic dialectically speaking — namely: the reduction of the 'world' and 'mind' to each other. The question, stated in the terminology of the present discourse, is: Are these categories *in the mind* as preexisting moulds into which the stream of pure experience is poured and shaped thereby, or, are these 'categories' *in the world* as the structural matrix of all possible objects?

This question evokes the dialectical interplay between epistemology and ontology — the last great theme of any serious realism. On the one hand, every being, insofar as it presents a possible object of knowledge for me, remains suspended in the medium of my consciousness (like a pigment particle in a jar of oil), so that every socalled material object is already a mental object. On the other hand, consciousness itself (*Bewusstsein*), already contains an intentional reference to being (*Sein*), so that *to be conscious* is already *to be conscious*-of a being.

Does being, then, *occasion* the thought of being, or, is being *evoked* by the being of thought?

For one can argue dialectically: that epistemology itself is, in the last analysis, but the ontology of the knowing-process; and, at the same time, that we know nothing of ontology (including the ontology of the knowing-process) without assuming an epistemological matrix of knowing.

"There are *a priori* conditions of human knowledge certainly," writes a philosophical colleague, "but there are also a priori conditions of the modes of being, without which human knowledge would be hardly possible."[21] Perhaps. But the question, how to give each its proper due, remains.

My fundamental hypothesis is therefore: *that being awakens consciousness, and the awakened consciousness then shapes being.*

The dialectical answer to the question stresses the *relation* between the two dimensions rather than the dimensions taken separately. What does this mean precisely? It means that (ontologically speaking) being precedes consciousness and its thought of being; but that (epistemologically speaking) consciousness determines the form in which it will encounter being.

§ 12

What is a Real Thing?

How may the question, "What is real thing?", be answered from the perspective of dialectical realism? We must evoke the categories of the actual and the possible, and their interplay, in order to elucidate the 'real thing' in the world dialectically. This will present the 'real thing' as a *doppelgänger* — as a blending of two realms of being as it were.

Dialectical Elucidation of the 'Real Thing'

I see a black spot.

It is my afterimage; and, after a while, it fades away. I know I have not seen this particular spot before; and also that I will probably never see it again. I know, too, that this spot could not have been seen by anyone else.

Was this spot a 'real thing'?

Consider, by constrast, the building I call my house. I designed it, and prepared a blue-print that could be read by everyone, and hired workers to build it. It has been there for several years, and it will continue to be there for years to come; and, not only I, but others as well see it (giving me visible evidence that they do). No one (excepting, perhaps, a philosophical skeptic of Humean genre) doubts its being a 'real thing'.

An object is 'real', we say, if (and only if) it occupies a locus in the ontological field. The ephemeral spot in my phenomenological spectrum, and the solid building on my land, both have a status in the ontological field. Both are 'real', in this sense, their striking differences notwithstanding. This is the preliminary eludication of the concept of a 'real thing'.

And then we look at the building again: we see that it is not one thing but really two things. As *this* particular building it has a *structure,* a gestalt, reflecting its blue-print. But as *a* building, in space, it has a *metastructure,* a geometrical matrix *without* which it could not have been intelligible as a possible structure. Something similar may be said of the black spot I call my afterimage — though, to be sure, there are some critical differences between the two things.

The dialectic of the concept of 'reality' is, then, twofold: firstly, it represents (at the intuitive level) the *structure* of the things; and secondly, it represents (at the transcendental level) the *metastructure* of things: i.e. the invariant matrix of their possibility. Call these two concepts Reality$_1$ and Reality$_2$. The relations between the two levels of reality will become clear presently.

However, not every object need necessarily be presented in order to be, nor be necessarily as it is *presented* — and only a naive realist would take exception to this critical proposition.

'Naive realism' is the view that takes things to be as they appear — a view which leads to phenomenalism as its consequence. As an illustration of the fallacy of phenomenalism, consider the following case (suggested by H. Heidelberger): A man perceives an object to be yellow, and he also sees a yellow light shining upon that object; but he remembers having perceived the same object sometime ago as being white, and that at that time there was no colored light shining upon the object. It would not, then, be reasonable for him to believe that the color of the object is what it appears to him to be. Merely from the fact that one perceives something to have a given property, it does not follow that it has that property in reality; for one may have access to other evidence which might correct the illusory evidence of a momentary perception.[22] Yet, it must be borne in mind that phenomenal properties, even if they are assumed to "adhere" in objects, are conditioned by our perceptual framework.

In an early treatise on epistemology, I wrote these lines, which are relevant here:

> Experimental science has demonstrated that there are colors in nature that we never see, and that there are sounds that we never hear. Our color perception is confined to the range of 20-20,000 cps. We never see the ultraviolet and the infrared hues (and we must see Röntgen rays in the dark with dark-adapted eyes); nor do we hear the cries of travelling bats at night. The world, as it appears without colors to the lowly crab, or with a displaced color spectrum to the tiny bee, or with an extraordinary rich

sensory experience to the dog, is not the world that appears to us, and could never be, being precluded by our a priori framework of perception. We are spectators this side of the epistemological screen, as it were, and feel but a fleeting phase of phenomena presumably representing the external world.[23]

It is evident, then, that 'being' and 'being presented' are far from being one — and this disposes of the theses of phenomenalism and naive realism.

(I will not even discuss the doctrine of *esse est percipi* (Berkeley) accordingly. That it presents a *non sequitur* should be evident: If 'to be' is 'to be perceived', then 'not to be perceived' is 'not to be'. But, from the absence *of the presentation of* the object X, one cannot logically infer the absence of X *in the ontological field*. And, further, the doctrine rests on the unwarranted assumption that the category of 'being' is not more extensive in its range than the category of 'sensible': i.e. denying the existence of other objects which may be knowable through other modes of presentation. And Berkeley's hidden theological motive for this anti-realist thesis adds insult to injury.)

A Bergmannian Analysis of the 'Real Thing'

A 'real object' represents an *occasion* in the transition of a possible state into an actual state. It remains, as it were, suspended in the matrix of existence. What, then, is the character of a 'real object' — i.e. what does its invariant structure consist of? We now have an 'epistemological lens' — thanks to Bergmann[24] — through which we may inspect the invariant structure of real objects.

Let us look through the Bergmannian lens at a single dot in the spectrum of existence:

I see a black spot.

There are three things here: (a) a bare particular (the spot), (b) its property (black color), and (c) the relation (nexus) by which the particular is "tied" to the property.

That the particular and its property are "tied" is evident, directly, as a self-presenting phenomenon. The question is: Do I, through my act of perception, connect the particular and its property; or, are these presented to me as interconnected already? The phenomenon must be grounded ontologically. There are two alternatives: either the ground lies in me (the observer) or it lies in what I observe (the object). Bergmann takes the latter alternative. And this he does on the assumptions that: firstly, what is presented must (in some form) exist; and secondly, a relation represents an internal affair inherent in the structure of the thing.

In what sense are relations, then, 'inherent' in their relata?

When some entities appear to be related to others, then this possibility must have a structural basis in the entities themselves. Hence (according to Bergmann) form determines function — ontologically speaking. Consider two musical notes: we say that C is higher than E (in a certain context). Therewith we are presented with five entities: two particulars (notes), two pitches (properties), and a second-order relation (higher-than). The apparent form (C > E) is a function of the relation; and the relation is to be grounded internally, i.e., in the character of the notes. Change the character of the notes, and their relations to each other would also change. That is what is meant by saying that relations are 'inherent' in the character of their relata.

We are committed, in the context of this ontology, to the recognition of 'bare particulars'. A particular is 'bare' in the sense that no property is inherent in it, but can only be exemplified by it: any particular would "wear" or "unwear" any property as it were. Yet — as Bergmann observes — "all individuals presented are qualitied; all characters presented are exemplified; (while) things never stand alone."[25]

Things never stand alone: then we must see them as aggregates of one kind or another.

Seeing things as 'aggregates', which are susceptible of groupings, involves the recognition of classes. Classes and functions represent higher categories—with ontological status of their own — as they provide the matrix for lower entities. Concrete collections of entities represent extensions of classes and not their essences. Thus the Bergmannian world contains levels of integration — and levels of necessity among logical forms. E.g. while it is analytically true that the spot X is either green or red allover, it is categorically impossible that a particular should 'exemplify' another particular, though both say something about the world.

How meticulously Bergmann distinguishes a *'thing'* from a *'fact'* is illustrated in the following passage:

> Ontologists do not just either catalogue or classify what exists. Rather, they search for 'simples' of which everything that exists 'consists'. These simples, and nothing else, they hold to 'exist', or to be the only existents... If, for instance, the tones in a symphony were simples, they would 'exist'; the symphony, though of course it exists, would not 'exist'... What is 'simple' is so simple indeed, that in speaking about it (directly), the best or the most one can do is to name it, that is, attach a label to it (though not necessarily, as we saw, a mere label). We may and do call an entity a thing and say that it exists even though, in a certain ontology, it may not be a 'thing' and therefore not 'exist'. As for 'thing', so for 'fact'. We naturally call what a sentence refers to a fact (state of affairs) and, if the sentence is true, say that it exists. But again, in a certain ontology it may not be a 'fact' and therefore not 'exist'. An ontologist unaware of the ambiguity is likely to get into trouble.[26]

Does Bergmann mean, then, to imply that the 'nature of things' is to be conceived on the basis of an *a priori* model of an 'ideal language'? Yes — with the provision that it be understood that this language, which contains designators which tie it to the world of 'real objects', also provides a "significance pattern" which gives us a "picture of the world". Further, the *a priori* form of the 'ideal language', which represents the 'logical form' of the world, is to be ontologically grounded. This last point underlines the *realism* in Bergmann's ontology.

Such is the Bergmannian analysis, then, of a 'real thing' in the web of existence. It answers to the Bergmannian question: "What are the (real) constituents of an ordinary thing?" He assumes (as we must also) that some entities exist *in* others as parts within wholes. And this demonstrable assumption constitutes the cornerstone of his "complex ontology". The philosophical merit of this ontology, beyond its formal complexity, lies in its explanatory power. And, by this criterion, the Bergmannian schema succeeds where others have failed recently.

Let us now set aside the Bergmannian lens — and turn to look at the genesis of the 'real thing' in the light of the dialectic of its structure and metastructure.

Dialectical Relation of Actuality and Possibility

Let us return to the character of the 'real thing' as a *doppelgänger:* i.e. as a blending of two dimensions — possibility and actuality — abstract metastructure and concrete structure.

When things occur and change, it must have been possible for them beforehand — as Aristotle observed in the *Metaphysica* already — otherwise nothing could actually occur or change. But the occurrence and changing of actual things take place in the matrix of space and time. And 'space' and 'time' themselves may be defined as the modes of possibility. Indeed, this is how Leibniz did define them: "For *space* is nothing but the order of existence of things possible at the same time, while *time* is the order of existence of things possible successively."[27] Thus the very receptacle of actuality, i.e. space and time, represent but two categories of possibility. And even though we may not agree with Leibniz, that "actual things are nothing but the best of possibles",[28] we must agree that there can be no *actualia* which were not prefigured in *possibilia*.

What is 'possibility' then?

We may distinguish from the outset — and apart from the empirical notions of possibility (probability, etc.) — two forms of 'ideal possibility': (a) *logical possibility* (where X is possible in the context of a thought system when its assertion does not involve contradiction), and (b) *transcendental possibility* (where X is possible in the context of a thought system when the conditions for its intelligibility are available). And, consequently, by an 'impossible world' we would mean a world which has an inconsistent and/or unintelligible form.[29]

To say that something is 'possible' is to say that it 'can be' (logically or transcendentally); and to say that something is 'actual' is to say that it already 'is'. It is clear that the 'can be' must precede the 'is' — otherwise what *is* would *not be* for it *could not be*. What is 'potential' or 'probable' is empirically possible; but what is empirically possible must first be ideally possible (i.e. possible on logical or transcendental grounds); for what is not ideally possible, could not be intelligible to us as being empirically possible. Thus, e.g., while a "golden mountain" is ideally possible, even though hardly probable, a "slopeless mountain" is ideally impossible (as a logically inconsistent concept) and, consequently, unintelligible to us as an empirical possibility.

The 'real thing' remains suspended in the ontological realm between the syzygies of two worlds: the possible and the actual. The 'possible world' represents a transcendental ground for the 'actual world'. And the 'actual world' represents but a crystallized occasion in the context of space and time; or, as we say, it represents an exemplification of a 'possible world'. The 'possible world' is ontologically prior to the 'actual world': the former instantiates the latter. Hence, the 'logical form' of the *possible world* defines the limits of the *actual world*.

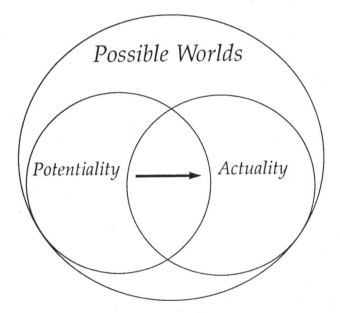

However, a deeper question remains: Why was *this* actual world realized rather than *another*? "Every eternal possibility is at every time available for instantiation, but where no causes are assembled, the material possibility that one or another shall be instantiated is the same for all; it is zero" — writes one contemporary philosopher.[30] But such an explanation does not tell us what are or might be the causes which might occasion the instantiation of possibilia in actualia. And this question of ontology — which generates the cosmological question of the origin and formation of the universe — opens up its own prospects: whether the world came into being by cosmic accident, or by cosmic design, or by the latter through the former? We shall discuss this question, in the context of the hypothesis of cosmic harmony, later.

CHAPTER V

Beyond the Kaleidoscope of Science

The kaleidoscope of science discloses to us the architecture of the universe. Looking *through* it, man has discovered the world of quanta and gazed into the realm of the galaxies. But we must look *beyond* it, in order to see the philosophical framework of science and its meaning for human life. For natural science harbors theoretical assumptions concerning reality and truth; and pragmatic consequences pertaining to the quality of life. We must turn to philosophy as 'metascience' and as 'worldview' — or the *philosophy of science* in its widest sense — for the examination and justification of these.

We must augment our scientific vision with a philosophical vision. The latter handles the metaquestions which haunt the former. For science and philosophy — the twin branches of inquiry which were nurtured by the goddess of reason — have complementary roles.

I think of two concentric circles: the inner circle representing empirical knowledge, and the outer circle its transcendental framework; the latter illuminating the foundation and the horizon of the former.

Consider, then, three important propositions — propositions which constitute the basic assumptions of scientific inquiry:
(a) that the world exists independent of the observer;
(b) that the world represents an architecture of order;
(c) that the order of the world is intelligible and, by rational inquiry, we can attain a true picture of the world;
These themes, and their ramifications, interest us here.

§ 13

A Dialectical Theory of Truth

Let us imagine that 'Reality' is (metaphorically speaking) a crystal with a multidimensional configuration. Then no single perspective would be able to grasp its entire character adequately. So the question arises (a question which this author has introduced into philosophical debates recently[1]): Are there different 'types of truth' corresponding to the multidimensional structure of reality?

The perennial tension between the objective conception of 'Truth' and its subjective conception continues to haunt modern epistemology. One needs only to recall the confrontations between neopositivism and phenomenology, or between formalism and intuitionism, in metascientific debates. We need not retrace the tedious history of these debates; but we must remember their lesson: that unidimensional approaches to the question of truth lead inevitably to an eclipsed theory of knowledge.

We ask therefore: Is it possible that the idea of 'Truth' might represent a multidimensional concept, such that the character of truth might be determined by the modes of cognition, and that consequently we may speak of the 'types of truth'? The answer to this question, from the perspective of dialectical realism, will be articulated here.

Logical Approach to the Question of Truth

All knowledge consists of propositions; and propositions represent truth-claims — as to what is or is not the case. We need, then, a logical criterion for distinguishing true propositions from false propositions. Is there such a criterion?

From the logical point of view, there can be one, and only one, concept of truth. And this concept, defined adequately, would serve as the criterion for assigning a truth-value to a proposition. This *concept of truth* may be defined as follows:

A proposition (p) is true *iff* it is verifiable by some criterion (K) of evidence.

Symbolically: ($\forall$ p) True (p) $\approx$ K:p

Correspondingly, one may formulate a logical definition of the *concept of falsity* as follows:

A proposition (p) is false *iff* its negation is verifiable by some criterion (K) of evidence.

Symbolically: ($\forall$ p) False (p) $\approx$ K: $\sim$ p

And, lastly, one may define *indeterminacy*:

A proposition (p) is indeterminate *iff* there is not a criterion (K) of evidence by which its assertion or negation is verifiable.

Symbolically: ($\forall$ p) Indeterminate (p) $\approx$ $\sim$ K: (pv $\sim$ p)

The above observations are corroborated by the depictions of the *concept of truth* by the epistemologists of the realist persuasion: e.g. a proposition is true *iff* "what it means is the case" (Bergmann), or it "obtains" (Chisholm), or it is in "agreement" with the evidence (Bunge). However (as Professor Chisholm has noted) only in the case of the directly evident the criteria of evidence and the "obtaining" of truth coincide; in other cases it is a question of inference. I interpret these depictions as assigning an *epistemic status* to propositions (with respect to their truth-value) which meets the requirement of rational inquiry.

Nor does the superficial doctrine of "truth by convention" present any refutation of the logical approach to the concept of truth. Consider, e.g., the Wittgensteinian *lying game*: The inhabitants of an island agree always to utter false propositions (instead of true ones) with the understanding that they are meant to be false. Could they, then, make themselves understood by such an inverted language? Possibly. But can we say that, therefore, they have eliminated the reference to 'truth' in their language? No. They have merely exchanged the labels, while leaving the underlying concepts untouched. For, if by " $\sim$ p" they mean "p", and what they mean is verifiably the case, then " $\sim$ p" in their language names the "true" and not the "false". Thus the "true", as the *negation* of the assertion of the true (in the lying game), will shine through as the *assertion* of the negation of the true. For, it is only by assuming the objectivity of 'truth' (i.e. its intersubjective cognition) that they can speak the 'false' and consistently mean thereby the 'true'. And, without the assumption of the concept of 'truth', even 'lying' (i.e. masking and/or misrepresenting the truth) would be meaningless in their language game.

The logical approach to the question of truth provides us a stark and clear elucidation of the *general concept of truth*. It requires a criterion of verification, but it leaves the criterion undefined. And herein lies both the strength and the weakness of the logical approach: its strength in that its open criterion represents an *epistemologically neutral* category; and its weakness in that its open criterion tells us little about the *character* of truth.

Epistemological Approach to the Question of Truth

'Truth' is a property of propositions — the Oxford philosophers notwithstanding[2] — according to epistemological realism. To say that a proposition is 'true' or 'false' is to assign it an *epistemic status*. And this status of propositions must be determinable by some criterion of evidence.

The "linguistic philosophers" (at Oxford and elsewhere) do not adhere to the realist thesis *that truth is a property of propositions*: they hold that the predicates 'true/false' do not qualify propositions, but merely serve as "performative signs" indicating the intent of the speaker — for to say that "p is true" is merely to announce that "I accept (or I insist that) p", and they are dispensable as such, for I could simply say "p". The assumed premise of this argument — that the propositions "p is true" and "p" are identical in meaning — is logically false: the one proposition *contains* the other.

The question remains: when I claim to know the truth about X, what is the ground for my claim?

The only possible grounds for claiming that *I know X* are: either that X is presented to me directly, or that I infer the existence/character of X from what is presented to me. There is no other possibility. And the essential terms here are 'presentation' and 'inference'.

To be 'presented' means to be the intention of a mental act. But not everything is presented in the same way. Some objects are presented in '*perception*' (i.e. the prehension of concrete objects in the matrix of space/time); other objects are presented in '*intuition*' (i.e. the prehension of abstract objects in the matrix of logical space). One may speak, then, of the *modes of cognition*, and correspondingly, of the *modalities of evidence*.

There is an implicit relation between 'truth' and 'evidence'. If we take *knowledge* to be 'true belief based upon evidence', then *evidence* constitutes the ground for knowing the truth of a proposition. And the criteria of evidence, corresponding to the modalities of cognition, are field-dependent.

Consider the following set of propositions as truth-claims:

(1a) My afterimage is a black spot.
(1b) I see clouds in the sky.
(2a) Water freezes at 32 degrees Fahrenheit.
(2b) Planets move in elliptical orbits.
(3a) $(5 + 7) = 12$
(3b) $N = n(n+1)/2$
     (Gauss Formula)
(4a) Nothing is black and white allover.
(4b) Every phenomenon has a cause.

How do we know that these propositions are true? What is the evidence for their truth? Evidently, these propositions cannot be verified in the same way. They represent, not only different modes of cognition, but also require different kinds of evidence for their verification.

One says that the evidence for *1a* consists of the intuition of a private datum of consciousness; and for *1b* it consists of the perception of a public datum of experience. And one says that the evidence for *2a* and for *2b* is not directly given but must be constructed on the basis of empirical induction. The evidence for *3a* and *3b*, however, appears to be of a radically different order: here the evidence consists of the assertability of the proposition within the formal system (in the case of *3a*); or the construction of a coherent pattern within the formal system (in the case of *3b*). Analogously, the evidence for the truth of *4a* and *4b* is independent of experience entirely: it involves the logical analysis of the meanings of the concepts themselves (in the case of 4a); or dialectical argumentation involving a transcendental category (in the case of 4b) explaining the very intelligibility of experience.

Clearly, the evidence and the criteria of verifiability for the truth/falsity of the above set of propositions vary widely. Do these classes of propositions, representing different kinds of truth-claims, also represent different *kinds of truth*? I will argue that they do. Hopefully, this line of thinking (whatever its shortcomings may be) has the merit of advancing beyond the hitherto global grouping of all true propositions into the two classes of "factual truths" and "rational truths" — a dogma which is still adhered to in some circles.

Dialectical Approach to the Question of Truth

We have seen that, in logical perspective, there is one and only one concept of truth; and that, in epistemological perspective, there are several distinct kinds of truth-claims. Is there, then, a relation between the one and the other?

We assume (as realist epistemologists do) the principle of the correlativity of the *modes of cognition* and the *modalities of evidence*. The varieties of truth-claims (exemplified by propositions 1, 2, 3, 4 above) represent the modes of cognition which remain grounded in their respective modalities of evidence. Nor are these propositions (as truth-claims) *reducible* to each other. To reduce them to one another would require reducing their modes of evidence. But their modes of evidence remain irreducible (ontologically); and, consequently, the propositions themselves remain irreducible (epistemologically). Hence the criteria of verification — i.e. cognitive access to their truth/falsity — remain different in each case.

The *hypothesis of the types of truth* may be stated as follows: That the range of cognitive propositions exemplify distinct kinds of truth-claims such that the epistemic status of each kind is to be determined by a unique criterion of evidence and verifiability.[3]

I distinguish four types of truth:

(I) Phenomenological Truth

A proposition is *phenomenologically true* when it is verifiable by the immediate intuition of a subjective datum of consciousness.

Phenomenological truths are self-presenting to the perspective of the observer. Thus, e.g., propositions 1a ("My afterimage is a black spot") and 1b ("I see clouds in the sky") represent phenomenological truths. Or, imagine walking on a path that winds around a hill: as one passes to the farside of the hill, a whole new scenery unveils itself before one, which a moment earlier lay completely hidden from view. And here the meaning of the Greek word for 'truth' ($\alpha'\lambda\eta'\theta\varepsilon\iota\alpha$) — which denotes 'what is no longer hidden' from view — becomes evident.

But the phenomenological truth is not always subjective merely.

The objectivity of phenomenological truth is evident in this: that anyone can see what I see — provided that they stand where I stand. But can anyone really stand where I stand? Rarely — and then perhaps only partially. And this shows the subjective (and the original and the creative) character of phenomenological truth.

There are also higher level phenomenological truths which transcend the elementary truths represented by the propositions concerning black spots and clouds in the sky. The truths of aesthetic and moral experience, in the context of a reflective *Lebenswelt*, have a phenomenological character. The phenomenology of aesthetic and/or moral experience is indeed inherent in all the literature of high realism: Thomas Mann and Hermann Hesse for example. These texts all require for their understanding, besides critical reflection, another level of mental operation — *verstehen* — a form of understanding wherein the *gestalt* of a situation is intuited through its happening and being-so: the phenomenological experience of truth however vicariously.

(II) Empirical Truth

A proposition is *empirically true* when it is verifiable by experimental observation, directly or indirectly, admitting of degrees of probability.

Empirical hypotheses are represented by the propositions 2a ("Water freezes at 32 degrees Fahrenheit") and 2b ("Planets move in elliptical orbits"). The higher the level of abstraction attained by empirical hypotheses, the greater the degree of their certainty. Complete certainty is attainable at the level of purely conceptual construction — e.g. theoretical physics. "It may even be said," as Poincaré remarked once, "that the object of science is to dispense with direct verifications altogether."

The hypothesis enables us to proceed from the visible to the invisible, as it were, or from the present to the future. I see footprints in the sand, and I infer that there must be some animal around; I see discolored skin on a person, and I infer the presence of some disease; or I raise the temperature of the burner, and I expect the water to come to a boil. "The essence of a hypothesis is, "as Wittgenstein has observed, "that it engenders an expectation..."[4] The logical form of the empirical hypothesis may be described as follows: two independent series of empirical data — $(a_1, a_2, ... a_n)$ and $(b_1, b_2, ... b_n)$ — may lead to the formation of a pair of concepts (A, B); then creative thought may relate these concepts on the basis of some intuition and/or observation (ArB); and deduce the consequences of this insight for further observation or praxis.

A hypothesis is a pencil-sketch by the thought of an aspect of reality as it were. The connecting lines it draws between the points of experience are initially tenuous and tentative; later they starken and present a clear configuration. The transformation of the hypothesis displays a unique aspect of dialectical thinking: it emerges as an *overbelief*, a belief which transcends its empirical base, and which haunts the thinker; and only later, after the conceptualization of the phenomena by the thought, it acquires the form of a conceptual *Gestalt*. It is at this stage that the deduction of consequences from the hypothesis becomes possible; and a cluster of these deductions, verified, preclude the credibility of alternative hypotheses. But it is at this stage, too, that the challenge of a single counter-example proves how vulnerable and fragile the hypothesis is. And then the thought, left with a fractured hypothesis, must resume the creative project of theoretical reconstruction.

Equally intriguing is the dialectical relation of the hypothesis to its evidence. That empirical hypotheses represent "degrees of truth", is shown by the fact that their probability varies as a function of their evidence.[5] How precarious is the epistemological status of empirical hypotheses is clear: while it may require a thousand cases of confirmation to lend it a reasonable degree of probability, a single negative case will suffice to cast doubt upon its truth, or even pronounce its falsity. (This is the import of Karl Popper's thesis of falsifiability.) And then the question is: what can the empirical hypothesis do, when confronted with the dreaded counter-example, to save its own truth? It must redefine itself or rearrange itself—like an amoeba as it were — either by restricting itself sufficiently to exclude the counter-example or by generalizing itself sufficiently to include the foreign body in its explanatory range. Otherwise the hypothesis must die. The dialectical life-cycle of the empirical hypothesis mirrors, in microcosm, the life-cycle of the giant organism science itself—with its capacity for self-critique and self-corrigibility.

(III) Logico-Mathematical Truth

A proposition represents a logical/mathematical truth when it expresses a necessary relation between its concepts, and, it is coherently assertable in the context of a formal system.

Logico-mathematical truths (to use Kant's expression) have the character of "inward necessity": i.e. a necessity derived from the very meanings of the concepts involved. Hence Tarski argues that: in a formal system, given its set of axioms and given the logical truth of its basic theorems, there is no false proposition that can be derived from it; and, consequently, any proposition derived from it (and assertible in it) must be necessarily true.[6]

The languages of logic and mathematics, in this sense, represent a genre of the 'ideal language'. Within this language there are levels of construction: (a) the level of *analytic propositions* which can be proven by the laws of identity/contradiction alone: e.g. the proposition $(5 + 7) = 12$; and (b) the *level of synthetic propositions* which cannot be proven by the laws of identity/contradiction alone but require some additional postulate: e.g. the proposition $N=n(n+1)/2$ which also requires the postulate of mathematical induction for its demonstration.

Higher mathematical constructions involve creative reasoning: abstractions, generalizations, and reasoning beyond recurrence. And the characteristic of reasoning beyond recurrence is that—as Poincaré aptly observed — it contains, in condensed form as it were, an indefinite number of microarguments. Because of the coalescence of logic and mathematics in these constructions (in topology, in set theory, in matrices especially) the question of the distinction between 'logical truth' and 'mathematical truth' arises. If they are different, then the difference lies in their semantics, not in their formal character.

However, logic is more basic than mathematics: since the axioms of the former are presupposed by the latter. But it does not follow — Russell notwithstanding — that mathematics is reducible to logic. Indeed, even within the realm of mathematics, the higher levels of construction are not reducible to the lower levels. Moreover, the applicability of logico-mathematical laws to the world of experience — ranging from architecture to astronomy — provides sufficient evidence that they are far from being mere tautologies. The realist handling of this thorny issue has engendered a new wave of epistemological debates.[7]

(IV) Philosophical Truth

A proposition represents a *philosophical truth* when it involves transcendental entities — i.e. 'invariant concepts' or 'paradigms' — and is susceptible of dialectical demonstration.

By 'invariant concepts' I understand those concepts which lie at the foundation or horizon of our thinking, so that their meanings are presupposed in the contexts of various nonphilosophical discourses. And by 'philosophical paradigms' I understand those higher level theoretical models which serve in ordering the lower level models of our thinking. Thus 'philosophical truths' represent a class of 'metatruths': i.e. truths about the conditions or the possibility of other truths; and truths about the interrelations of other truths. This explains why the elucidatory and the integrative functions of the philosophical thinking constitute a transcendental inquiry.

There are three levels of philosophical truth — and to these correspond three kinds of philosophical propositions:

(a) *analytic propositions*, which derive their truth from the meanings of the concepts involved, and consequently, can be proven by the laws of identity/contradiction alone.

(b) *transcendental propositions* (or, *synthetic propositions a priori*, as they are commonly called), representing truths which are *a priori* (i.e. independent of experience) and yet applicable to the world of experience: they assert something about the logical/dialectical form of the world, and consequently, provide the transcendental matrix for the intelligibility of empirical knowledge.

(c) *dialectical propositions*, which represent truths attained by conceptual generalization (intuitively or inferentially), as in the construction of paradigms which are applicable to human thinking and life.

The last kind of philosophical truths represent the truths of the perspectives of different philosophical systems, insofar as they are true, dialectically speaking.

At least one philosophical colleague, Walter Watson, taking as his starting point the assumption "that the 'truth' admits of more than one valid formulation", has inquired into the kinds of truth *within* the realm of philosophy proper. He approaches the range of philosophical inquiry from the viewpoint of a set of "archaic variables", and their relations of "reciprocal priority" (in the sense that each, *from its viewpoint*, includes the other viewpoints), in the contexts of different philosophical movements. The archaic variables consist of 'pure modes' of philosophical reflection and critique — resulting in existential, substrative, noumenal, or essential truths, respectively — which remain nevertheless, in the larger context of philosophical inquiry, complementary modes.[8]

However, from the fact that the idea of 'Truth' represents a multidimensional concept, it does not follow that a definition of the general concept of 'Truth' is not possible. But our definition, as we have seen, must be an open definition as it were: it must contain an open variable susceptible of acquiring different criteria as its values — thus allowing for the multidimensional character of the concept of 'Truth'. What applies to truth in general, also applies to philosophical truths.

Concluding Remarks

The *dialectical theory of truth*, sketched above, has implications for the relations between the arts, the humanities, and the sciences. Under the dialectical 'ideal of truth' the complementarity of the different genres of truth in these inquiries is displayed. And this implies an attitude of interdisciplinary dialogue and appreciation.

Perhaps now we may envision an end to the relentless campaign of reductionism in the 'philosophy of science'. The history of this campaign is all too familiar: Recall the attempted reduction of empirical truth to logico-mathematical truth by Descartes; or the proposed reduction of empirical truth to phenomenological truth by Hume (and by Husserl later); or, conversely, the attempted reduction of phenomenological truth to empirical truth by the Vienna Circle (and Carnap in particular); and so on. And then there are, within each field of inquiry, proposed reductions of higher level truths to lower level truths. Yet the same 'reductive fallacy' lies at the base of all these attempts: i.e. identifying two truths at different epistemological levels *by means of* the arbitrary substitution of one perspective for another.

Picasso says: "Of a thousand possible lines there is one true line for me." Riemann might say the same thing in the context of his geometrical system. But they do not mean to assert the same proposition: the one is concerned with logical coherence, and the other with aesthetic harmony.

We may evoke, then, the *principle of complementarity*, not only relative to the genres of truth *within* philosophical inquiry, but also *between* philosophical truths and the truths of the other arts and sciences. We can bypass the Scylla of reductionism and the Charybdis of nihilism. This consequence too — i.e. philosophical tolerance toward the genres of truth — we owe to the perspective of dialectical realism.

The metacritical question (speaking in the context of a metalanguage) — i.e. How can we be certain that our propositions concerning the concept of 'Truth' are true themselves? — this question also belongs to, and may be handled in, the ideal language of philosophical discourse.

§ 14

Truth and "Marginal Philosophers"

The discourses of 'marginal philosophers' are overcrowding, even if not overpowering, the contemporary philosophical scene. How do their claims fare when confronted with the central philosophical question of 'truth'? I will attempt to depict the confrontation, and explain its dialectic, as seen by a dialectical realist. And I will argue that this confrontation may be taken as the critical test of the validity of their claims; for, if they fail here, then they are bound to fail elsewhere.

The designation "marginal philosophy" is mine.[9] It refers to the recent fascination with surface issues, by rhetorical means, rather than conceptual inquiry into the deeper issues. That this trend arises from, and in return gives rise to, an *epistemological crisis* is evident: what was taken to be the object of inquiry is no longer accessible to the inquirer. But what is less evident is the clarity and/or validity of the theses of the marginal philosophers in response to the crisis.

I shall focus on the dialectic of the epistemological crisis; and then show, in the light of that dialectic, that the responses of the 'marginal philosophers' represent, not a philosophical solution, but a philosophical disintegration or (to borrow a harsh expression from Nietzsche for whom ironically they retain an oblique admiration) a new form of "philosophy as decadence"...

Wittgenstein's Linguistic Prescription

The epistemological crisis began with the Wittgensteinian dilemma: *i.e.* the recognition of the indispensability of 'logical form' at the cognitive level, and yet the negation of its status at the ontological level; and, consequently, abjuring its articulation in language. Eliminate the 'logical form' from discourse, and nominalism remains as the residuum. Such was the transition from the *Tractatus* to the *Investigations*; or, as Bergmann has depicted it, from the "glory" to the "misery" in Wittgenstein's philosophical pilgrimage.

The passage that indicates this transition occurs on the very last page of the *Tractatus*: "The correct method in philosophy would really be the following: to say nothing except what can be said...and then, whenever someone else wanted to say something metaphysical, to demonstrate to him that he had failed to give any meaning to certain signs in his propositions" — meaning, that is, in "ordinary language". The passage that transfers the burden of 'truth' from the realm of reality to the domain of language occurs in the *Investigations*: "Grammar tells us what kind of object anything is" — (a proposition, be it noted, which is inconsistent with an earlier proposition in the *Tractatus*: "Only by being a picture of reality can a proposition be true or false.")[10] The two passages, taken together, constitute what may be called the 'linguistic prescription' for doing philosophy.

How faithfully the "linguistic philosophers" (at Oxford and elsewhere) followed this prescription is now familiar history. And, in this connection, one representative pronouncement is worthy of being quoted: "A philosophical answer is really a *verbal recommendation* in response to a *request* with regard to a *sentence* which lacks a *conventional use* whether there occur situations which could conventionally be described by it" (my italics).[11] Similar assertions abound in the writings of J. L. Austin, A. J. Ayer, and others. Here, then, 'language' is made to be everything, while 'conceptual reality' is reduced to nothing. A radical response from the continental philosophers was then inevitable.

Hermann Wein — in a critical essay in the *Zeitschrift für Philosophische Forschung* — challenged the "linguistic philosophers" to answer a critical question: "Where and how can *philosophical insight* result from a preoccupation with the state of symbols/signs in cognitive language?"[12] But there was no answer; nor could there be any answer. For it was not certain that the "linguistic philosophers" were certain that they really understood the meaning of the question: they were not clear as to what the expression 'philosophical insight' was to mean. The "grammar" of their ordinary language (Professor Wein implied) apparently could not enlighten them on this crucial point.

The dialectic of the issue held a hidden aspect. And it was to be revealed, later, by the examination of the presuppositions of "linguistic philosophy". The epigones of Wittgenstein were hard pressed to have a conception of 'philosophical insight', when they remained in the dark as to their conception of the 'concept' of anything. Indeed — as Professor C.W.K. Mundle has demonstrated[13] — they usually failed to articulate the meaning of the expressions, '*the concept of*' and '*the logic of*', which they continued to use. But it would be tedious to rehearse this critique.

This (dialectically speaking) was the *first movement* in the history of the epistemological crisis. It was accompanied by another, not entirely unrelated, movement: what I shall call the "nominalist interlude". But they differed, in principle, over the question of truth: the one reducing it to an issue of the "usage of language"; the other, to an issue of "elementary cognition". The two movements, taken together, prepared the way (again dialectically speaking) for the final movement: the "marginal philosophies" and their programme of deconstruction.

The Nominalist Interlude

I do not intend to examine the character of the new nominalism generally — but only wish to focus on a contemporary moment of it as an interlude in the dialectical scheme which I am about to disclose.

'Nominalism' is the view whose ontological repertoire includes only one kind of objects, i.e., concrete objects. It does not recognize the need for — not to mention the reality of — abstract objects. Nominalism represents a "book of simple truths", written in a language whose variables are of the lowest order. It was once the dream of the Vienna Circle to write such a book; but the staggering developments in the recent philosophy of science shattered that simplistic dream...

How does the new nominalism — which reproaches realism for

complicating the question of truth — itself approach the question of truth?

Nominalists, both the less and the more sophisticated, stumble over the paradox of Pegasus. To assert that "Pegasus does exist" would be (on their grounds) false; and to assert that "Pegasus does not exist" would be (again on their grounds) meaningless. Thus they are in a predicament: they can neither affirm nor deny the existence of "Pegasus". Yet nominalists are obligated, by the requirements of their ontology, to take an unequivocal stance on the issue of the existence/non-existence of objects. For the dialectical realist, however, the paradox of Pegasus presents no crisis. Here the proposition "Pegasus does exist" translates into the proposition "There is an abstract object in the *possible world* which is the designatum of the word 'Pegasus' in our language"; and the proposition "Pegasus does not exist" translates into the proposition "There is no concrete object in the *actual world* exemplifying the concept of 'Pegasus'." Thus, in the context of realism, the paradox dissolves. And the reason why nominalism fails to handle such paradoxes of truth is that it negates the reality of 'logical space', and therewith, the possibility of the construction of abstract forms therein.

However, some contemporary nominalists believe that an abstract reconstruction — providing a true picture of the real world — is still possible within the matrix of nominalism. Nelson Goodman is a representative of this group.[14] He evokes a program of ontological reduction — (which recalls how Carnap built his world in 1928!) — and he utilizes formal logic in his reconstruction. He also avoids, successfully, 'naive realism' (the view that takes things to be what they seem to be).

Here we are presented with a particularistic world — presumably undisturbed by the problems of abstraction, concretion, and exemplification. The 'structure of appearance' is explained on the basis of a set of 'simple elements' plus a set of postulates of propositional logic. Here 'functions' are taken as indefinables; 'categories' are defined as classes; and 'classes' are reduced to their extensions. And, in the absence of a real categorial matrix, classes remain suspended, as it were, as accidental clusters of properties in a vacuous space. Further, given Goodman's definition of 'quality' (as a given space/time locus) it could *not* be exemplified by more than one individual. Yet a 'quality' (by its standard definition as 'character') *can* be exemplified by more than one individual. This awkward situation is but one consequence of this system of unreal classes and homeless individuals.

Consider a sample of Goodman's ontological inventory: given the elements (a, b, c, d), and two systems, A (wherein the pairs a/c and b/d are discriminated) and B (wherein the pairs a/b and c/d are discriminated); then for a complex realist (like Bergmann) such a world would contain ten entities (4 individuals, 2 pairs of subclasses, and 1 pair of classes) which are *not* identical in character; but for a nominalist (like Goodman) there would still be, after all the reconstruction, only the four entities (a, b, c, d) with which he began.

And because classes are unreal, and categories absent, it is to be expected that, in this fragmented "world", such counterfeit properties as "grue" and "bleen", *etcetera*, would make their bizarre appearance. The epistemological principle of color incompatibility would rule out their existence *a priori* in any ideal world; and, in the actual world, they represent but commonplace phenomenological hues. Yet they "exist" in Goodman's artificial world as exemplars. And so the problem of 'concretion' arises anew in this system: i.e. how can 'qualia' (not to mention bare particulars) congregate? In response to this problem, Goodman introduces such extra-logical concepts as "affiliation" and "overlapping" (the only combinator terms in his system); but we note that these are merely *descriptive* rather *explanatory*. And the idea of "concurrence", which Goodman evokes to *explain* his "explanation", does not solve but only suppresses the problem. Thus the "world" of the new nominalism, for all its apparent formalistic finesse, remains a fragmented and eclipsed world.

In what sense, then, can the new nominalists claim to present a 'true picture' of the real world? It appears that Goodman, for one, no longer makes that claim. We read his confession in his last major work: "I began by dropping the picture theory of language and ended by adopting the language theory of pictures. I rejected the picture theory of language on the ground that the structure of a description does not conform to the structure of the world. But I then concluded that there is no such thing as the structure of the world for anything to conform or fail to conform to."[15] The conclusion (as I see it) is more a consequence of the failure of its author's conception than of the failure of language. But to demonstrate this would be another issue.

The issue that concerns us is: that, in the context of the new nominalism, the "picture of the world" is taken *to be* the "world", for (to them) there is no world *beyond* the picture. This explains also why Goodman and his colleagues speak (arrogantly) of their project as "world-making", *rather than* making a picture of the world. And this, in turn, implies an even more arrogant claim: *i.e.* that we (the observers) by *making* our world, also *make* (and not discover) our "truths" about the world.

Then, too, Quine enters the troubled scene and, in an effort to save 'nominalism' logically, places an important proposition before us: "One ontology is always reducible to another when we are given a proxy function f that is one-to-one."[16] An ingenious formulation of ontological relativity. But is it valid? Let, then, a given world (U) be reduced to another world (V) by means of a proxy function (f), such that all the entities in the one are accounted for by entities in the other. But there is a hiatus in this thesis: we would need a third world (W), conceptually inclusive of both U and V, wherein the function (f) is to be grounded, serving as the ontological matrix of the reduction. This last world (W) would represent then our true and irreducible ontology — relative to the worlds U and V — and so on. Admittedly, this is a transcendental critique of ontological relativity. In the Oxford/ Harvard circles it would be regarded in bad taste to present them with a transcendental critique — but, then, why remain absolutists in matters of taste, while remaining relativists in matters of ontology?

At a symposium of the recent World Congress of Philosophy (XVII) in Montréal/1983, Professor Quine reasserted his thesis of ontological relativity: "There is no difference between holding one ontology and holding another..." Did this mean that the 'reference' and the 'sense' of philosophical propositions no longer mattered? If so, then the objective basis for the possibility of intersubjective understanding, and therewith the intelligibility of philosophical and scientific discourse, would vanish.[17] But apparently Quine and his associates either do not see this point, or seeing it, do not care. Why? Perhaps because they seek to focus their energies on the 'picture' (language) rather than on the "pictured" (reality) — as their nominalist programme requires them to do. Herein then lies the blindspot in their brilliance: the very brilliance, which originally led them to the lure of formalistic elegance at the expense of philosophical significance, would now lead them to embrace ontological nihilism.

This recalls a story which Bertrand Russell tells: when he was a boy he had a clock with a pendulum; and he discovered that, by lifting off the pendulum the clock went much faster, giving him a gratifying sense of temporal speed. It could no longer tell the time, of course, but that did not matter if one could teach oneself to be indifferent to the passage of time. So the new nominalists have acquired a clock which has lost its pendulum; and they have managed to teach themselves to be indifferent to the events in the real world.

The logical consequence of the abandonment of the knowledge of 'reality' by the new nominalists is clear. In the absence of any genuine truth-claim for any 'picture of the world', there would be no longer any point in critically comparing *the truth of* competing hypotheses, theories, or paradigms. And with this negative outcome the *second phase* of the epistemological crisis, the dialectic of which I am examining here, comes to a close.

"Phantom of Truth" as the Ideal of Marginal Philosophers

The third (and last) phase of the epistemological crisis begins with an overt abandonment of the search for 'truth', and ends with a covert aspiration to capture some semblance of truth — or, metaphorically, the 'phantom of truth'. To that end is elaborated a programme of "conversation" and/or "marginal discourse", which disclose, not 'truth' but its shadow. But, one may ask, why bother about the "semblance of truth" when "truth" itself is an illusion? (And if 'truth' be illusion, would not any "semblance of truth" be even more of an illusion?) Herein, then, lies the paradoxical intention, and the *mauvaise foi*, of the marginal philosophers.

The movement of their thinking, from the abandonment of the concept of 'truth', to the renunciation of 'epistemology', is quite understandable. The failure of the new nominalism, resulting in the breakdown of the *connection* between the 'real world' and the 'picture of the world', implied that thenceforth any talk about a 'true/false picture' (and therewith any talk about knowledge and its truth conditions generally) would be pointless. Since these thinkers had tacitly assumed the nominalist programme, they also fell victim to the epistemological failure of that programme.

Where did this leave 'philosophy' and 'philosophical inquiry'?

Let us heed, momentarily, the exhortations of Richard Rorty as a spokesman for the retreat of reason:

Starting with a dubious rhetoric *against* 'epistemology', *per se,* Rorty urges that the time has come to leave behind this vestige of European culture, and to pass "from epistemology to hermeneutics". And what is 'hermeneutics'? We normally take 'hermeneutics' to be the art of the interpretation of literary texts. Not so for Rorty and his colleagues; they have in mind something far more amorphous: "In the interpretation I shall be offering, 'hermaneutics' is not the name for a discipline, nor for a method of achieving the sort of results which epistemology failed to achieve, nor for a program of research ... it is an expression of hope that the cultural space left by the demise of epistemology will not be filled ..."[18] No comment is necessary to exhibit the inane character of the notion depicted in this passage. There is an embryonic metaphor there, but it cannot be unpacked. And metaphors that cannot be unpacked (as Gustav Bergmann once observed) are the source of the greatest evils in philosophy. That marginal philosophers are abundantly contributing to the stockpile of non-philosophical metaphors is to be seen in the proliferation of "bad literature" in philosophical journals in recent years ...

Eventually — (and not consequently) — Rorty identifies 'philosophy' and 'hermeneutics' with what he calls "edifying conversation", as a kind of intellectual melange:

"To see edifying philosophers as conversational partners is an alternative to seeing them as holding views ... One way of thinking of wisdom as something of which the love is not the same as that of argument ... is to think of it as the practical wisdom necessary to participate in conversation ... I want now to enlarge this suggestion that edifying philosophy aims at continuing a conversation *rather than* at discovering truth ..."[19] But can one engage in meaningful "conversation" *without* holding any "views"; or, would there be even any point in engaging in any "conversation" if it were not *for the sake of* "discovering truth"? These questions arise in the wake of the suppression of truth as the ideal of discourse.

Let us focus, then, on the character of the "conversation" proposed by marginal philosophers: Are there to be any restrictions as to the meaning and import of these "conversations"? Only (says Rorty) that they are to be congenial in the "context of the culture" in which they take place — only the gentlemanly business of "keeping the conversation going" — but without ever challenging the underlying beliefs of the participants in any serious manner. Nor any references to 'reality' and to 'truth' are to be made; or any compliance to 'rationality' (in the sense of reasoned discourse) is to be required. And such a community of intelligentsia would resemble a social rehabilitation center, whose inhabitants are in desperate need of "talking-to and being-talked-to", but without being sufficiently healthy- minded, or intelligent, to engage in any real dialogue over the critical questions of the world or of life. Moreover, the very notion of "conversation", remains murky: if 'understanding' be the presumed end of 'conversation', and 'understanding' would *not be possible* without the elucidation of some 'truth', or, the recognition and/or articulation of some 'viewpoint', then 'conversation' would be reduced to nothing more than mere babble.

Nor is Mr. Rorty alone among "professional philosophers" in the English-speaking world who are gnawing away (in the manner of termites) at the foundations of their own discipline. I mention two others here: Kai Nielsen and Peter Unger.[20] They propose to replace 'epistemology' by what they loosely call "critical theory". Have they really forgotten that 'epistemology' is *already* a critical theory, the most radical critical theory, and perhaps a critical theory of the highest order? Apparently — for they no longer acknowledge the possibility of foundational theory. Indeed, they openly insinuate that foundational theory rests upon a "mistake" (Nielsen), or, that it rests upon our "arbitrary choice" (Unger). But in vain do we peruse their wordy discourses in search of any cogent counter-argument which might be taken as a viable critique of foundational inquiry. This phenomenon too — i.e. taking a philosophical stance, *in the name of truth*, but without presenting any serious philosophical argument — must be taken as being a part of the style of the marginal philosophers. So they reject the validity of foundational theory and question the possibility of transcendental arguments — (and cast

aspersion upon the good name of Kant)[21] — *without* understanding
either *and* merely as a *façon de parler*... Yet they could not possibly
understand these issues so long as they themselves are not prepared
to recognize the truth/falsity of philosophical propositions. For this
recognition (as we have noted) is requisite for any 'understanding'.

And when we pose the question concerning 'philosophy' and
'philosophical truth' to the most original of marginal philosophers,
Jacques Derrida, we encounter a novel puzzlement. At the opening
of his main work we read these seemingly lucid queries: "Does
philosophy answer a need? How is it to be understood? Philosophy?"
And then we read what he writes in response:

"Ample to the point of believing itself interminable, a discourse
that has *called itself* philosophy — doubtless the only discourse that
has ever intended to receive its name only from itself, and has never
ceased murmuring its initial letter to itself from as close as possible
— has always, including its own, meant to say its limit. In the
familiarity of the languages called (instituted as) natural by
philosophy, the languages elementary to it, this discourse has always
insisted upon assuring itself mastery over the limit... (*peras, limes,
grenze*). It has recognized, conceived, posited, declined the limit
according to all possible modes; and therefore by the same token, in
order better to dispose of the limit, has transgressed it..."[22]—*etcetera*
— a seemingly interminable rhetoric which, as the underlying
concepts lie eclipsed in the background, is preoccupied only with
savoring the nuances of words at the surface.

Are these contortions of mental agony, struggling to articulate a
single idea and yet failing, to be taken as a fragment of 'philosophical
discourse', or, as a piece of linguistic fantasy? Further, as if by
coincidence, alongside the already obscure text of the commentary,
runs a marginal text, a reflexive linguistic narrative, touching it only
at tangential points, and presenting a cognitive baffle as it were. Thus
the ideology of deconstruction, camouflaged, continues its gnawing
at the roots of *reason* — even when the deconstructionist follows the
labyrinth of his own warped *reasoning*.

In Derrida's depiction of 'philosophical thinking' we see a
depiction of his own style of thinking: for how something is said also
says something. He stands, like Narcissus, before a mirror, engaging
in a verbal pantomime. I (as an author given to the conceptual style

of expression) find it rather awkward to depict his philosophical posture, which is *thesisless*, as it were. Thesisless, that is, excepting the negative assumption that "there is nothing outside the text"; or, by implication, that "the text is everything". But, tragically, this text, which is everything, is (as Derrida says) "undecidable" as to its meaning; for its propositions lack objective reference. It articulates, therefore, no objective truths.

Why then bother with the "text" and its interpretation?

Evidently, in order to disclose — despite the author or the reader of the text — its supposedly "suppressed meanings", which it harbors between its lines and in its apparently blank margins, in the context of an undisclosed ideology and culture . . . Thus, while Derrida closes with one hand the door to the world of objective and verifiable meanings, he opens with the other hand the door to a world of subjective and indeterminate meanings.

Reading Derrida recalls what Jorge Borges was to say of the fictional "Metaphysicians of Tlon", namely: "They seek neither truth nor its likelihood; they seek astonishment; they think (philosophy) is a branch of literary fantasy." Yet every mirror requires a tain. So Derrida has to confess (in a parenthetical note) that there is no sense in doing *without* the "concepts of metaphysics" *in order to* discredit metaphysics — and thereby "the grand deconstructionist" falls in the very snare he has taken pains to set up for 'philosophy proper'. For the project of the destruction of reason, by means of the use of reason, results inevitably in the demise of the reasoner.

Motive, in theoretical inquiry no less in praxis, is of critical importance. What, one may ask, was Derrida's motive for the assumption of such an opaque view of philosophical inquiry? He aspires, it seems, to level the genre distinction between *philosophy* and *literature* — thereby rendering philosophical texts accessible to literary criticism *by means of* the distillation of philosophical discourse into rhetorical discourse. But precisely here Derrida makes a momentous mistake: Taking the poetic function of language to be the essential function of all language — symbolic/literary as well as conceptual/philosophical — he then overgeneralizes by denying the genre distinction between these two extraordinary spheres of discourse. This is a heuristic blur. But it is through such a heuristic blur that Derrida could possibly claim to assign to rhetorical art the problems and projects which are the unique prerogative of philosophical inquiry. This might indeed please those literati who in their own thinking remain frustrated by the abstract character of philosophy. But the aspiration fails by failing to accomplish the tasks of philosophical thinking, for which rhetoric *per se* lacks the requisite conceptual means. As a consequence, the great tasks of philosophical inquiry would remain untouched and undone. Who should then perform those important tasks of inquiry — or should we neglect them and relapse into a new mode of intellectual barbarism? For the special functions of philosophy — as we have examined them in some detail earlier in this work — are essentially of a dual nature: to inquire into the "foundational questions" on the one hand, and into the "horizon questions" on the other — and to pursue such inquiries at the conceptual niveau rather than at the linguistic niveau merely. To insist on the heuristic blur would mask the dialectical struggle of philosophical thinking in its truth-disclosing process: it would misrepresent it (to use the appropriate phrase of Jürgen Habermas) merely as "the flux of interpretations beating rhythmically between revolutions and normalizations of language". Then the Yes and the No of dialectical thinking, recurring in all serious philosophical inquiry in the course of its search and research for Truth, would vanish along with the capacity of discourse for reality-disclosure. Instead, we should wallow in rhetorical morass, hoping that by happy accident we might attain enlightenment about the greater issues.

Concluding Remarks

The dialectical process, underlying the 'marginal philosophers' receiving their nourishment from the very epistemological crisis to which they have contributed, is intriguing. For what was taken to be the object of inquiry — i.e. truth — becomes no longer accessible to the inquirer. Hence, I have argued that, in their encounter with the question of 'truth', the marginal philosophers fail and fail inevitably. And their rhetoric of self-justification fails to cover up their epistemological failure. What is true in their rhetoric is not philosophical; and what is philosophical in it is not true. But they themselves do not make the distinction; and that, too, is symptomatic of their predicament.

Yet the epistemological crisis which they have generated (dialectically viewed) has a heuristic value: it enables us to see, through the fog of debates as it were, the *shadow of philosophy* — against the gestalt with which we have been familiar. The shadow harbors the negative motive for the "deconstruction" of philosophy and the "destruction" of reason. And just beyond the shadow are awaiting the spokesmen for irrational mythologies, with their inflated baggage, eager to enter the "house of reason" and present anew their distorted worldviews and their bizarre wares as remedies for the intellectual malaise of modern man.

Either that — or something else:

For the programme of the elimination of 'truth' and the destruction of 'reason' holds many an ugly promise. Some of these have already come to pass; but others are yet to come. The abandonment of philosophical inquiry and its replacement by exercises in rhetoric; the blind groping for the 'phantom of truth' instead of the search for 'true' hypotheses and paradigms; the deterioration of genuine dialogue and understanding (on the basis of the possibility of the recognition of truth) into superficial conversation and/or cross-talk; and, lastly, the degeneration of ethical discourse (in the absence of ethical concepts) into amoral exhortations — i.e. the destruction of 'practical reason' *as a necessary consequence of* the destruction of 'theoretical reason' — *etcetera* ... Consequently, the entire realm of 'applied philosophy', with its concern for the actual problems of our civilization — ecological, social, and cultural — would also disappear.

It would be naive to suppose that the lowest ebb of our modern culture lies safely behind us. It lies before us — if the programme of the destruction of the 'ideal of truth' and 'reason', and therewith, the highest hope of mankind for progress — were to be carried out. For the same process of the 'destruction of reason' that led to the rise of fascist ideology in the recent past — (the dialectic of which has been explained by the masterly pen of Georg Lukács) — now under the sophisticated label of the 'deconstruction' of philosophy would give rise to an era of unprecedented intellectual and moral destruction — and, consequently, cultural decadence. This would come to pass if the recent ideology of nihilism were to succeed in attaining its dream: the worldwide movement of *une grande alliance rhétorique contre la raison philosophique.* Then 'philosophy', which alone can rightfully claim to be a 'cultural healer', would become merely a 'cultural pastime' — and it would *no longer* be worth pursuing.

But 'philosophy' *is* worth pursuing: it alone leads the psyche, along the dialectical path of reason, to higher enlightenment and to the critique of our ailing culture. For — as Karl Jaspers observes at the end of a thousand page discourse on the question of 'truth' (*Von der Wahrheit*) — the aim of philosophy is to prepare the human psyche "to experience the outer reality" and to reflect upon its meaning and significance.[23] And if one were to believe that that were not what 'philosophy' were about — i.e. to put us on the way to 'truth' (about the psyche, the world, and life) — then 'philosophy' would have lost its relevance to human existence.

Philosophy must lead to human enlightenment — or it leads to nothing.

Ironically, however, the marginal philosophers do harbor a 'humanistic motive' as well: they seek, in their oblique way, to restore the credibility of a "humane philosophy" (after Nietzsche or after Heidegger), and to offer resistance to the trends of neopositivist reductionism in the human sciences. But, deplorably, they themselves lack the power and the gumption (unlike those two thinkers) — and unlike Lukács or Habermas — to articulate any 'truths' about the deeper humanistic concerns, which might generate critical/ constructive philosophical debates.[24] For that would require — what is anathema to marginal philosophers — a belief in the *possibility* of 'true knowledge' *and* in the serious character of philosophical inquiry.

Thus (to resume the dialectical thread of our argument) the path of inquiry — from the linguistic prescription through the nominalist interlude to the recent genres of marginal philosophies — represents a distorted path which may be depicted (borrowing the words of the German poet) as: *vom schönen Traum zum bösen Trauma* — and therefore, by their own methods and objectives, the marginal philosophers are quite justified in speaking (as they habitually do) of "the end of philosophy" — *only they should speak for themselves merely* and not for the transcendent project of thinking we call 'philosophy'.

§ 15

Is the External World Only a Dream World?

A basic assumption of dialectical realism is the existence of the "external world" as a precondition of the possibility of the truth/ falsity of any "picture of the world". This assumption is to be made, however, in the context of an interpretational matrix of understanding. We shall now examine the philosophical grounds for this assumption.

Question of the Existence of the External World

I recall, at the dawn of my philosophical studies, how overwhelmed I was in reading the opening pages of the *Meditations* of Descartes. There he articulates, with indelible lucidity, his doubts and worries concerning the existence of the external world. I recall, in particular, the following passage:

> ... I must remember that I am a man, and that consequently I am in the habit of sleeping, and in my dreams representing to myself the same things or sometimes even less probable things, than do those who are insane in their waking moments. How often has it happened to me that in the night I dreamt that I found myself in this particular place, that I was dressed and seated near the fire, whilst in reality I was lying undressed in bed. At this moment it does indeed seem to me that it is with eyes awake that I am looking at this paper; that this head which I move is not asleep, that it is deliberately and of set purpose that I extend my hand and perceive it; what happens in sleep does not appear so clear nor so distinct as does all this. But in thinking over this I remind myself that on many occasions I have in sleep been deceived by similar illusions, and in dwelling carefully on this reflection I see so manifestly, that there are no certain indications by which we may clearly distinguish wakefulness from sleep, that I am lost in astonishment. And my astonishment is such that it is almost capable of persuading me that I now dream ... [25]

And yet (as a great scientist confesses): "The belief in an external world independent of the perceiving subject lies at the foundation of all science."[26] For, *either* we must be able to convince ourselves rationally that the external world has an objective existence (in some form) independently of our mind, *or* we must abandon the claim that we know anything outside our mind — and thereby collapse into solipsism. Those appear to be the only two dialectically viable alternatives on this issue.

Some philosophers (phenomenalists in particular) are not overly worried about the question. They simply take a thing to be what it appears to be. So they are inclined to admit into their "world" anything that crawls up, however momentarily, from whatever depth of unknown darkness, into the fringe of their consciousness. For they assume, tacitly, that *esse est percipi*. And yet (as we have seen earlier) there *are* distinct cases of phenomena where a thing may have a character *other* than it seems to have in a given circumstance.

Other philosophers (neopositivists in particular) ascribe to objects in the external world properties which are presumed to be independent of the matrix of the human mind and understanding. They assume, tacitly, that there can be "protocol facts" *without* there being "sense data". They claim that there are such things as "unowned experiences": they envision a world *without* an observer.

Both viewpoints suffer, dialectically speaking, from a philosophical illusion. The illusion, in the one case, of imagining the observer as a spider which weaves the web of its own world. And the illusion, in the other case, of imagining the world as a quicksand wherein the differences of the perspectives of various observers are eliminated without any noticeable trace. Yet, the existence of the external world, without the observer, would mean nothing as a possible (and actual) object of experience. And, correspondingly, the "world" of the observer, without the objective existence of the external world, would be a mere dream world.

Both viewpoints ignore the dialectic of the observer/world interrelation:

I form a picture of *the* world, but the world and its picture are not one. I form hypotheses to guide me in the unexpected universe; and the unexpected waylays my expectations of the world. Yet my picture of the world provides a shelter for my hypotheses concerning the world. The shelter, however, might be ill-built: this is the point of any critical realism. For although I am *in* my world, I am *other* than my world. I am the observer: the interpreter and the rebuilder of *my* world.

Argument of Naive Realism

Can naive realism (which claims to be a "realism") demonstrate the existence of objects *in* the external world? Perhaps it might propose a demonstration. But a vicious circle—that in order to claim that our perceptions are veridical, we must also claim that we have a direct access to the objects in the external world, which we can only know through our perception — would lurk beneath every such demonstration.

In recent philosophy, a quasi-empirical version of the argument has been articulated by G.E. Moore. Taking as a clue (and taking it out of context as well) Kant's depiction of 'externality' — i.e. "the situation in which things are to be met in space" — he proceeds to argue as follows:[27]

Waving one hand in the air, in front of his own and his audience's eyes, and saying "this is a human hand", and then waving the other hand similarly and saying "here is another human hand"; and further observing that, not only he encounters them in space, but also he encounters their encountering (clapping) in space; and reminding us that "human hands" are analytically definable as "physical objects"; he concludes that two "physical objects" exist. Further, given the web of possible relations among physical objects, he infers that numerous other physical objects exist. And therefore the "external world", as a congerie of physical objects, exists.

What is wrong with such a "common-sense" argument? It begs, and begs unwittingly, the point at issue. Could one ignore the fact that the word 'is' occurs in its premises already? And could one ignore also that the existence of 'space' as the receptacle of physical objects in the external world — i.e. the world as 'wherein' — is assumed throughout? But the weakest link in Moore's argument consists in its facile transition from the *perception* of objects to their *existence*. For, how do I *know* that my perceived hand is not actually a dream-object, which I perceive in my mind only, without its having any objective existence in the space/time matrix of the external world? In vain do we await for an answer. For this argument demonstrates, at best, the existence of *'my world'* and not *'the world'*; at worst, it blurs the line between reality and illusion.

Thus Moore's proposed "proof" of the existence of the external world turns out, upon examination, to be no proof worthy of the name. Its only appeal would be to those who subscribe to the naive realism assumed by common-sense philosophy. I regard, accordingly, Moore's essay (with due respect to the British Academy before whom it was read originally) to be the worst essay worthy of note in recent philosophy.

Argument of Conceptual Constructionism

A more cogent argument concerning the existence of the 'external world', has been presented by Bertrand Russell. The very formulation of his question is incomparably better than that of Moore: "Can the existence of anything other than our own sense data be inferred from the existence of those data?"[28] We look at the external world, Russell observes, as the representation of the objective properties of things, through the medium of our senses; much as we look at a landscape through colored eye-glasses. We may differentiate, then, our subjective *picture of the world* from the objective character of the *external world*. Consequently, an object in the "external world" can be seen in n-number of ways by n-number of observers. And, given the multiplicity of observers, an n-number of "private pictures" are formed as a function of their subjective perspectives. Yet, it is the totality of all the aspects, both actual and possible, relative to any object X, which represents the real "thing" in the external world. Hence Russell's definition of a "thing": "Things are those series of aspects which obey the laws of physics." Substitute "science" for "physics" and the definition would hold even better. The main point being that Russell's concept of a "thing" is a *conceptual construction*, only particular aspects of which are reflected in momentary phenomenal things, perceived by particular observers.

Such an argument, evoking the matrix of perspectivism, assumes the postulate of critical empiricism. Its merits lie in its transcending "naive realism"; and in its recognition of the degrees of subjectivity/objectivity (the latter being measured by a scale of intersubjectivity). However, the weak point of the theory — especially from the standpoint of a consistent empiricist — lies in its recourse to the construction of 'ideal objects' in order to establish the existence of 'actual objects'. And Russell, with characteristic keenness, saw this point. Seeing it, he chose to change his strategy, rather than abandon his empirical commitment. That explains the sharp contrast between the two theories of knowledge articulated in his two most important works: *Our Knowledge of the External World* (1926) and *Inquiry into Meaning and Truth* (1940). In the latter work, he redefined the "thing" as a "bundle of qualities" (à la Hume); but insisted that it was empirically verifiable. Where once the "real object" represented a constructed concept, now it represented only a shadow lurking behind the sense-data. Thus Russell buried, as it were, the "ideal object" of his early thinking — but not without repercussions.

Reviewing Russell's work, Albert Einstein found it to be disturbing philosophically. While finding Russell's overcoming of "naive realism" admirable — on the grounds that it is inevitably undermined by science — he rejected his redefinition of the "thing". In the later work of Russell, Einstein saw reflected a "malady" of contemporary philosophy, i.e. an inveterate "fear of metaphysics" (ideal objects, etc.); and he reproached Russell for the "bad intellectual conscience" which shone through the lines of this, his recent, treatise in epistemology.[29] Einstein's disappointment with the views of the *late* Russell is poignant, all the more, since his own theory of the "external world" displays a marked affinity with that of the *early* Russell.

Einstein suggested that our "concepts" of objects, which cannot be inductively derived from sensory experience (as Hume had demonstrated already), are "free creations" of thought. And he proposed that the only requirement for their validity would be that the "conceptual system" be linked at some point with "sensory experience". Thus Einstein sought to restore the concept of the 'thing' as an "ideal object".

How did Einstein, as a natural philosopher, propose to establish the existence of the "external world" and the objects contained therein?

This much stands out prominently in Einstein's chain of reasoning: (a) the forming of the "concept" from the review of a series of phenomena in thought, and (b) the attributing to this "concept" a significance which is (to use Einstein's expression) to a "high degree" independent of the sense impressions which occasioned it. This transcendental objectivity of a "thing", as represented in its constructed concept, is what he means by its real '*existence*'. And the reality of this ideal object is even greater than that of the sense data related to it. Writes Einstein: "These notions (concepts) and relations, although free mental creations, appear to us as stronger and more unalterable than the individual sense experience itself, the character of which as anything other than the result of an illusion or hallucination is never completely guaranteed."[30] But the concrete evidence for the "reality" of these conceptual systems and ideal schemata lies in their operational applicability to experience, or (to use Einstein's expression) in their guiding us in the "labyrinth of sense impressions". Thus, we proceed from the phenomenal *structure* of objects to their conceptual *metastructure*, in order to form an intelligible picture of the world. Hence, Einstein acknowledges it to be a great discovery of Kant to have demonstrated that the question of the *existence* of the world would be meaningless *without* the question of the *intelligibility* of the world. And our conceptual systems constitute the only viable basis for the intersubjective understanding of the "external world" between observers living in their different subjective worlds.

The constructionist theory of objects provides an answer to Hume's skepticism with regard to the objective reality of the external world. It should allay the Humean worry that, when we leave the room, we are uncertain whether its furniture continues to exist. The Humean "impressions" (in the refined sense of that expression as elucidated by Professor H.H. Price who perhaps understood Hume better than anyone else) remained suspended in the medium of consciousness, as it were, and dissolved in time, apparently with no constancy or permanency. What the early Russell (and the later Einstein) tells Hume is that there are, beyond the momentary "impressions" of things, some formal constancies; that these formal constancies provoke us to construct *in* thought "concepts" of objects; and, lastly, that these "concepts" constitute the reference of our discourse, whenever we speak of "objects" *in* the external world.

Yet this, for all its merit, appears to be a paradoxical answer. It highlights the indispensability and yet the insufficiency of experience; and it reintroduces the constructive role of thought in the formation of our "picture of the world". Whereas it was formerly believed that *experience* determines the *thought* about the world, now it appears that the thought gives form and meaning to experience. A passage written by Schrödinger (not altogether independently of this debate), depicts the paradoxical truth in these words: "While direct sensual perception of the phenomenon tells us nothing as to its objective physical nature (or what we usually call so) and has to be discarded from the outset as a source of information, yet the theoretical picture we obtain eventually rests entirely on a complicated array of various informations, all obtained by direct sensual perception. It resides upon them, it is pieced together from them, yet it cannot really be said to contain them . . ."[31] It is worth noting too that this paradoxical truth was recognized already by the first critical scientist, Democritus of Abdera, who opened the mathematical path to the understanding of reality. And it is highly significant that the philosophical scientists of our time have arrived at the same realization too: *i.e.* that it is the *thought*, and not merely experience, which builds a 'picture of the world' and then infers the existence of the world.

Dialectical Argument for the Existence of the External World

The metaquestion concerning the relation of the observer to the world haunts us still: how is the observer to know, given his thought system (and his rhapsody of impressions), that he might not be submerged in a "grand dream" as it were? A dream within which we are bombarded by sense impressions; a dream within which we may conjure and build conceptual systems by the transient power of thought; a veritable "grand dream" which may contain within itself all the moments and vicissitudes of our conscious existence (including our nocturnal dream life) . . . Such a hypothesis is still viable — unless we are able to disprove the hypothesis of solipsism.

My dialectical strategy, accordingly, will be twofold: firstly, I will present a formal argument for the existence of the external world, independently of my mental acts, by evoking the distinction between intentional and non-intentional events; and secondly, I will demonstrate that the hypothesis of the dream-world entails the paradox of multiple observers, and consequently, that solipsism collapses on its own grounds. Nor, as will be evident to the discerning reader, are the two phases of the argument unrelated.

Sketch of the dialectical argument:

(P1) My world exists.

(P2) My world is a changing world.

(P3) The changes in my world represent two classes of phenomena:
   (a) phenomena of which I am the cause
   (b) phenomena of which I am not the cause

(P4) I am able to distinguish the two classes of phenomena (*a* and *b*) by epistemological criteria.

(P5) The changes in my world, of which I am not the cause, must be caused by a reality outside my being.

(∴) The 'external world', as the reality which lies outside my being and which is the cause of some changes in my world, exists.

Commentary:

The first premise (P1) is verifiable by the immediate data of my consciousness — regardless of whether 'my world' might or might not represent 'the world' adequately. The second premise (P2) is verifiable by my memory beliefs — allowing for the limitations attending the epistemological status of memory beliefs. I submit the third premise (P3) as an analytically true proposition. The truth of the fourth premise (P4) rests upon the possibility of the distinction between intentional acts and non-intentional events on the basis of epistemological criteria. And the fifth premise (P5) refers to the *existence* of a 'reality' (world) outside the observer, without any presumption as to the *character* of that 'reality' (world). The conclusion follows from these premises, logically, but not without some assumptions.

Assumptions of the argument:

(A1) the principle of causality — i.e. that every phenomenon has a cause — which I submit as a synthetic *a priori* proposition required for the intelligibility of the causal propositions of our experience.

(A2) the epistemological criteria for distinguishing between 'intentional acts' and 'non-intentional events' in the world — which will be discussed in § 23 below.

(A3) the distinction between 'phenomena' (the world as it appears to the observer) and the 'noumena' (the world as it may be in itself) implicit in any serious realism.

It is noteworthy that the solipsist does not, and cannot, make the last assumption. He does not distinguish the phenomenal world and the noumenal world. For his world consists of a 'dream world' whose range includes the phenomena only. That the consistent solipsist remains a pure phenomenalist, therefore, goes without saying. Here, then, lies the implicit connection between the two phases of my dialectical argument.

As the second phase of my argument I present a thought-experiment:

Imagine the solipsist playing a chess game. But could the solipsist play a chess game? He could play (from his point of view) an 'imaginary game' only: on a dream board, against an imaginary "person", who happens to be but a character (among other characters) in his dream world.

Suppose, then, that the solipsist makes a wrong move; and suppose, too, that his opponent makes an appropriate counter-move, and checks him; and supposing that the solipsist fails to revoke the check, despite a desperate attempt, and he is checkmated … Thus the solipsist is confronted with an improbable situation: this "person" and these "chessmen", mere characters in his dream, display a power which lies *outside* the range of his own power.

Then the solipsist who believes in the correlativity of the two acts — world-dreaming and world-making — is rudely startled by the event of the checkmate in the chess game. Ought he then retaliate by confronting his adversary in the imaginary game with the ultimate truth? Suppose that he does retaliate and utters: "You are *a mere character* in my dream!" This utterance would engender an existential "moment of truth", as it were, between the presumed dreamer and the presumed figure in his dream. And suppose that the figure in the dream counters the dreamer with a reply: "But *you* are a character in *my* dream!" Are there, then, two dreamers (at least) and one world, or many dreamers and many worlds? The scenario could be developed further — with multiple observers and their "worlds" cancelling each other's claim to ontological priority.

The solipsist must then confront the dilemma: Either he believes himself to be the sole creator of his dream-world, and then he must have power over his world; or, if he does not have power over his world, then he cannot believe himself to be the sole creator of his dream-world. The "world-dreamer" (in the most refined sense of that expression) must also be a "world-maker". For the analogy is between his dream and our world *rather than* between his dream and our dream. Unlike our dream, which is *contained* in our world, his world is contained in his dream, from which there is no awakening.

The paradigm of the chess game shows that: *neither* can the solipsist prove the truth of his original assumption of a single observer, nor can he handle the paradoxes of multiple observers in the context of his worldview.

The dialectic of the case is intriguing:

The basic proposition of the solipsist is: "*The* world is *my* world — and (implicitly) I am the only observer." This proposition implies that there are no objects or persons in the world which are not mere figures in his dream. That reduces the "external world" to a "dream-world" ontically. Therefore, when *his* world ends (as in case of his death) then *the* world would also end. But this is not the case. Imagine, then, that the solipsist upon being checkmated resigns from the game and leaves the scene. Then, as he abandons the chess-game, the possibility of the chess-game would vanish for everyone. But the solipsist would be startled, and unable to explain, upon re-entering the scene to find a new game in progress between the old and a new challenger. Evidently, the world of chess did not vanish for others. On the contrary, from the point of view of the other players, only one player (the solipsist) left the scene — while everything else in *their* respective dream-worlds remained the same. Any claim of the solipsist about the world, given the multiplicity of observers, is canceled by a counter-claim. Thus the thesis of the solipsist, if true, entails a consequence which is falsifiable on the grounds of its own assumption. This demonstrates the transcendental impossibility — nay absurdity even — of solipsism.

CHAPTER VI

Hypothesis of Cosmic Harmony

Perhaps the deepest assumption of modern science is the idea of 'cosmic harmony'. The very expectation of discovering the laws of natural phenomena implicitly rests upon this assumption. And, without this belief, the intelligibility of the cosmos would remain questionable.

The question before us is: Can the metascientific assumption of 'cosmic harmony' be justified philosophically?

By 'cosmic harmony' I understand that the universe — as an object of intelligible experience — consists of a megasystem, comprising systems and subsystems, within which there are levels of order, periodicities, and equilibria.

We know that the ancients — the natural philosophers of early Greece — took the idea of 'cosmic harmony' as the startingpoint of their approach to nature. The very word *kosmos* meant, to them, "a great being of order and beauty". Even their one "philosopher of conflict", Heraclitus, ultimately subsumed the principle of phenomenal conflict under the ideal of an overriding rational order: it is out of the interplay of strife (*éris*) and reason (*lógos*) that evolve the universal patterns of phenomena.[1]

The idea of 'cosmic harmony' was resurrected — after two thousand years of darkness — by the thinkers of the Renaissance (and developed further by the thinkers of the Enlightenment) on philosophical grounds. *Ubi materia, ibi geometria* — was the word-magic that gave to Descartes, Kepler, and Spinoza the intellectual courage to shun the medieval heritage and usher the dawn of the modern worldview. So the vision of the "Kosmos" by Leibniz (the one thinker to whom the designation "microcosm" applies uniquely) assumed the harmony of the universe on purely rational grounds: for the principle of sufficient reason, which he called his "grand principle", states "that nothing happens without a reason why it should be so rather than otherwise".[2] And, on this basic point, Leibniz and Newton (despite their interminable disagreements on other critical points) agreed. Nor did Kant question, though he questioned nearly everything else, the hypothesis of cosmic harmony; but, on the contrary, was to defend it on *a priori* grounds.

However, it was not until Henri Poincaré, and later Albert Einstein, that the ideal of 'cosmic harmony' was evoked on the basis of new mathematical and scientific arguments, causing modern cosmologists to take a new look at the universe. "Our experience hitherto justifies us in believing," wrote Einstein, "that Nature is the realization of the simplest conceivable mathematical ideas."[3] Whether Einstein derived this belief from the natural philosophers of the Renaissance, or whether it originated in his own creative mind, the fact remains that this belief constituted the main philosophical motive, the *télos*, of his scientific inquiries. Subsequently, Henry Margenau was to formalize this metascientific belief into an epistemological principle: *i.e.* that the very possibility of formulating scientific hypotheses requires the assumption of an invariant order, a constancy and continuity underlying phenomenal processes, without which there could be no 'science'.[4] There could be no 'science', I interpret these scientific thinkers to say, without the *assumption* of 'cosmic harmony' as a philosophical hypothesis. Let us then examine the meaning and ground of this grand assumption.

§ 16

Order and Disorder

A mere cosmic accident would have been sufficient to prevent us from even thinking about the question of order/disorder in the cosmos. If, for example, the amount and distribution of the water vapor in the atmosphere of the Earth had been slightly greater than what it happens to be, then a thick blanket of clouds would have enveloped the Earth continuously, forming an opaque screen as it were, veiling the clear sky and its population of stars from our view forever. We would then have lived our lives, and thought our thoughts, under an all-encompassing and perpetual fog, totally unaware of the existence of celestial phenomena — except possibly, the vague awareness that there might be something like a "Sun", whose light would seem to vaguely penetrate the canopy of fog and enable the plants to survive. And its movement would also explain the diurnal periodicity of light and dark, as well as the succession of our meager seasons. Our earthly existence would then have resembled that of cave-dwellers who are unable to leave their dismal habitat; and our science would then have remained crippled and been reduced to the knowledge of earthly phenomena only.

But, fortunately for mankind, this did not happen to be the case: an insignificant accident (from the cosmic point of view) did not alter the constitution of the atmosphere for us which would have been a catastrophic event (from our point of view) and we were able to look beyond the *earth* and attain a glimpse of the *cosmos*.

And, now, when we turn our eyes (granting the limitations of our epistemological goggles) toward the cosmos that surrounds us, we experience a "sense of awe" (of which Kant was to speak); for what we confront baffles us, by its enormity and complexity, and by its invisible lines of undisclosed harmony:

Our galaxy contains (as estimated by astronomers) approximately 100 billion stars. Of these we see, with our bare eyes on a clear night, about 3000 stars only. And, with the aid of the 100-inch Schmidt telescope, we could see about 1500 million stars in the skies. Some of the stars we perceive now have perished a long time ago — being many light years away (a "light year" being defined as the distance travelled by light with its constant velocity c in one year) — resulting in the retarded perception of their last rays which reach us belatedly. By contrast, there are other strikingly bright stars (the novae) which suddenly appear in the sky, changing the appearance of a whole constellation dramatically, and then disappear. Further, beyond the stars known to us, there may exist skies filled with stars, surrounding "island universes" which remain unknown.

Our giant telescopes magnify our epistemological problems:

They locate no less than 500 million galaxies in space (out of an estimated number of 100,000 million galaxies in the universe) — but locate them in an altered perspective. E.g. they show us the Andromeda galaxy, the youngest and the nearest, not as it is today, but as it was some two billion years ago (for it has taken that time for its light rays to reach us on earth). Nor, therefore, they can tell us anything about the origins of the galaxies (much less the cosmos). We only know some scattered facts about our cosmos: we know that the lighter elements were formed first, and that the heavier elements were formed later; we know something about the celestial chemistry of the first "three minutes" of our own galaxy; and we know our cosmic time scale (5 billion years for earth and 10 billion years for our galaxy). But the question of the origin of our galaxy remains shrouded in mystery and controversy. Did it originate in primeval nebula or in primeval matter? Did it arise from gradual condensation or was it formed by sudden explosion? Which theory of cosmogony approximates the truth: the theories of Kant and Laplace (and their revised version by C.F. Von Weizsäcker) or the theories of Lemaître and Gamow?

In view of these problems, it is audacious, to say the least, to talk about the "state of the cosmos", whether in terms of its harmony or disharmony.

And yet some authors, reviewing the "history" of our galaxy, deduce conclusions which portend total disharmony. Noteworthy in this connection is the theory of "worlds in collision" advocated by Velikovsky and others. Velikovsky argues that, since "two series of cosmic catastrophes took place in historical times" (precisely, thirty-four and twenty-six centuries ago, respectively), to which some ancient historical documents bear testimony, this evidence constitutes a sufficient demonstration of cosmic disharmony.[5] But such evidence — quite apart from its dubious character owing to its being derived from apocryphal documents of human history — cannot be taken (as its author intended it to be taken) as implying the negation of the hypothesis of cosmic harmony. For, in view of the range of cosmology which estimates events in terms of millions and billions of years, it would be naive to derive one's picture of the cosmos from a few centuries of earthly existence. Moreover, the transitional instability of cosmic events might imply the idea of 'cosmic evolution'. And the hypothesis of cosmic harmony is not contradicted by the idea of cosmic evolution; on the contrary, viewed from a dialectical perspective, it may require it.

Let us review, then, three cases of the "hidden harmonics" of the cosmos, as recorded in the history of science:

Consider the problem of planetary motion. Johannes Kepler, operating on the Aristotelian assumption that the orbits of the planets describe a circle, encountered insurmountable difficulties in explaining certain celestial phenomena. He was puzzled, in particular, about the shape of the orbit of Mars against the background of fixed stars. And he has described his mental agony in *De Stella Martis*: Should he admit irregular and erratic facts in his picture of the cosmos, and abandon the elegant idea of circular orbits, and therewith shatter the ideal of cosmic harmony? But Kepler believed too deeply in the ideal of cosmic harmony to be daunted by the problem. He reasoned that, if this particular pattern failed to represent it, then another pattern might succeed in representing it. He then formulated, with a brilliant stroke, an alternative hypothesis for planetary motion: that a planet moves around the Sun on an elliptical orbit (with the Sun at one focus of the ellipse). Then all the collected data (what he had inherited from his predecessors and what he had collected himself) fell into place; and all the celestial phenomena (including the shape of the orbit of Mars) could be explained. Further, on the basis of this new hypothesis, Kepler was able to formulate his great law of planetary motion: that the straight line, connecting the center of an orbiting planet and that of the Sun, sweeps equal areas in equal intervals of time. This law was, and remains, surely one of the most important discoveries in astronomy — (it also implies another law, correlating the period of a planet and its distance from the Sun, which Kepler was to formulate later) — as it revealed that the harmonics of the motion of planets, based upon the ellipse, were far more complex and elegant than their being based upon the simple circle. And Kepler (who already believed in geometrical order of the cosmos) took this law as a further evidence for the harmony of the cosmos.

Or, consider the problem of three-bodies in motion: it is complicated by the fact that there are 3 bodies, hence 9 degrees of motion in 3-dimensional space, and 18 independent integrals. Reflecting over this problem, J.L. Lagrange the mathematician proposed an astronomical paradigm: Let the Sun (S) and two planets (A and B), attracting each other according to the law of gravitation, be arranged so as to occupy the corners of a triangle, and let the triangle (ASB) be equilateral, so that the distances between the three bodies are equal; then (Lagrange concluded) the two planets (A and B) would describe identical elliptical orbits around the Sun (S), with their axes inclined to each other at an angle of 60 degrees. No one assailed the validity of Lagrange's reasoning on mathematical grounds; but it was generally doubted that this ideal paradigm could be actualized in nature; and so the theorem was regarded as a pipe-dream. It was argued, however, that if the sides of the ideal triangle varied in length *slightly*, the motions of the planets (A and B) would be such that *nearly* the same orbital distances between them would persist indefinitely. Suppose, within our solar system, that A is the planet Jupiter, and L one of the two ideal Lagrangean points (two points because they would be located on the curve of their common orbit 60 superior and 60 inferior to the given planet respectively), so that ASL represents an equilateral triangle, then if another planet B be located close to the point L, the subsequent elliptical motion of B will always be close to L. Now (since Lagrange's time) astronomers have discovered two clusters of planets: the Trojan Group (numbering 5 planets) and the Greek Group (numbering 10 planets) which, by their proximate positions and varied velocities (their orbiting time being from one to twelve years), fulfill the requirements of the Lagrangean hypothesis: their patterns of motion are analogous either continuously or periodically.

Or, again, consider the phenomenon of the Sun. What now the

astronomers call by the familiar name of "Yellow Dwarf" represented, until recently, a great puzzle as to its continued radiation at such a high intensity. Veiled by its blinding light, its "inner rhythm" remains invisible to us. It sits 30,000 light years away from the mysterious core of our galaxy. "If the comparison were not insulting to the Sun-god," Flammarion once observed, "one might say that it is like a giant spider sitting near the center of its web."[6] For the Sun takes a central place in the galaxy, and by the powerful gravitational field that it spreads around it, it holds other planets in their orbits; and they, in turn, simulate the eastward rotation of the Sun around their own axes. The puzzle, why this gigantic mass of fire did not grow cold gradually as other planets did, and thereby lose its flow of energy radiation, embarrassed the cosmogenic theory for some time. Then it was discovered that the Sun is actually a giant reactor which chemically generates its own energy from the nuclear interaction of its internal atoms. It converts, with its core temperature of 20,000,000 degrees centigrade, hydrogen into helium, thereby producing a continuous flow of radiant energy. Yet its corona (or its halo) has a cooler temperature of 1,000,000 degrees centigrade. As the Sun rotates on its axis, there appear across its surface "sunspots" — dark or red blemishes — seemingly irregular in shape and appearance. Are these sunspots mere arbitrary epiphenomena? So it was believed to be the case for a long time. But they display a rhythmic cycle, of appearance and disappearance, occasioned by the magnetic cycle of the Sun itself: for the Sun reverses and regains its polarity on a 22-year period. And other planets (including our earth) display their own periodic process, either imitating or complementing those of the Sun. Thus the Sun, symbolically speaking, holds the mirror to our universe.

Patterns of harmony are not limited to the macrolevel of phenomena; they are to be found at the microlevel as well: Recall that the "Periodic Table of Elements" represents an arrangement of chemical elements by family groupings, i.e., elements with similar properties recur at regular intervals when listed in the order of their increasing atomic weights (and the gift of Mendeleyev consisted in that, while only a third of the number of elements known today were known to him, he inferred a pattern which predicted the position and properties of unknown elements). Or that the hexagon pattern is reflected in the structure of the benzene molecule which represents a substantial family of organic compounds; that it is also reflected in the structure of the ice molecule, from which the snow flake (which comes in a dozen patterns) derives its basic structure; and that it also recurs in a grosser form as the basic pattern of beehive; *etcetera*. Or that the structure of the simplest atom, with the proton at its center and the electron at its orbit, suggests a model of the planetary system in microcosm . . .

Other cases illustrating the harmonics of the cosmos could be gathered from the realms of mathematics and the natural sciences. But we are less interested in amassing the empirical evidence than in elucidating the dialectic of the issue. Accordingly we shall turn to examine the counter-evidence to the hypothesis of cosmic harmony.

In recent scientific debates, the idea of "chaos" has emerged from an array of chaotic phenomena, and has acquired a mathematical significance. Does it threaten to turn the dream of science, with regard to the harmony of the cosmos, into an existential nightmare? The phenomenon of 'chaos' represents a class of non-ordered dynamics, *i.e.*, an apparently acausal and aperiodic process. A classic example of the chaotic phenomenon is the Brownian movement: look at a particle of dust in the air, through a magnifying lens, and it displays a movement which may be described as a continuously erratic jiggle (perhaps owing to the invisible bombardment of vapor molecules in the surrounding atmosphere). Or observe the continuously random movement of water splashed by rain across the window of a car in motion. Or, again, consider the random motion of a turbulent river: a non-summative phenomenon, which cannot be adequately assessed through the analysis of the separate motions of its waves, for it involves a complex torus. On the face of it, the flowing river represents a state of phenomenal chaos. Yet, we know that the direction of the current determines the wave-line of the meander-formation; that the area of the cross-section of the river is correlated to the strength of its wave-line; that its general torus moulds its total structure. Our knowledge is not sufficient to give us a complete picture of what is happening in these cases.

It is less surprising that there are instances of disorder than that there is often some order implicit in the apparent disorder. For the phenomenon of chaos may also be seen as a *fringe phenomenon*: lying between the boundaries of one stable pattern and another. If so, then the attractor centers of the two potential patterns will, in time, pull the chaotic waves toward them (or toward one of them) and incorporate them into a pattern. That this in fact happens is illustrated by the discovery of the Lorenz attractor: a twin-figure, resembling the rings on a moth's wings, wherein the trajectory line never intersects itself (in the matrix of the three-dimensional space), and hence it is never iterative at any point, and yet the resulting pattern is confined to a definite boundary. The Lorenz attractor may serve as a paradigm for the phenomenon of chaos. That apparently chaotic phenomena may reveal, *in the long run*, some underlying geometrical pattern and/or an unsuspected causal connection is intriguing. It is not surprising, then, that the students of the "science of chaos" are beginning to speak of "order in chaos" and (with some diffidence) of "chaotic harmonies".[7]

As we encounter the phenomena of "chaos" and "chance", we must remember — as Poincaré has observed already[8] — that they usually have a long and complicated "anterior history" and do not emerge *ex nihilo*. And the "anterior history" represents the causal continuum wherein an "event" is but a moment. The "event" must be seen, then, not as an isolated dot on the scattergram of statistics, but as the manifestation of underlying continuities. And the inquiry into a new field of phenomena — (as Bohr observed in the course of his epistemological discussions with Einstein) — may pass through a developmental phase wherein the perception of *chaos* is gradually replaced by the recognition of *order*.

Our dialectical conclusion, concerning the phenomenon of chaos in the world of experience, is threefold then: that what we perceive to be "chaos" may be (a) the result of the limited perspective of the observer; or (b) a transitional phase in the natural history of the given phenomenon from one stage of equilibrium to another; or (c) the apparent mask of a hidden order. Here, then, we must introduce the suggestion that there is a *disparity* between our "first vision" and "second vision". And the unforgettable philosophical lesson which we may learn from the dialectic of order/disorder is that we must take the disparity between our "first vision" and "second vision" as a measure, not only of the limitations of our "epistemological goggles", but also of the complex character of cosmic harmony.

§ 17

Contribution of the Theory of Relativity to the Hypothesis of Cosmic Harmony

The theory of relativity (and its cosmological generalization) provide important philosophical insights concerning the hypothesis of cosmic harmony. We encounter three great ideas in Einsteinian cosmology: (a) the idea of geometrical form *as a* structural representation of objects and their modalities in the world, (b) the transformation laws interrelating the dimensional values of different world systems, and (c) the 'cosmological constant' as the symbolic expression of the equilibrium of field forces in the universe. Since these three ideas have significant implications for the hypothesis of cosmic harmony, we shall dwell on them here.[9]

Does Geometry Represent the Form of the World?

The very title of Einstein's essay — *Geometrie und Erfahrung* — was pregnant with the implication (to be demonstrated subsequently) that there *was* a connection between the abstract configurations of geometry and the experience of the world.

Einstein writes: "Experience, of course, remains the sole criterion of the physical utility of a mathematical construction. But the creative principle remains in mathematics. In a certain sense, then, I hold it as true that pure thought may grasp reality, as the ancients dreamed."[10] This represents his methodological approach.

Geometry as a formal science, which appears to be irrelevant to the world, can be shown to be actually relevant to the world. Einstein proposed to accomplish this by introducing a basic postulate: that rigid bodies in the world are verifiably interrelated, with respect to their possible dispositions in space, as are the configurations of geometry.[11] Thus we are able to convert "formal geometry" into "practical geometry". And such an "emended and completed" geometry (as Einstein calls it) would represent the character of things in space: it would reflect the geometrical form of the world. This means that abstract explorations in geometry would *provide* us an understanding of imaginable possibilities in the actual world of experience.

Consider two great geometrical systems, which compete with each other, in representing the form of the world. In Riemannian geometry we encounter properties of space which are radically different from those with which we are familiar in Euclidian geometry. Here, e.g., more than one straight line can be drawn through two fixed points; the sum of the angles of a triangle are always greater than two right angles; and the ratio of the circumference of a circle to its diameter is always less than the π (and it decreases as the area of the circle increases); etc.

Which geometry represents the true form of space?

The Euclidian schema represents the form of the *perception* of space. But, since the space-time continuum of relativity cosmology has a mega-curvature, its *conception* requires the Riemannian schema. The question, as to which kind of geometry (whose axioms are "free creations" of thought) truly reflects the form of the world, must ultimately be answered by the realm of "experience". In the realm of the *perceptual world* (as Kant observed) the laws of Euclidean geometry hold; but in the realm of the *conceptual world* (as Einstein observes) the laws of Riemannian geometry hold. There is accordingly no contradiction — some commentators notwithstanding — but only complementarity between the two geometries.

However, "experience" is acquired and processed by physics, and not by geometry; and consequently, the metaquestion of decidability between systems of geometry, must lie outside the science of geometry. Thus, for example, the ray of light, which must travel along the shortest path, follows the curvature of space, and describes a Riemannian line (and not an Euclidean line); and, further, it is the Riemannian geometry which provides us a set of quadratic coordinates for the representation of space-time continuum; and the structure of this continuum explains, as a corollary, the curvilinear orbits of the planets; *etc.* Such empirical considerations would determine which geometrical system (given the fact that each is endowed with rationality and internal coherence) we may take to represent our world — or a level of our world — and its harmonics.

Are There Constancies Behind Relativity?

The main thesis of the special theory of relativity (STR) is: That in the universe there are an infinite number of systems of reference, moving uniformly relative to each other, in which all physical laws assume the simplest identical forms; but (while the velocity of light remains constant in these systems) the local lengths and times measured by the same rods and clocks appear to be different in each system; and yet the results of all these measurements can be meaningfully interrelated by means of a set of transcendental concepts.

Within this universal matrix matter and time lose their constancy: bodies in motion "contract" and clocks in motion are "retarded" (owing to the "compression" of their mass atoms, in the direction of the motion, as a function of the intensity of the gravitational field within which the motion takes place). Yet light travels with a constant velocity (c = 300,000 kilometers per second) regardless of the relative motion of the system of reference. The Michelson-Morley experiment, indirectly and unintentionally, provided the empirical evidence for this proposition.

Consider the experiment:

The experimental interferometer failed to determine the motion of the Earth, relative to the velocity of light, by failing to record any change in the to-and-fro velocity of a projected ray of light between two points on Earth. Let a pulse of light be projected simultaneously from a stationary point (O) to two mirrors (M_1 and M_2) located eastward and westward, as the Earth continues to rotate on its axis with a velocity (v), then (according to classical physics) the time (t) required for it to arrive at M_1 will be greater by a fraction than the time (t') required for it to arrive at M_2, so that $\partial t = (t-t') > 0$; but the result observed in the experiment was: $\partial t = 0$. Because of its startling negative result — which would shake classical physics out of its dogmatic slumber — the experiment was repeated, again and again, on the floors of the valleys and atop the hills, hoping to discover the trace of an infinitesimal difference, but there was to be none.

But the negative result, in the hands of Einstein, produced a positive reconstruction. Einstein proposed the postulate of the constancy of the velocity of light as an assumption of physics: i.e. that the time required for a ray of light to travel from a point A to another point B equals the time required to travel from B to A (from the point of view of an observer at rest) *regardless* of the relative motion of the given reference system.

Now there are an infinite number of reference systems in the universe: their hypothetical observers might view the world from their relative perspectives of rest or motion—none of which represent the objective state of rest or motion in the cosmos. Is there, then, beyond the constancy of the velocity of light, any formal constancy which might interrelate these reference systems? In response to this question, the theory of relativity proposes a set of transcendental laws (disclosing formal constancies) by means of which we might describe the structural interrelations between various systems in the world.

Specifically, we may transform the coordinates (x and t) of any world-point (P) in a reference system (S) into coordinates (x ´ and t´) of the same world-point (P) in another reference system (S´), by means of a pair of Lorentz formulae.

However, the harmony of the cosmic picture at the conceptual niveau does not preclude the undulations at the phenomenal niveau. The surface structure of curved space may be intercepted by local discrepancies of matter and energy concentration; but they do not disrupt the general picture. Consider (to use Einstein's analogy) the rippled surface of a lake which leaves the structure of the lake unaffected.

Thus the discrepancies between the systems of things in a relativistic universe can be integrated, epistemologically, by means of a set of invariant concepts in cosmology. The "observer" is introduced, in this cosmology, in order to enable us to relegate ordinary observations to the realm of "relativity" — but only to transcend it conceptually and attain an objective vision of "reality". For "reality", as Einstein conceived it, represents a continuous manifold characterized by invariance and harmony. It was no mere accident, then, that the resulting cosmological model of the universe represented a state of equilibrium. It is worth noting here—as Henry

Margenau has noted already[12] — that students of the theory of relativity have usually concentrated on the dramatic aspects of the relativity of phenomena and ignored the constancies of nature implicit therein.

The question arises then: Do the phenomena of the quantum realm present an irrevocable challenge to the idea of cosmic harmony implicit in the theory of relativity?

In response to this question it is instructive to read the following passages from Einstein's commentary:

> I wish to adduce reasons which keep me from falling in line with the opinion of almost all contemporary theoretical physicists... One arrives at very implausible theoretical conceptions, if one attempts to maintain the thesis that statistical quantum theory is in principle capable of producing a complete description of an *individual* physical system. On the other hand, those difficulties of theoretical interpretation disappear, if one views the quantum-mechanical description as the description of *ensembles* of systems... (the ψ-function is to be understood as the description not of a single system but of an ensemble of systems)...
>
> For me, however, the expectation that the adequate formulation of the universal laws involves the use of *all conceptual elements*, which are necessary for a complete description (and explanation), is more a natural (way of thinking). It is furthermore not at all surprising that, by using an *incomplete description*, (in the main) only *statistical statements* can be obtained out of such description. If it should be possible to move forward to a *complete description*, it is likely that the laws would represent relations among *all conceptual elements* of this description which, *per se*, have *nothing to do* with statistics...
>
> We are here concerned with 'categories' or schemes of thought, the selection of which is, in principle, entirely open to us and whose qualification can only be judged by the degree to which its use *contributes to making* the totality of the contents of consciousness 'intelligible'.[13]

Evidently, Einstein is concerned, not only with the *order of the cosmos*, but also with the *conceptual matrix for the intelligibility of the order*. Herein lies the philosophical affinity between Einstein and Kant (to whom he makes repeated references in this connection). In particular, Einstein cites Kant on the question of 'presentation': that 'reality' is not merely 'given' (*gegeben*) to us, but rather 'posed' (*aufgegeben*) to us for interpretation. The theory of relativity represents, then, an interpretation of the order of cosmos — an interpretation which is grounded in a conceptual matrix. And the challenge of the quantum theory — which in the absence of a conceptual matrix resorts to statistical index — falters on epistemological grounds.

Moreover, there are some indications of order in the realm of the quanta itself: Had not Bohr himself proposed a "planetary model" for the elucidation of the structure of the atom — consisting of a proton at the center and an electron at the orbit—simulating the sun and its planet? Had not Einstein explained to Bohr, that although it may not be possible to predict with certainty at what *point* a projected electron hits a photographic plate (owing to the diffraction of the microwave connected with the motion of the particle) it is nevertheless possible to predict with certainty in what *region* of the plate it will be found? And did not (according to Dirac's dialectical hypothesis of particle/ antiparticle) some groups of quanta (i.e. the baryons and the mesons) arrange themselves in space according to a hexagon pattern wherein the positive and the negative particles occupied opposite points diametrically? Rare instances of order within a sea of apparent disorder in this realm — but sufficient to warrant an epistemological revision.

The very "comprehension" of the world, Einstein argued, is made possible by the construction of a conceptual system which imbues the rhapsody of perceptions with order and meaning. Hence our "picture of the world", to be possible, must be a rational construction; but the construction must be confirmed by the world of experience. To empiricists who attacked this conceptual realism as "idealism", Einstein pointed out that they themselves suffered from a "positivistic attitude" which rested upon the simple fallacy of *esse est percipi* (i.e. for x to be real it must be observed empirically only). On the contrary, Einstein argued, the ontological issue (*i.e.* what we must take the character of "reality" to be) is to be resolved in terms of the epistemological issue (*i.e.* what we can take to be "intelligible" to us). Therefore we must ask the critical question: Are the apparent uncertainty and indeterminacy of the quantum realm owing to an inherent disorder in nature, or, are they an indication of the inadequacy of our level of understanding? This brilliant move adequately checked the challenge posed by the quantum theory to cosmology.

For these (and other) reasons, Einstein believed that the quantum picture of "reality" was incomplete and inadequate; and he regarded it to be a "weakness" of the theory to invoke explanations involving non-rational notions like "indeterminacy". The character of "nature" — he told Bohr and others[14] — was not such as to require "ugly" constructions (e.g. "statistical theory") for its intelligibility and comprehension. And the "intelligibility" of nature remained the ultimate challenge — and the ultimate wonder — in cosmology.

The Cosmological Constant

And so we must ascend, from the special theory of relativity to the general theory of relativity, in order to attain yet another view of cosmic harmony. The main thesis of the general theory of relativity (GTR) is: that the space-time continuum, providing a four-dimensional matrix of all possible world-lines, has the form of a positive curvature (wherein particular instances of + curvature may occur locally) resulting in a universal energy field. In this matrix "things" are described as points on continuous functions, field variables, of four coordinates. Too, within this matrix, matter and energy are interrelated — as depicted by the Einsteinian formula: "$E = MC^2$" (i.e. that matter is condensed energy). This law, assuming the constancy of the velocity of light (c), demonstrates the interconvertability of matter as mass (M) and energy (E) measured in ergs. It is applicable, not only at the macrolevel of physical phenomena, but also at the microlevel of quanta. In the latter context, the masses of particles represent enormous concentrations of potential energy enclosed within very small volumes — "the millionaire in beggar's clothing" (to use Einstein's metaphor). The correlation (indeed equilibrium) between matter and radiation — demonstrated by the Compton Effect — confirmed Einstein's hypothesis concerning the *photon* which challenged the traditional corpuscular theory. One can imagine that Benedict de Spinoza — the favorite philosopher of Einstein — would have appreciated this, the finest, mathematical expression of monistic ontology.

In this universe, the gravitational field is governed by the "cosmological constant" (symbolized: λ): i.e. that the forces of attraction/repulsion among physical systems balance each other owing to the general structure of space. Where the force of attraction dominates over repulsion, there is condensation; and where the converse is the case, there is expansion. But, given the cosmological constant, the universe will neither collapse nor dissipate in the long run. Hence, the "cosmological constant" implies that the gravitational force (g), which tends to diminish the radius, is countered by a cosmic force (f), which tends to augment it. And the process approaches the ideal of an "equilibrium" sufficient to allow for cosmic expansion (and evolution) and yet to preclude cosmic collapse or dispersion. Whether the cosmic equilibrium is static (Einstein) or dynamic (Lemaître) will be depicted by different cosmological models.

Let us then look at the model of the universe as conceived by Einstein and DeSitter: It is a universe in a permanent state of unstable equilibrium. Its function in the space-time continuum has a value of " $\lambda \geq 0$ ". Originally the cosmological constant was evoked to maintain its equilibrium; subsequently it was dropped to allow for expansion. Is this universe static or dynamic? It lies on the borderline between the two states; for the value of λ is only slightly greater than O; allowing for some degree of evolution and expansion but without losing its basic equilibrium. The beauty of this cosmological model, then, lies in that it depicts the simplest form of cosmic equilibrium.

Consider the comparative schema of the two cosmological models:

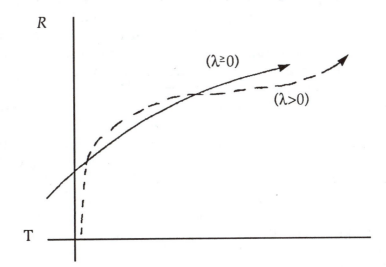

where: R = radius of space curvature
        T = time
        Solid Curve = Einstein-DeSitter Model
        Dotted Curve = Lemaître Model

How does the Lemaître model look by comparison to the Einstein-DeSitter model? Its function in the space-time continuum has a value of " $\lambda > 0$ ", or more precisely, " $\lambda > \lambda$ E" (where λ E denotes the value of λ in the Einstein-DeSitter model). Hence the curve of this model begins markedly lower at the initial phase, and rises higher at the final phase, while nearly overlapping the curve of the other model during its long hesitation phase (which has been calculated to be longer than the Hubble period of 2 billion years). The form of the curve in this model allows for the internal equilibria of the galaxies over a very long period of time. Thus the Lemaitre model retains the merit of its competitor (i.e. its cosmic equilibrium to a significant degree), and yet explains the origin of the universe by the "big bang" hypothesis, while allowing for cosmic evolution and expansion to a greater degree.

That the universe is expanding there is no longer any doubt — it has been demonstrated by the Doppler effect (and its phenomenon of "redshift" radiation) — but this external expansion does not negate the continued integrity of galaxies and the field forces within them. And that the universe may have originated in an explosion of primeval matter (the "big bang" hypothesis) is indicated by the pervasive existence of "cosmic rays" — those extraordinary, superradioactive, waves which may harbor the prehistory of the universe. "The radiation produced during the disintegrations (of the primeval atom), during the period of the first expansion, could explain cosmic rays . . . " writes Lemaître, "They are truly cosmic, they testify to the primeval activity of the cosmos. In their course through wonderfully empty space, during billions of years, they have brought us evidence of the superradioactive age; indeed they are a sort of 'fossil rays' which tell us what happened when the stars first appeared."[15] But does original explosion imply continued expansion, or, expansion at a given rate? No matter — so long as it takes place in the context of cosmic equilibrium.

The universe, viewed from the perspective of the theory of relativity, is isotropic. Certain cosmic rays and elements (particularly the hydrogen/helium related elements) are pervasive throughout the universe; the curvature of space is uniform at all places; and the same cosmological laws hold good everywhere. But isotropy does not mean homogeneity; and, consequently, the idea of an "evolving universe" or an "expanding universe" (the latter demonstrated by the Doppler effect) is not contradictory to the idea of isotropy.

Except for one disquieting thought: it was once observed by James Jeans that the occurrence of events in the matrix of time is somewhat similar to the way in which "the pattern of a tapestry is woven out of a loom"; but — from the viewpoint of the early cosmological model of a 'static universe' constructed by the young Einstein in his pre-DeSitterian phase — the tapestry of events is already woven in the universe as in the spherical world there is not absolute demarcation between past/present/future; and it is we, the observers, who must discover its successive parts, bit by bit "in time" as it were, with the groping hand of a blind explorer . . .

Whatever the discrepancies between these two cosmological models — the Einstein-DeSitter model and the Lemaitre model — it is evident that the idea of the "cosmological constant" plays a critical role in both pictures.[16] Both world pictures, accordingly, envision a cosmic harmony based upon the ultimate equilibrium of cosmic forces. That Einstein, in later years, was to set the "cosmological constant" aside, seeking to dissolve it in the context of a new "unified field theory" as it were — the finest dream perhaps of modern science (with even further implications for the hypothesis of cosmic harmony) — is a theme for another occasion.

It is clear that Einstein — who disagreed with Kant in relying upon *a priori* principles in explaining the intelligibility of the world — eventually based his own scientific picture of the world upon one great *a priori* postulate: the idea of cosmic harmony. This postulate also rendered the world intelligible. And 'intelligibility' for Einstein consists of the susceptibility of phenomena to being ordered by general concepts which are themselves "free creations" of the mind. The only requirement for these concepts is that they must be connected by "relations of some kind" with sense experience. The concepts of science, then, are neither merely *empirical* nor *a priori*: they represent a creative interplay between thinking and experience: they are the very fiber of our "picture of reality". For concepts serve as guides in the "bewildering chaos of perceptions" (to use Einstein's expression) so that we come to apprehend general truths from particular observations in experience. But the resulting "picture of reality" must above all be intelligible — as Kant believed and Einstein regarded that belief to be a "great insight" of the philosopher — a belief without which there can be no motive for natural science or natural philosophy.

§ 18

Nemesis

> " . . . for things make amends and give
> reparation to one another, for their
> injustice (disequilibrium), according to
> the order of time . . ."
>   —Anaximander: Fragment
>   (Peri Physios Istoria/c. 580 BC)

The above words from the oldest extant text in the history of European natural philosophy — remaining buried in the archives only to be referred to as a relic of prescientific thought or as an object of scholarly curiosity — those ancient words can no longer be ignored or taken lightly in view of the philosophical import of discoveries in modern science . . .

For, if by the *hypothesis of cosmic harmony* we understand — that the universe consists of a megasystem encompassing systems and subsystems, within which there are levels of order, periodicity, and equilibria — then the evidence in its favor is considerable. The evidence, however, does not erase the counter-evidence of asymmetry, of aperiodicity, of chaos. And so the question may be asked anew: "Is the universe characterized by harmony or disharmony?" And, we might note, what a presumptuous question that is — unless we assume that we already have before us a complete picture of the 'cosmos' in all its complexity and infinity — a picture which we do not have.

We are barely able to estimate the age of our own galaxy (the Milky Way) to be 15 billion years, the age of our planet (the Earth) to be 2 billion years, and the origin of life on earth to have been 1 billion years ago. Our neighbor galaxy, the Andromeda, lies 2,000,000 light years away. And our "cosmological horizon" — i.e. the domain of the cosmos from which light can reach us — defines for us a woefully limited 'observable universe': its diameter is no greater than (10^{25}) kilometers, which is yet sufficiently great to bedwarf our imagination, and beyond that lies darkness (from our point of view and not the point of view of the cosmos) and not 'dark matter' merely.

Moreover, the very origin of the 'cosmos' remains shrouded in controversy and mystery. Was it nebulous and gradual or was it hot and chaotic? Some contemporary astronomers question the hypothesis of the chaotic origin of the universe: they cite the phenomenon of regional isotropy (i.e. that the black-body radiation surrounding us is relatively uniform) as evidence against it. And they argue, further, that the early evidence of nucleosynthesis — which took place presumably within the "first three minutes" after the Big Bang — indicates that the chaotic forces were early overcome by harmonic forces. Thus, the original chaos subsided eventually, or assumed novel manifestations, occurring as intermediary events amidst spheres of harmony. And this oscillating history, too, implies the idea of "cosmic evolution".

And yet we know of the persistent existence of "dark matter" in the background: an inert form of matter (or antimatter) which, owing to its depleting energy state, is characterized by contraction and inverse spinning, generating magnetic whirlpools — "black holes" — which swallow up neighboring celestial bodies without leaving any trace of their previous existence. And we also know that the "law of entropy" — i.e. that in any physical system energy tends to disperse itself evenly as a function of time — continues to gnaw at the body of the universe, resulting in imperceptible but measurable erosion of its being. Thus the challenge to order and harmony by disorder and chaos cannot be ignored.

However, the "law of entropy" has a limited range: it is confined to physical systems primarily; and it has a partial application to organic systems which synthesize energy. The latter are governed (as Albert Szent-Gyorgyi has suggested[17]) by the opposite "law of syntropy". This law states that, in the natural realm, syntheses occur which generate a higher level of energy concentration than before. Indeed, without any form of synthesis, the very origin of the universe itself would remain inexplicable. For, if the "law of entropy" always held, then no synthesis would have taken place, and the universe could have not gotten "started". So the advocates of universal entropy, predicting the ultimate and inevitable "running down" of the universe, cannot answer the question as to why (contrary to the law of entropy) the universe got started to be formed with its enormous and varied energy systems.

The astronomical evidence for the "law of syntropy" can no longer be denied. Especially noteworthy is, not only the phenomenon of "star formation", but also the phenomenon of "star clustering". Thus the Pleiades, which appears to the bare eye to comprise 7 to 9 stars at most, it reveals to a large refractor telescope a cluster of several hundred stars. And about 350 similar star clusters are known to exist in our galaxy alone. These range from relatively "open clusters", wherein the individual stars are distinguishable, to the more densely organized "closed clusters", which appear as one great mass with extraordinary illumination. Also there are levels of clustering: that beyond first-order clusterings, there are second-order clusterings, and even a third-order clustering — altogether ranging in diameter from 10 to 100 to 1000 million light years. This evidence warrants, then, that we may speak of a "hierarchical universe"; and that we may imagine "island universes" suspended in a sea of background magnetic field and light radiation . . .

And within *our* "island universe", there exist structural affinities between the highest and the lowest terms of the cosmic hierarchy. Consider, for example, the form of the motion of a single electron in a liquid medium and the spiral form of our galaxy: both represent the same geometrical pattern. Or consider the homology between the pattern of the radiation curves of the Crab Nebula (which derives its extraordinary luminosity from a rotating pulsar at its center) and that of a hen's egg broken on a plane surface. Or consider the phenomenon of clustering in the atomic realm (which prompted Bohr to propose a "planetary model" for the atom): The simplest atom, *hydrogen*, has a proton (positive charge) at its nucleus and an electron (negative charge) at its orbit. And *helium* has two protons, and correspondingly, two electrons. But add a third electron to the original orbit, it will be rejected, and accepted only at a secondary orbit, drastically changing the atomic structure, and creating a new element (*lithium*); and so on for *boron, carbon*, etc. The resulting series of the complexification of structure can be represented by the equations of wave mechanics (as formulated by Schrödinger): these equations take into account, not only the actual structure of the microsystem, but also the potential energy involved, and hence they are applicable to the grosser astrophysical phenomena as well.

Too, it has been discovered recently that—against the background of a mild magnetic field which fills the cosmic space between the galaxies—the sun, the earth, and most of the other stars in our galaxy function as "colossal dynamos".[18] They generate their own magnetic fields, which in turn determine their interaction with other stars. The intensity of a planet's magnetic field is proportional to the mass of its core and the rate of its rotation. The origin of these magnetic fields is not yet known; but it is known that they provide counter-forces which serve as "cosmic agitators" vis-a-vis universal gravitation and degradation.

As a result of these two great discoveries — *i.e.* the phenomena of clustering and of magnetic fields in the cosmos—our understanding of the traditional laws of *uniformity* and *entropy* must be revised: "If, then, the deepest and most encompassing surveys of faint galaxies do not begin to approach the required statistical uniformity; if clustering forces still operate strongly on a scale of hundreds of megaparsecs; what is the evidence for large-scale homogeneity and isotropy?" — asks a contemporary astronomer.[19] It is evident that the traditional laws cannot be universal; and, therefore, they must have only a regional range of application. The law of *entropy* must be complemented with the law of *syntropy* in order for us to envision a more realistic picture of the cosmos.

Is it possible, then, to advance a *philosophical explanation* for the discoveries of science relative to the harmonics of the cosmos?

Here we may invoke the *hypothesis of ontological strata* — referred to earlier (§7) — which provides a philosophical explanation and interpretation of our empirical picture of the world. This hypothesis, which conceives the world as a "grand organization", states: (a) that the world of phenomena comprises strata such that every being belongs to one stratum at least; (b) that the higher strata, having emerged from the lower strata, acquire their own special qualities and organizational laws; and (c) that the strata of reality are continuous *from below* but discontinuous *from above*. This hypothesis provides an ontological grounding for the empirical picture of the world.

I see the hypothesis of ontological strata as providing the conceptual matrix for the recent *theory of natural systems* which is emerging as the philosophy of science of our time. For the systems-theory conceives the world as a network of interrelated "natural systems" which display levels of organization. The beauty of the systems-theory lies in that it renders the phenomenal world intelligible without any curtailment of its complexity.

The logical form of the 'natural system' — (following Laszlo's exposition)[20] — may be depicted as follows: $S = f(\alpha, \beta, \gamma, \partial)$ where S = natural system, α = the *interactive relation* of parts within S; β = responsiveness to disruptive stimuli resulting in the *restoration* of the previous state of equilibrium; γ = responsiveness to environmental stimuli resulting in the *reorganization* of the structure of the system and the *acquisition* of a new state of equilibrium; and ∂ = the dual structural/functional *adaptation* of the system S relative to subsystems and supersystems, i.e., the attainment of an ecological niche or a "place in nature". Thus 'natural systems' represent dynamic configurations (*Gestalten*) which are: (a) open to adaptation, (b) irreducible qualitatively to their constituent parts, and (c) capable of interaction with other systems within the natural hierarchy.

The dialectic of 'natural systems' may be stated in this way: that the lower level properties are continuous throughout, but that the higher level properties, which emerge as a function of advanced organization, are discontinuous. Emergence and reduction are then complementary phenomena.

The idea of 'cosmic hierarchy' may be represented schematically: Atom — Molecule — Cell — Organism — Earth (Ecosystem) Solar System — Extragalactic Nebulae — Megasystem.

Our conclusion, concerning the hypothesis of cosmic harmony, is twofold:

Firstly, that the order of the cosmos has a dialectical character: wherein matter and antimatter, entropy and syntropy, expanding and clustering occur alternately. Nor, in this complex and evolving universe, does the existence of sporadic disorder prove the nonexistence of order. The conflict of order and disorder, on the contrary, represents the dialectic of cosmic evolution.

Secondly, that our encounter with the cosmos (as a megasystem) is already conditioned by our limited framework of understanding. Our "first vision", accordingly, must ever be emended by our "second vision", to reveal hidden order. We may recall, in this connection, the lessons of the history of science: nature has again and again surpassed the expectations of the human mind, compelling man to abandon premature pictures of the world, in favor of more whole pictures revealing greater harmonies.

And now, as we reflect over the staggering phenomena of the cosmos, discerning therein but fragments of a hidden "grand design" — thanks to the limited scope of our epistemological goggles — we might imagine that this very encounter, between man the *microcosm* and his habitat the *cosmos*, this grotesque disproportion between the powers of the *observer* and the magnitude of the *universe*, may elicit a smile of irony from the goddess of cosmic equilibrium — Nemesis.

Imago Dei:
A Note on the Possible Existence of the Author of the Universe

The ideal of 'cosmic harmony' — if assumed to be true — poses another, deeper, question: Does cosmic harmony imply the existence of an intelligent 'Author of the Universe'?

We can no longer say — as the modern materialists say — that the cosmos (this "great thing of beauty and order" as the Greeks called it) might have come into being by mere accident, and so we no longer have any need for an explanatory hypothesis concerning cosmogony.

The very notion of 'accident' is problematic: If by an "accidental event" we mean something that occurs *without* the order of nature, then it is an unintelligible notion; and if we mean by it something that occurs *within* the order of nature, then it is no longer an accident.

Looking at an apparently "accidental event", we must remember that it usually has a long and complicated "anterior history" and that it has not emerged *ex nihilo*. The anterior history represents a continuum of process wherein the "event" is but a moment: it must be seen, not as an isolated dot on the surface of existence, but as the terminus of underlying continuities.

The mathematical probability of the cosmic order having been generated by accident, merely, approaches zero: it is the probability that a magnificent ice-castle might be generated, accidentally, by a snow avalanche on the mountainside; or the probability that a portrait of Rembrandt or a composition of Mozart could be created, accidentally, by a chimpanzee playing with the same materials for an indefinite period of time; or the probability that a pair of dice figures might recur ninety-nine times in a hundred cases.

Philosophically speaking: the emergence of *order* without any *ground for order*, i.e. the emergence of actuality without its possibility, would be unintelligible. I make, then, a dialectical move from the *intelligibility* of the order of cosmos to its *ground of intelligibility*. My philosophical argument for the existence of the "Author of the Universe" may be stated as follows:

The order of the cosmos as an "ensemble of possibilities" requires, for its intelligibility, a ground which may be taken as its sufficient reason for existence. For the intelligibility of the cosmos requires that we ought to be able to answer the ground-question: why is there order rather than non-order? This ground for the order of cosmos as an "ensemble of possibilities" can be none other than an intelligent Being as its author. And the negation of the existence of this intelligent Being, as the author of the ensemble of cosmological possibilities, would mean the negation of the intelligibility of the order of cosmos. Therefore, we must either assume that the order of cosmos must remain *unintelligible* to us — in the absence of a ground for its "ensemble of possibilities" — or we must assume that an intelligent Being must exist as the 'Author of the Universe' (i.e. as the author of the ensemble of the cosmological laws of order) *even though* the "grand design" of the cosmos might remain to us something less than completely visible.

Some remarks concerning the interpretation of the above argument are in order:

This is a transcendental argument — i.e. one that proceeds from the possibility of X to the *a priori* conditions for the intelligibility of X — and, as such, it bears a similarity to an earlier argument proposed by Kant as the "only possible" argument for the existence of "God".[21] There is, however, a critical difference between the Kantian argument and mine: in the former it is the concept of "possibility" which carries the burden of the argument; while in the latter it is the concept of "intelligibility" which carries the burden of the argument. Yet both arguments make use, implicitly, of the two correlative concepts. Both arguments are radically different from the traditional "cosmological arguments", which argue from the "grand design" of the world, while the "grand design" remains to us unknown in its entirety.

Lastly, it may be noted that the Imago Dei envisioned by our argument is similar to that envisioned by the philosophers of the Renaissance and Enlightenment: it presents the image of an intelligent 'Author' of cosmological laws and cosmic order, allowing the natural processes in the world to run their course accordingly, along a scale that overlaps but transcends our intelligence — an image which is starkly different from that of any anthropomorphic being who presumably makes the world, and interferes with everything therein, piecemeal as it were.

CHAPTER VII

Psyche

We have viewed the cosmos — in order to discern its dialectical order — but what would the cosmos be without the observer? The observer, however, is the psyche: it harbors an image of the cosmos in itself. What, then, is the character of the human psyche — and what is the place of man in the cosmos?

By *psyche* I understand the infrastructure of consciousness: it is characterized by the integrative functions of self-reflection, self-determination, and self-realization, at the conscious as well as subconscious levels.

We shall focus on the epistemological aspect of higher consciousness. But we shall recognize, in the background as it were, the ineffable reality of the darker region of the psyche: the subconsciousness (and the dream life). Thus I seek to retrieve the nigh-forgotten word 'psyche' (ψυχή) — from the natural philosophy of Ancient Greece — but with a renewed meaning.[1]

§ 19

A Philosophical Reading of the "Cosmic Calendar"

Modern science has reconstructed an intriguing picture of the origin and evolution of our world: it has given us a "cosmic calendar". The calendar displays an analogical view of the emergence of life-forms from a background of original matter. But it harbors some philosophical questions — questions which we shall articulate in the following pages.

The "Cosmic Calendar" as a Scientific Picture

Let us then read this extraordinary calendar — an overview (based upon the original version presented by Carl Sagan)[2] — in order to see the gestalt of the scientific view of the world and the emergence of man:

If we assume that the Big Bang occurred on 1 January, then the origination of protogalaxies took four months, resulting in the formation of the Milky Way on 1 May. It is significant that for the next four months (May — August) our calendar is blank: it is to be marked "unknown events". Earth itself is born in mid-September. Only in late September do we see the stirrings of the chemistry of life, giving birth to bacteria in October, and to eukaryotes (complex living cells) in November. Then comes December, the last month of the calendar, pregnant with all forms of life in succession: aquatic plants, fishes, terrestrial plants, amphibia, reptalia, mammalia, birds, primates, hominids, and lastly homo sapiens.

It may be noted that the "year" of the cosmic calendar represents a time span of 15 billion years — assuming that the life of our universe began with the Big Bang — and, consequently, a month of the calendar would represent a time span of 1.25 billion years. Moreover, there remain huge periods of "unknown events", eras of darkness, periodically intersecting the continuity of our calendar, wherein the universe must have done its hidden work as it were. Presumably, the age of our galaxy (as indicated by the character of the radioactive waves resulting from the Big Bang) is about 15,000,000,000 years. And the age of our Earth (estimated on the basis of the analysis of radioactive materials) is about 5,000,000,000 years. The first sign of life (bacterial life) appeared about 3,000,000,000 years ago; and Man walked on earth about 1,000,000 years ago.

It is significant that Man emerges on the scene during the late hours (10:30 PM approximately) of the last day of the last month of the cosmic calendar. And the entire history of civilization — exploration, discovery, technology — falls in the span of the last hour (11:00 PM to 12:00 M) of the 31st day of December. Thus, viewed in the context of the cosmic calendar, human existence appears to be a mere dot on the vast canvas of existence which was apparently painted in endless time. Accordingly, Carl Sagan, who constructed the "cosmic calendar", confesses that it has been a humbling experience. It is, however, also an inspiring experience: that Man should emerge at all represents the last cosmic wonder.

It would be naive to suppose that the "cosmic calendar" explains, or even reveals, everything. As a scientific picture of nature, it remains grossly sketchy and incomplete. For, though it reveals some startling truths, it hides other underlying truths. It hides the fact that the various phases of the natural history of our cosmos are not in reality as isolated and fragmented as they might appear. It hides the dynamics and harmonics, as well as the gaps and levels, of phenomena. And the recurrence of patterns throughout the universe — as depicted by the hypothesis of cosmic harmony previously — remains invisible here.

A thought-experiment in this connection — suggested by Professor E.S. Ayensu and his colleagues at the Smithsonian Institution — would be worth describing here: Imagine a demigod in another galaxy curious about the character of ours. And suppose that she is able to sweep away, by means of her gravity-warp, a goodly sample of plants and animals from the face of the Earth. Could she, then, infer anything from this sample about the character of the world from which it came? Perhaps. They would reveal, by their temperature

138

sensitivity, that their life-world on Earth had a climate range between -10 degrees and +40 degrees Centigrade; they would display, by their activity/rest phases, a circular rhythm of 24 hours (and possibly day/night alternation); the marine creatures in the sample would show a twice diurnal as well as a 14-day or 28-day periodicity corresponding to the time patterns of the tides; and the longer-lived specimens would display a seasonal rhythmic period of about 350 days. The intelligent demigod would then conclude, from the observation of this earthly sample, some astronomical truths: that the planet X, from which the sample came, rotates about its own axis once every 24 hours; that it completes its solar orbit in about 350 days; and that it has a single satellite moon, with an orbital period of 28 days around X, producing tidal waves in the planet's large water masses; etcetera. Thus conclude Professor Ayensu and his colleagues: "Each of the 10 million species that has evolved and now swarms on the Earth's surface, carries the time-signature of the planetary motion of our world indelibly stamped within it."[3]

In the light of such cosmological considerations, scientists are already proposing to redefine the idea of *life*, as a generic concept, to include not only 'dynamism' but also 'rhythmicity' as its essential qualities. These qualities place living beings in stark contrast to the phenomena of the inorganic world which form the background for life and its evolution.

Herein arises the question of emergence: as we view the larger picture, we discern two great gaps, each separating two strikingly different qualitative realms:

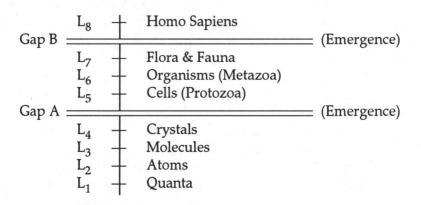

Indeed the very "tree of life" itself is overwrought with lacunae — repeating, as it were, the qualitative leaps and gaps of the larger picture of the universe — and a modern scientist has depicted it in these words:

"Now we see the tree of life standing before us... We could call it the negative of a tree, for contrary to what happens with our great forest trees, its branches and trunk are revealed to our eyes only by ever-widening gaps; an almost petrified tree, as it appears to us, so long do the buds take to open. Many that are half-opened now we shall never know in any other state. A clearly drawn tree, nonetheless, with its superimposed foliage of living species. In its main lines and vast dimensions, it stands before us covering all the earth... From a merely external contemplation of it, there is a lesson and a force to be drawn from it: *the sense of its testimony.*"[4]

Thus the scientific picture of the living world, as it is represented by the cosmic calendar, is an intriguing picture which raises a pair of philosophical questions.

Our First Philosophical Question

We ask: *How could life, with its dynamic properties, arise from the primeval matter which was originally lifeless?* Specifically, how could living cells (and protozoa) arise from inorganic crystals (however refined their molecular structure might be) which were their immediate predecessors? There would be no explanation, it seems, unless we accept the phenomenon of *emergence* and reject reductionism.

But what does 'emergence' mean?

It means that when a set of elements combine, integratively, a compound results which displays some new properties. It means that the whole is something more than the sum of its parts. It means, in a word, that there are genuine *Gestalten* in nature.

Examples of natural *Gestalten* may be seen in the realm of chemistry: a pair of gases (hydrogen and oxygen) combine to produce a molecule of liquid (H_2O); two toxic/corrosive elements (chlorine and sodium) combine to produce a beneficial substance (salt) in our nutrition; or, again, a pair of elements in varying proportions result in radically different substances: N_2O_5 (solid crystal) and N_2O (laughing gas). Similarly, natural *Gestalten* recur in the biological and psychological realms.

What, then, is the nature of 'life': what is it to be a 'living being'? If we view 'life' as an emergent phenomenon, in the context of an evolving cosmos, then a 'living being' represents a new kind of natural system — a dynamic system with a relative degree of self-awareness and self-determination. These qualities, we shall see, preclude the reduction of living systems to mechanical systems.

"Life," writes Professor A.I. Oparin of the Academy of Sciences of Russia, "is a special form of the movement of matter, qualitatively different from that of the inorganic world..."[5] He argues, on biochemical grounds, that the 'living organism' displays properties and behavior patterns which do not merely reflect the laws of inorganic nature. The 'living organism' is characterized by: (a) metabolic processes, (b) purposive behavior, (c) dynamic equilibrium. Hence 'living organisms' represent open systems, in contrast to machines which are closed systems. Accordingly, Oparin regards the analogy between 'combustion' and 'respiration' — proposed by mechanist thinkers — as being superficial from the point of view of physiology. The conclusion arrived at by this scientist, owing to its philosophical import, is worth quoting here:

> It is therefore completely wrong to try to characterize the *line of life* simply on the basis of one point, whether that point lies at the beginning, the middle, or the end. In fact, if we try to define life in terms of the characteristics which arose at the very beginning of its emergence on the Earth, we have to exclude from among its features, not only consciousness but also respiration, which obviously did not occur among the earlier organisms. On the other hand, if we define life on the basis of phenomena which are typical only of the more highly developed living beings, we shall risk relegating the anaerobic amoeba, as well as many other primitive organisms, to the category of non-living bodies belonging to inorganic nature.[6]

Discontinuity — and yet continuity.

And yet, the same inexorable law of entropy, which governs the condition of physical systems, seems to haunt living beings as well. This law predicts eventual atomic disorder for everything in the universe. Energy seems to seek its lowest denominator. Or, to express it in terms of the Schrödinger equation: (Entropy = k log D) where k is a constant and D is a quantitative measure of atomistic dispersion. This law predicts, given indefinite time, nothing less than the "running down" of the universe — resulting in a stagnant pool of low energy in which nothing *does* happens because nothing *can* happen.

However, happily for our universe, there are some exceptions to the law of entropy. Some natural systems (like the Sun) generate their own energy; others (like the stars) are generated anew out of the cosmic ashes of old ones. Atomic disorder and energy dispersion, in special cases, seem to lead to atomic regrouping and reconcentrations. And nowhere is this reversal of the law of entropy more evident than in the realm of organic and living systems. "Life," observes Erwin Schrödinger, " seems to be an orderly and lawful behavior of matter, *not* based exclusively on its tendency to go over from order to disorder, but based partly on existing order that is kept up."[7] The characteristic of a living organism is to hold the state of maximum entropy at bay, as it were, and to postpone the inevitable death. And here the process is more significant than its end. For the process of life counters entropy by extracting order from disorder in its environment. The living being effectively counters "positive entropy" with "negative entropy" — to use Schrödinger's expression — defying death and decay for some time. Thus life, which rises from the soil of disorder like a flower, after a time disintegrates and dies, and is absorbed by the same soil again. Does, then, in the end entropy prevail unopposed? Perhaps not. The term "syntropy" (suggested by Albert Szent-Gyorgyi), rather than "negative entropy", depicts the positive character of life *versus* death, of order *versus* disorder, and of evolution *versus* devolution.

Thus we must recognize the *law of syntropy* as the dialectical complement of the *law of entropy*.

We may conclude that the concepts of physics are not sufficient to explain the phenomenon of life. For the law of entropy depicts but one aspect of the natural universe. To assume otherwise — to grant to entropy a universal range — would render it impossible to explain the very emergence of living systems. For the same law that predicts the inevitable dissolution of all existing systems, would certainly have precluded the formation of such systems (as special concentrations of energy) *ab initio*. For, *if* the law of entropy were universally and unqualifiedly true, *if* it were true that the universe is doomed to eventually "run down", *then* it would also be true that the universe neither could nor would have "gotten started". Such is the inexorable dialectic of the case as disclosed by our first philosophical question.

Our Second Philosophical Question

And so we must ask: *How could the human psyche, with its powers of higher consciousness, emerge from the chemistry of the body?* How could this being — which Goethe depicts as "*Zum Sehen geboren, zum Schauen bestellt...*" — (*Born to see, destined to behold...*) — how could this being emerge from the inert earth? How could a non-material *psyche* emerge from a material *body*? But this same question is asked by idealists and materialists, rhetorically, and with opposite intentions; both giving the same answer: impossible.[8] We shall handle the question from the perspective of dialectical realism.

When we turn to natural science to see what we might learn about this question, we find that the very empirical facts themselves are being constantly revised by new discoveries. And the latest discovery, e.g., indicates that man did not "descend" from the ape. Thus writes Bjorn Kurten the eminent Scandinavian biologist: "The appearance of modern man in Europe about 35,000 years ago is very sudden: There is no known transition from the Neanderthals to those essentially modern-looking people who have been called Cro-Magnon men... These Europeans are definitely not some kind of "generalized" *homo sapiens*, but clearly belong to the Caucasoid or white race. At this early date, then, man had already split up into distinct races..."[9]

And the ethologist Konrad Lorenz remains utterly baffled by the emergence of the human psyche: "...the gulf between the physical and the spiritual is of a fundamentally different kind from that between the organic and the inorganic, and between man and animals. These latter gulfs represent transitions... (they can be) bridged by a theoretical continuum of intermediate forms... The 'hiatus' between soul and body, on the other hand, is indeed unbridgeable..." he writes and, after deliberation, concludes: "The autonomy of personal experience and its laws cannot in principle be explained in terms of chemical and physical laws or of neurophysiological structure, however complex."[10]

One may suppose that *consciousness*, in its most general sense of awareness (including instinct), permeates the entire realm of living beings. Evidence for this supposition is to be found in abundance everywhere. Even the lowest forms of life display some measure of awareness of, and correspondingly responsiveness to, their environment. But it is *higher consciousness* — as a function of the self-reflecting, self-determining, and self-realizing psyche — which appears to be a characteristic of man exclusively.

It appears that, as we ascend the levels of being in the living world, a shift of polarity occurs between the lower and the higher: hitherto sensation and perception predominated the life forms, but henceforth memory and reflection predominate the highest form of life. Even though Julian Huxley regards the distinction between the "lower" and the "higher" to be a matter of degree — the degree of the complexity of organization and the specialization of functions — he recognizes that the shift is radical: in his terminology, "psychometabolism" comes to predominate over "physiometabolism", at the level of homo sapiens.[11] This inversion of the polarity of life — from sensation/perception to memory/reflection — is a remarkable phenomenon. And its consequence is noteworthy: while animals continue to live in their *environment* only, man strives to live in the *world*, as he harbors in his psyche a sense of history, a picture of the world, a culture.

Dialectical materialism assumes a critical and subtle approach to the question of consciousness. Herbert Hörz articulates an interpretation of the emergence of consciousness from this perspective. 'Consciousness' is defined by Hörz as "the specifically human quality of reflection", i.e., as "the imager of what exists outside and independently of the subject *as well as* the imager of what goes on within himself."[12] And, on the basis of this definition, he proposes the thesis that: Consciousness represents "the highest developmental stage" of the evolution of matter. With characteristic brilliance, Hörz puts his finger on the nerve of the issue: that there are qualitative 'stages' in the evolution of matter, and that the 'higher stages' are not, and could not be, identical with the 'lower stages'. And thus the mind/brain identity thesis of naive materialism is overcome.

From dialectical materialism to dialectical realism is but a critical step:

The *hypothesis of ontological strata* provides the only adequate explanation of the phenomenon of consciousness.[13] The 'large picture', according to this hypothesis, appears as follows: The ontological structure of reality, admitting a hierarchy of interrelated systems, displays ranges of continuity and divergence. And the relations between the strata present a dialectical character: that, while the lower strata retain the potential possibilities of the higher strata, the higher strata harbor emergent properties which are not reducible to those of the lower strata. Thus, for example, while everything organic is also material, not everything material is also organic, and so on. We see then, in the light of the general picture, the emergence of man at the apex of earthly existence. Man represents a manifold of the three basic ontological strata: biogenesis — psychogenesis—noogenesis. Man emerges as a veritable microcosm. And the *human psyche* represents a phenomenon at the highest level of ontological reality.

Nicolai Hartmann—whose ontological theory we have discussed —regarded this "yawning gulf" of the psycho-physical divide in the structure of reality analogous to that which exists, far below, at the level of organic/inorganic division in nature. He depicts its dialectic as follows:

> The genesis of consciousness from unconscious life is a fact, which in the process of the growth of every individual person is brought before our eyes, *regardless* of whether or not we understand it. What has once been accomplished by the evolution of organisms in the grand system, and on a geological time scale, is here recapitulated on a small scale — according to the universal law of ontogenesis... The important point is that the autonomy of the consciousness is thereby *in no way* prejudiced. If, in fidelity to the facts, we regard its genesis as belonging among the morphogenetic process of the organism, *this does not mean* that it is exhaustively determined by the laws of organic matter. What actually takes place is the rising of the form... *beyond the limit of* the stratum in which it originates. This again involves its integration into the higher stratum so

that it then belongs under *different* categories.[14]

Thus the human psyche may be seen as a phenomenon at the higher level of being — or (to use Hartmann's expression) *das höchste Seinsmoment*. Does this present a third alternative beyond mechanism and supernaturalism? The answer is evident. And even if an "explanation" of the phenomena of consciousness, in terms of the mechanisms of the brain, were possible, this *per se* would not negate their reality: Explained emergence remains still an emergence.

Moreover, the reductive program of neopositivism (and naive materialism) involves a vicious circle: It proposes to reduce 'mental states' to 'brain states', while it assumes that 'brain states' are to be known only through 'mental states'. Conversely, subjectivism proposes an opposite reduction — resulting in the paradox that the 'mind', which emerges from the 'brain', turns to negate its reality. To overcome this epistemological predicament, we must *overcome* reductionism by dialectical realism: we must give each its proper due.

§ 20

A Commentary on Kant's Theory of Man's Place in the Cosmos

In view of Kant's philosophical perspective, which sees man in a cosmological setting, it would be relevant to ask: What did Kant understand by 'human psyche' and what place did he assign to 'man' in the cosmos?

Kant's theory is of special interest to us because he sees man in a dialectical perspective. He assigns man a naturalistic position in the world, while at the same time, he grants him a spiritual dimension which has a transcendental character. He depicts human nature in the hues of naturalism and idealism, showing that the two aspects are complementary, indeed necessary to each other. Nor are the internal tensions of the Kantian philosophy of man to be underestimated: the polarities of noumenon/phenomenon, of being/representation (or inner/outer), and of reason/feeling — these complicate the plot, as it were, and call for a dialectical interpretation. It is perhaps owing to these complexities and subtleties, that Kant's theory of man has remained the least understood part of his philosophy entire.

Man is a special being who displays a higher awareness about his existence. This concern — as Kant himself was to articulate in the last pages of the *Kritik der reinen Vernunft* (A805/B833) — is expressed in these questions: "What can I know? What must I do? What may I hope?" It is in terms of man's 'higher consciousness', then, that Kant defines man's place in the cosmos. He notes, in particular, three modes of consciousness:
(a) self-reflection (including aesthetic, moral, and personal reflection)
(b) self-determination (i.e. freewill in a world of alternative modalities)
(c) cosmic reflection: understanding and interpreting the cosmos by means of reason and creative imagination (*Einbildungskraft*) — resulting in the creations of art, science, and philosophy.
Requisite for the understanding of the Kantian view of the

essence of man is the interrelation of the *noumena* (things-in-themselves) and the *phenomena* (things-in-appearance). Man has access to the phenomenal aspect of things in the world, but he has never access to their noumenal aspect. And this applies to everything — *except* man's relation to himself. Man stands, toward himself, in a dual relation:

He sees himself as a natural phenomenon, conditioned by the forces of nature, among other natural phenomena. And, again, he sees himself — through the "window of intuition" — as a transcendental noumenon which provides the wellspring of his actions. Through outer perception he is aware of his *body* (as a phenomenon); but through inner intuition be becomes aware of the deeper resources of his psyche. He can draw, then, from the "spiritual well" within him, his unarticulated feelings of the good and the sublime, his deeper reasons, and his power of freewill.

Noumena are the ground of the phenomena — ontologically speaking — and herein lies the hidden source of human freedom: as a *phenomenon*, man's existence is determined by the laws of the natural world; but as a *noumenon*, his essence determines his existence. And this pertains not only to the formation of the picture of the world; it pertains also to man's capacity to use his reason (and his moral conscience) as motives for his actions. The manifestation of this existential self-determinism may be called personal *freewill* properly. Moral responsibility, Kant argues, assumes the freedom of the will without which it would become meaningless. And moral responsibility—involving the employment of practical reason toward a higher purpose above material needs — distinguishes man from other living beings.

The power of the inner reality over the outer reality becomes evident in a twofold way: Firstly, that man's picture of the world is determined by his mental schemata which constitute the *a priori* forms of all possible experience. I have explained this thesis above (Section § 11) and elsewhere.[15] And, secondly, that man is a being whose character and actions are self-determined, i.e., as a result of his freewill — and this thesis may be explained in the following.

The noumenon is not — as usually assumed — merely a black-box. It is evident — (and on this point I agree with Professor Erik Stenius)[16] — that the noumenon/phenomenon distinction is to be seen, not only as *consequence* of Kant's epistemological theses, but also as a *source* of his philosophical anthropology. For the 'inner' determines the 'outer' in human experience.

What does man see when he looks *within* himself, through the "window of intuition", as it were?

Man sees his immediate data of consciousness — or "impressions" as Hume called them — but he also "sees" something beyond these. He sees the infrastructure of the seer. For we have two things here: the empirical data and the transcendental categories. What brings the two together? "A third thing is required," says Kant, "wherein alone the synthesis... can originate."[17] This *tertium quid*, however, is the 'transcendental unity of apperception' — which must be assumed as the necessary ground for the possibility of subjective experience — and which is Kant's name for the *psyche*.

"'I am' is not a statement of experience, rather I take it as the basis of every perception, and in order to bring about experience" — writes Kant, concerning 'inner sense', in a fragment which has been recently discovered.[18] And here the two aspects of 'inner sense' emerge: 'I am' *simpliciter* (psychological consciousness of my own being); and 'I am in the world' (cosmological consciousness of my being). The latter defines man's existence in relation to other beings in the world.

The dialectical relation between the 'inner sense' and the 'outer sense' is significant. It is the 'outer sense', through which I experience the world, which causes me to define my own existence, through the 'inner sense', as being other than other beings. Though I experience the world through my 'outer sense', this experience is preconditioned by the *a priori* forms which I discover by my 'inner sense'. Thus, in the final analysis, the 'inner sense' is autonomous of the 'outer sense'. E.g. I cannot reverse the order of space/time by the 'outer sense', but I can do so by an act of my 'inner sense': I can imagine a river voyage in reverse, so that I move backward in space/time, instead of forward; etc.

The 'inner sense' is also a pathway to 'moral sense'.

"Two things fill the mind with ever new and increasing admiration and awe, the oftener and more steadily they are reflected on: the starry heavens above me and the moral law within me" — wrote Kant at the end of the *Critique of Practical Reason*.[19] Too, there is the 'aesthetic sense' — the sense of 'beauty' (i.e. an object pre-adapted to our faculty of judgment representing in itself an object of admiration) and the sense of the 'sublime' (i.e. an object which transcends our faculty of judgment and envelopes in itself an unfathomable dimension). Both the 'moral sense' and the 'aesthetic sense' are, then, awe-inspiring — elevating the human psyche above other living beings.

The 'moral sense' is the natural endowment of all normal human beings. It is, in its origin at least, autonomous of cultural milieu. Man drinks, as it were, from the spiritual well within. But not all men do. And therein lies the ontological gradation of human beings. In the tension between the "inner man" and the "outer man" — to use the Swedenborgian expressions in a Kantian context of discourse — the modality of human personality acquires its timbre and hue. Men are not morally equal.

However, the development of moral character — insofar as the feeling of 'sympathy' plays a role in the activation of moral behavior — requires moral education. And this education must involve the teaching of the 'sense of duty', so that the moral act may not be performed out of mere inclination or arbitrarily. It must also involve the development of the feeling of 'sympathy' — *Einfühlungsvermögen* — without which the *will* to act morally or to do good might remain lethargic or even inactive. Hence Kant would urge that young persons must be exposed to the experience of suffering (illness, failure, tragedy) — in real life or in high literature — so that they may have the occasion to activate their natural aptitude for moral sympathy.[20]

These two things taken together — the inner sense of moral duty and the aptitude for the feeling of moral sympathy — contribute toward the formation of *moral character*: i.e. the aptitude to act, *with* sympathy and *from* a sense of moral duty, in response to the existential problems of life.

The 'higher purpose', to which Kant alludes, is none other than the ideal of the 'Highest Good' — rather than the idol of 'happiness'. It constitutes the true incentive of human life. What, then, is the ideal of the 'Highest Good', and how may it be attained by man? It represents the last moment of the spiritual progress of man: wherein the two essential virtues (*die beiden Arten des Guts*) — i.e., 'moral character' and 'wellbeing' — find their union in the life of a person. Then 'happiness' will appear as an epiphenomenon. Consider the analogy of a butterfly and its shadow: wherever the one goes so does the other; and only when passing clouds blot the sun, the shadow disappears, but not the butterfly. Similarly, the "goodness" of personal character continues to exist, despite the passing clouds of adversity, and his potential for "happiness" continues to endure. And so, to the question of modern man, "What should I do?" (morally speaking), Kant would answer: "Do that, through which you would become *worthy* to be happy." The dialectic of this answer can be brought out — as John Silber has brought it out already[21] — through the interrelations of good acts, wellbeing, and happiness. For man to seek to be "happy" (or to pretend to be happy), without being morally good — even if such an anomaly were to be possible — it would be an aberration of his true nature. For man could never be truly happy without also being good. Thus Kant holds up the ideal of the 'Highest Good' before the eyes of mankind, not as a natural endowment (for man remains too imperfect a being for that), but rather as an ideal of practical reason. But, insofar as man possesses the freedom of the will (as a natural endowment) he has the power to pursue the ideals of practical reason. And herein lies the meaning of *human dignity*.

The realization of these aptitudes of man, these inherent powers of the psyche, constitutes the road to human 'enlightenment'. But how could modern man attain a state of 'enlightenment' when he is not quite prepared to understand his own 'place' in the cosmos? For the vast majority of men still trudge in a prephilosophical plateau of life. Kant asks: "Do we now live in an *enlightened age?*" — and answers: "No" — we merely live in the "age of enlightenment".[22] The subtle diagnosis is relevant to the conditio humane today. The *philosophical enlightenment* of modern man remains still an ideal condition rather than an actual condition of human existence. And Kant hopes, by holding up the ideal of 'higher humanism' before the eyes of mankind, to drag them out of the darkness of their habitual existence.

Human nature, seen in the light of 'higher humanism', represents a blending, a harmony, as it were — of reason and feeling and, correspondingly, of goodness and happiness. To this 'moral harmony' corresponds the 'intellectual harmony' of receptivity of the "rhapsody of perceptions" and the creative spontaneity of reflective imagination. Thus, according to the Kantian view, man unites in himself the two supreme principles of the active and the passive. This inherent dialectic of Kant's theory of man has prompted one contemporary scholar, Jacques Taminiaux, to ask: *"Mais n'est-ce pas la l'incarnation historique (grècque) du caractère total?"*[23] Not quite. What we encounter here, in Kant, is an image of man arrived at by a very different path from those of Plato and Aristotle — even if their resulting insights may display a partial convergence. This becomes evident, especially, when we read Schiller's reading of Kant: the central theme of *Kallias* (Letters on the Aesthetic Education of Man) consists of the dialectic of the two apparently antagonistic tendencies of human nature, and their ultimate harmony, in the light of the Kantian idea of 'personal freedom'.

That particular individuals may fail to achieve an inner harmony does not detract from the human potential for enlightenment. For, although man (in the collective sense) is not always rational or moral — and the two aptitudes are interrelated in Kantian thinking — rationality and morality constitute a norm for mankind nevertheless. And this *norm* will be rejected by *abnormal* persons only. Here, then, is the line which separates the healthy realm from the pathological realm, the realm of light from the realm of darkness, in human life.

Nor does this represent a complete portrait of the human psyche. There is here a dark side to the picture. Kant sees it — and bypasses it in silence. He only declares a person without any significant 'inner sense' — from which to derive his aesthetic/moral feelings — to be 'aesthetically blind' or 'morally dead'. For such a person would be no longer capable of aesthetic experience or of moral sympathy. He would live in an existential vacuum — in the absence of aesthetic/ moral ideals — and remain mired in human misery: *"Aber das Schrecklichste der Schrecken, das ist der Mensch in seinem Wahn"* (But the *most dreaded of the dreaded, it is man in his delusion*) — in the words of Schiller (who was the spiritual heir of Kant as far as human nature was concerned). Nevertheless, despite pointing the finger at the morbid side of human nature, Kant remains silent over the issue. It will remain for Hegel to depict the phenomenology of human 'consciousness' and 'bad consciousness' — and, in particular, the dialectic of the "noble" and the "base"; and it will remain for Nietzsche to propose to overcome the duality by the "will to power" which is inherent in the individual person; and it will remain for Heidegger to beckon the human psyche to the 'call of conscience'.

The Kantian theory of man, and his place in the cosmos, represents an attempt to depict the life of the psyche in the light of the ideal of higher humanism — and to this theme we shall return later.

§ 21

Three Eclipsed Views of the Psyche

There are three theses, concerning human mind, against which I shall argue on philosophical grounds — namely:

(1) That the mind consists of a set of dispositions and habits explainable by environmental conditions exclusively.

(2) That the mind represents a reservoir, mostly unconscious, of irrational forces which explain human behavior.

(3) That the mind is essenceless: it is merely a negative reflection of existence.

These three theses represent three contemporary theories of human nature: behaviorism, psychoanalysis, existentialism. They all assume reductive models of one kind or another; and they negate the reality of the psyche as the essence of man. Each theory, no doubt, has its own methodological reasons for doing what it does. Only their philosophical predicament concerns us here: that the 'higher consciousness', which is precluded by their reductive models, is reassumed in their interpretive discourses. They present, each in its own way, eclipsed views of the human psyche.

The human sciences seem to be caught in the middle as it were: they cannot ignore the contributions of reductive doctrines, and yet, they cannot go so far as to lose sight of their own objectives. What appears to be at stake here is none other than man's self-image *qua* human being. And when man is handed a distorting mirror, by the social sciences, to view his own artificial self-image, where may the humanist scholar turn for the means of rectifying that distortion?

It may be argued, too, that the resulting self-images of man have had a demoralizing effect upon the education and life of modern man. And the distortions of human character and spirit in the arts of our time — in painting, in music, and in literature — would provide abundant evidence for this argument. It remains a task for philosophical critique, then, to salvage the authentic sense of the 'human being' — from the camouflages effected upon it by the intellectual-cultural trends of our time.

Epistemological Error of Behaviorism

Far more provocative than the quasi-philosophical utterances of experimental behaviorists — e.g. B.F. Skinner's talk about going "beyond human freedom and dignity" into a robotic dystopia, etc. — is the philosophical apology for behaviorism: the apology for closing the door to the realm of higher consciousness *ex ante*. Such an apology has been provided by Gilbert Ryle;[24] and it is deserving of serious attention. After denouncing the mind/body dualism of Descartes as the theory of the "ghost in the machine", Ryle proposes an elaborate agenda for the dissolution of 'mind' into a set of "dispositional properties", accusing his mentalist adversaries of committing a "category mistake" *simpliciter*.

What, then, is a "dispositional property"? We say that X has a disposition when, under a given condition Y, X would display the property . Thus (to use Ryle's example) glass has a disposition to be brittle. To explain *why* glass shatters, when hit by a stone, we would say that it is disposed to be brittle. And to explain why glass happens to be brittle, we could only say (on Ryle's theory) that it has the dispositional property of being brittle. But this is clearly a circular answer. So we must explain (going beyond Ryle's theory) that glass is disposed to being brittle, because it has the structure (nature) which *makes* it brittle. Thus, in order to explain the *behavior* of X, one must refer to the *nature* of X, at least in such cases.

The same is true of psychological behavior. If the behavior of a glass vase cannot be explained adequately by reference to its disposition alone, much less can the behavior of man be explained by reference to his mental dispositions only. We need to inquire, beyond mental dispositions, into the structure (nature) of the mind and personality. Thus, e.g., when we say that a man is melancholic, there are three things involved: (a) the melancholic behavior, (b) the disposition of melancholy, and (c) the personality structure of the man. As *b* is required to explain *a*, so *c* is required to explain *b*. Ryle's error consists of ignoring *c*; and this renders his explanation of human behavior a quasi-explanation. But why does Ryle commit the error? Because, the recognition of *c* would entail the recognition of *mind*, as a metastructure beyond its set of dispositional properties; and that would commit him to mental realism.[25]

Nor is Ryle's charge of "category mistake" against mental realism convincing. Ryle presents the example of a visitor to a factory who asks, after being shown all its departments, "Now where is *the* factory?" Ryle implies that there is *nothing else* above and beyond the totality of the rooms of a factory. And yet it is evident that there is *something more* above and beyond the rooms of the factory: there is a master-plan (and the administrator) of the purpose, operating principles, and resources of the factory as an economic system.

It is interesting to note that A.J. Ayer carries the argument of philosophical behaviorism farther: In his first inaugural address (1947) he denies that, properly speaking, mental acts have any reality. Yet, in his second inaugural address (1960), he refers to introspective mental states which involve propositions of the form: "I know...", "I believe...", "I doubt..." — which express mental acts. And such references, insofar as they represent the self-negation of anti-mentalist assertions, render Ayer's analysis of knowing utterly unconvincing.

For behaviorists, however, mental dispositions can exist without *minds*— paradoxical as that may be— for their theory operates at the level of description, or, pseudo-explanation. Note the supposedly profound words of a grand behaviorist:

"I am a physical object sitting in a physical world. Some of the forces of this physical world impinge on my surface. Light rays strike my retinas; molecules bombard my eardrums and fingertips. I strike back, emanating concentric air waves. These waves take the form of a torrent of discourse..."[26]

On reading this extraordinary passage, a series of epistemological questions arise, which need to be examined critically:

Firstly, can there be *bare sense-data*, as it were?

We do not *experience* light rays and molecular bombardments. We experience *phenomena*— or the *Gestalten* of things — which are a function of physical stimuli and our mental schemata. There are no *sense-data* — only *sense-impressions*. But, evidently, the behaviorists do not seem to make the epistemological distinction.

Secondly, can there be "observations" *without* an "observer"?

The "forgotten observer" — and his mental acts — is the *a priori* condition of the possibility of empirical observations. Thus, for example, the behaviorist might say to himself: "*I* am reluctant to *accept* the truth of *my* phenomenological report, owing to *my doubts* as to the objectivity of *my observations...*" Such a statement contains *intentional terms* and *meanings* (including a reference to the "observer" and his states of consciousness) without which it would become unintelligible. Thus the discourses of behaviorists must *either* assume mental realism, in some form, *or* remain unintelligible in their own context.

Thirdly, we may ask: Who is the *narrator* of the passage quoted above?

The standard answer, that it is a robot who is playing back a conditioned response to a physical stimulus, would be questionable here. For such an answer would be relevant to *first-order* responses only; and the narrator of the report is clearly giving a *second-order* response. The difference between the two is qualitative (and no degree of mechanical complexity can bridge the gap). For the latter response assumes higher consciousness: consciousness, not merely of *what* has happened, but of the *meaning* of what has happened. Thus there is a contradiction between the role of the behaviorist as experiencer (wherein he may deny consciousness) and as *interpreter of his experience* (wherein he must assume consciousness). But the behaviorist remains oblivious to this contradiction which lies coiled at the heart of his programme.[27] It follows that the behaviorist must confuse (as he does) the two things: the *intellect* and the *mind* — and argue that, because computers are capable of intelligent responses, therefore a mind may be attributed to them.

Psyche and the Psychoanalytic Model

The merit of psychoanalytic theory, as compared with the behaviorist theory, consists of its commitment to mental realism. It seeks to explain human behavior by referring to the psychic dimension involving psychogenic variables. But it reconstructs the dynamics of mind according to the psychoanalytic model of human nature. Thus, while it explores the deeper roots of human nature, it does so in a highly restrictive and reductive manner. The very fact that this model was formed originally in a pathological context constitutes at once its strength and its weakness.

The 'unconscious' constitutes the "greatest part" of the psyche; so that 'consciousness' represents only the visible tip of the iceberg. The evidence for this (according to Freud) consists of the fact that the mass of symptoms in neurosis and hysteria spring from the forces of repressed memories. The unconscious is the abode of the libido and a repository of irrational drives. And though Freud admits that a "shadow" spreads over the realm of the unconscious, beyond the domain of biological desires, he does not pursue the issue. And, since the unconscious controls the consciousness, from below as it were, the "rationality" of conscious life becomes a superficial process.

Consider the droll scenario:

The *Id* (the giant hedonic octopus at the center of the unconscious) issues its demands. The *Ego* (the intelligent bourgeois servant) is ever ready to obey. But the *Ego*, not having a moral conscience of its own, must seek the approval of a higher authority. The higher authority, the *Superego* (a moral puppet of society) represents merely the dictates of culture. The *Superego* would normally acquiece with the petition of the *Ego*, unless it conflicts with the norms of society. In the latter event, the *Ego* meekly takes the matter back to the *Id*, who either reissues its demand or harbors the frustration with enormous resentment, piling repression upon repression. This fertilizes the ground for neurosis and psychosis. There is little cooperation between the parts of the psyche in this model — not to mention the Platonic idea of the harmony of the psyche. And the question of true morality, of right and wrong beyond the norms of society and culture, does not even arise in the picture. It is merely a political drama in which all the characters, lacking in moral conscience, blindly exert pressure against each other.

However, the façade of normality is maintained in the psychoanalytic model: The person acts and moves about, *as if* he were a free agent, but *in actuality* his "rational" behavior is predetermined by hidden "irrational" forces — analogous to the Japanese "Bunraku Theater", where the puppet "actor" is sustained by three figures draped in black, who determine his acts and movements, but themselves remain invisible in the background.

In this black-box model of human nature, the real-life dialectic of the rivalry between opposite kinds of motivations — between *éris* and *éros* — and the possibility of authentic action by the human person, is missing. It is known that the young Carl Jung had had an important dream — wherein he explored a house, from its attic to its cellar, where he found broken pottery and skeletal bones — a dream which he took to represent the history of his own mental development — but he feared presenting it to Freud lest he might read it as a "death wish" and thereby miss the main point of the dream.[28] The principle of psychological egoism, which permeates the psychoanalytic model, precludes the dialectical realism of I/World relationship.

Precisely here lies the significance of the contribution of Viktor Frankl which serves as a corrective to Freud's theory: he places the I/World relation in the foreground. Here *éris*, and not *éros*, emerges as the reigning principle. This implies that the view of human nature as a "closed system", specifically, a system operating according to the "pleasure principle", must be rejected. Instead, it is the "search for meaning" that determines man's relations to the world. As a "dynamic system", man's personality develops through the challenge and resolution of conflicts and tensions. And the levels of the development of the psyche represent the levels of "self-transcendence". To neglect this essential character of the human psyche — Frankl argues — would be to invite the disasters of "noogenic neurosis" which haunts the human condition in contemporary times.[29]

The opposition between Freud and Frankl is most evident in their views concerning the question of the 'meaning of life'. Freud once wrote: "The moment a man questions the meaning and value of life, he is sick..."[30] By that criterion, Goethe, Tolstoy, and Heidegger — to name but three of our healthiest human beings — were merely sick persons. In contrast, Frankl writes: "Man's search for meaning is not pathological, but the surest sign of being truly human"; and again: "For doubt about the meaning of life, the despair of a person because of the apparent lack of meaning in his life, is indeed not an illness, but a potential characteristic of the human being."[31] It appears to us — who have been reared in the heritage of Socrates — that, on the contrary, the man who never questions the 'meaning of life', or has never questioned it in his life, remains *something less than* a 'human being'.

In view of the great variation in the range of human personality and existence, the breakdown of the psychoanalytic model is to be expected. For it must be remembered that, originally, the psychoanalytic theory was derived from a pathological data-base: specifically, neurotic and hysteric human beings. Only later did Freud generalize his pathological theory into a theory of human nature. But it is evident that the anxieties which a young Einstein might suffer in his relation to the world would be of a radically different kind than those to be suffered by a young Baudelaire. The prejudice, that all human personalities are cast of the same mould, is a prejudice embedded in all reductive theories.

In connection with this last point, it is revealing to note a confession made by Freud in his old age (in a letter edited by Ernest Jones) concerning the unbridgeable gulf that separated his personality from that of Nietzsche the philosopher: "In my youth he signified a nobility which I could not attain." And Nietzsche—whose philosophy of life represents the nemesis of that of Freud — envisioned the human psyche, not as something static and predetermined, but as something dynamic and evolving. The conflict between Freud and Nietzsche is none other than the very conflict between psychoanalysis and philosophy.

Psyche and the Negatizing of Existentialism

It is by a negative definition of 'consciousness' that Jean-Paul Sartre approaches the human psyche. 'I am not the other which is not me' — that proposition is to describe the primordial experience of self-awareness. Thence follows a long concatenation of negatizing concerning human nature which terminates by reducing it, precisely, to *ens absurdum*.

But by this negation, that 'I am not the other which is not me', I am also affirming: (a) that I am; (b) that I am this person (and no other); and (c) that I know who I am. Hence the negative aspect of 'consciousness' is complemented by its positive aspect. Since Sartre remains oblivious to the latter aspect, and only focuses on the former, his thinking remains at a pre-dialectical niveau.

And this pre-dialectical thinking is illustrated in Sartre's critique of the so called "transcendental ego". He argues that the prereflective experience is not accompanied by the 'I'; that the 'I' is something which is added on in a postreflection which follows the original experience; and, consequently, that what we call the 'I' does not have a phenomenological existence. E.g. I can be reading a book, and turning its pages as I read them, without any awareness of the 'I' throughout the course of this experience; and it will be later, in response to the query (by myself or by another) as to who it was that was reading, that I shall answer: "It was I who was reading." Sartre concludes then: Since the 'I' is not given (not to ask: given to *whom?*) in the original experience, therefore it does not exist on phenomenological grounds.[32]

A twofold epistemological error vitiates Sartre's argument: *Firstly,* that the 'I' is *assumed* implicitly by every moment of prereflective experience even though it is not accompanied by it explicitly. Every moment of my experience is 'mine': 'I' am the bearer of my experience. And to speak of a moment of experience that does not belong to an observer would be a paradoxical assertion. *Secondly,* that the 'I' may be given in reflective experience. For the contents of secondary intentions ("I know that I am reading") are phenomenologically *as good as* the contents of primary intentions ("I am reading"). Therefore the higher phenomenological experience, and the *transcendental reflection*, coincide in affirming the existence of the 'I' as the complement of all experience.

Why does Sartre fail to recognize the reality of the 'I' *as assumed by* phenomenological experience and *revealed* by reflective experience? Because that would commit him to mental realism: it would commit him to the recognition of the *person*, as an ontological entity, and therewith the recognition of an *essence* in human beings. And that would be an anathema to an existentialist of his genre... And the philosophical plot, in the light of the ideological motive, unfolds itself: by negating the reality of the 'I' as the *thinker*, one negates the reality of the *person*, which in turn implies the negation of the *humanitas* of man.

Too, the philosophical consequences of this negatizing for human existence are noteworthy:

The same Sartre, who claims that "*l'existentialisme est un humanisme*", writes the following about a 'human being': "A human being is a useless passion... and to intoxicate oneself alone in a cabaret or to direct the course of nations is equally vain."[33] Ironically, while existentialists claim to be concerned about the *conditio humane*, they preempt their own human concern by negating the reality and the worth of the *human person*. For what is the moral force of a program for social reform when its philosophical premises preempt the very values it claims to serve? This paradox, too, may be taken as a manifestation of the *mauvaise foi* of the existentialist in relation to humanity.

Recall that when, in Robert Musil's *The Man Without Qualities*, the existentialist hero is asked, what he would do if he were in God's place, he replies: "I should be compelled to abolish reality."

As a commentary on this revealing passage, I quote Georg Lukács, who has studied the literature of existentialism critically: "Attenuation of reality and dissolution of personality are thus interdependent: in their magnitude they reciprocate each other. Underlying both is the absence of a consistent view of human nature. Man is reduced to a series of discrete experiential fragments; and hence remains inexplicable to himself as well as to others."[34] Lukács has further explored the effects of this anti-realist trend in philosophy in the areas of art, music, and literature. The existentialist writers and artists, he observes, are driven into believing that the caverns of psychopathology are their safest refuge; for playing with insanity is indeed the ideological complement of their own ahistorical/ nonphilosophical existence.

The tragedy of existentialism is that its view of the human psyche (and human existence) arises from an epistemological mistake. But one's epistemological stance determines one's ontological stance. And where "negative existentialism" fails, a positive philosophy of existence (as articulated by Karl Jaspers) might succeed in responding to the *conditio humane* more adequately.

§ 22

Higher Consciousness

To depict 'psyche' as the infrastructure of 'higher consciousness' means that it sustains the range of mental life. And, we have seen, the psyche and its higher consciousness remain inaccessible to the methods of reductive theories which have access only to the lower phases of mental life. What, then, is *higher consciousness*?

Consciousness represents a transcendental mental field within whose range objects fall, in relation to the observer, independently of the character of the relata.

Epistemologically speaking, the proposition 'I am conscious of X' means: *(I) R (X)* where 'R' represents 'intentionality' as a transcendental relation which is independent of the character of the object 'X'.

Higher consciousness involves (besides the consciousness of objects in the world) self-reflection *and* cosmic awareness in some measure.

'I' as Thinker

The question concerning the *I* arises since the picture of the world which I have formed is *mine*.

I enter the world, not merely as a part of it, but as an *observer*. I am aware of my own being, of the world as *my* world , and of the I / World relation.

'I' is the personal designator of the psyche. And the pronouns 'he' and 'she', too, are personal designators. If I say: the author of *Amerika* is a millionaire, and I happen to be the author in question, then I am merely naming myself by oblique reference.

Hence the 'I' serves as an epistemological operator in the ideal language. For the possibility of every first-person proposition is contingent upon the assumption of the 'I'. The epistemological priority of the 'I' lies in the fact that it constitutes the *a priori* condition of the possibility of *my* awareness that any given moment of experience (or thought) belongs to *me*.

'I' is prior to every thought-expression: "I think...", "I perceive...", "I believe..." And, if the 'I' represents an awareness *of* the experience-moment or of the thought-moment, then the 'I' itself can never be merely a moment *in* thought or *in* experience. Hence, I can conceive of myself, as 'I', only by reflecting upon the epistemological ground of the possibility of my experiencing or thinking.

"Mais les états de la conscience existent à titre des phénomènes" — so remarked Professor Jean Piaget of Geneva during the epistemological debates at the Institut J.-J. Rousseau — but we must remember that the 'transcendental unity of consciousness' is not accessible phenomenologically.

Do I then exist?

Were I to say: "I do not exist now" — I would be asserting a self-contradictory proposition. For the very possibility of that proposition presupposes that I exist as the thinker. And if I did not exist, I would not be able to utter that proposition. Therefore, I must say: "I do exist now" — is a necessarily true proposition.

(On this point Descartes was right in saying that *"je suis, j'existe, est nécessairement vraie, tout les fois que je la prononce..."* — in the opening argument of his *Méditations*.)

Besides the above logical consideration, there is a phenomenological consideration, concerning the existence of the 'I'. Here the elegant argument of Brentano — perhaps inspired by the Kantian distinction between noumena and phenomena — is worth noting:

"For what do we understand by a phenomenon? Something that appears to one. To say that something exists *as* a phenomenon, but there is nothing in itself *to* which it is a phenomenon, is thus a contradiction. If one were to say, of that *to which* the phenomenon appears, that it too is a phenomenon, then one must say that there must be something else in itself, *to which* it is a phenomenon, and this something is known in its own being."[35]

It must have been on the basis of such an argument that Brentano, on another occasion, confidently writes: "For in the case of self-awareness, one says 'It is evident to me that I exist'; it cannot be directly evident to anyone else that I exist"[36] — for it is only *I* who have direct access to *my* psyche.

That Hume failed, in searching to find the 'I' among the myriad of his "impressions", is understandable. Recall his confession: "When I enter into what I call myself, I always stumble upon some particular perception or other... I am but a bundle of perceptions;" and again: "The mind is like a theatre, where several perceptions successively make their appearance; pass, repass, glide away, and mingle in infinite variety of postures and situations... there is no *simplicity* in it... nor *identity*..."[37] Hume, it appears, did not take note that it was *he* who searched, as he stumbled upon *his* perceptions, looking for *himself* in the wrong places. His very assertion, that "I am but a bundle of perceptions", implies that his "self" *transcends* the congeries of his perceptions, as there exists *no* perception which can *refer* to the ensemble of perceptions, in order to render that assertion possible.

However, in recent philosophical debates, the levels of intentionality have been questioned, lending indirect support to Hume's skeptical conclusion. Consider, in particular, Wittgenstein's attempted logical reduction of intentionality. Wittgenstein writes: "At first sight it looks as if it were also possible for one proposition to occur in another... It is clear, however, that '*A* believes that *p*', '*A* has the thought *p*', and '*A* says *p*' are of the form '"*p*" says *p*': and this does not involve a correlation of a fact with an object, but rather the correlation of facts by means of the correlation of their objects."[38] It follows that '*p* says *p*' may be written as '*p*:*p*' and simplified as '*p*' thus completing the reduction of the "observer" to his object of "observation". However, Wittgenstein confuses the *intentions* of the two propositions: '*p*' and '*A* thinks/believes that *p*'. The latter proposition involves three things: (a) the thinker (A); (b) the mental act (thinking/believing) referring to *p*; and (c) the event described by *p*. It is clear that the intentions of the two propositions — '*p*' and '*A* thinks/believes that '*p*' — are not the same. The one proposition *contains* the other as its constituent. Therefore, epistemologically, the proposition '*A* thinks that *p*' is *not* reducible to '*p* says *p*' or '*p*'.

That second intentions are not reducible to first intentions is also evident in that the senses of the two propositions, '*A* believes that p' and 'p' are not identical. For, if they were, then the negation of either would imply the negation of the other. But the negation of 'p' is not at all incompatible with the assertion of 'A believes that p'. E.g. it is possible for one to believe that it is raining elsewhere while in fact it is not raining.

Similarly, tertiary intentions are not reducible to secondary intentions: the proposition 'I know that I know that p' cannot be reduced to the proposition 'I know that p'. Suppose a man, standing at the edge of a river, says: "I know that I can swim across the river." And, if he is successful in swimming across the river, he will say: "Now I know that I was right in saying that 'I know that I can swim across the river'." That the meanings (and intentions) of the two propositions are different, is evident in that this man could utter the one, but not the other, *before* the act of swimming.

Here arises the ontological question concerning the transcendental existence of the 'I'. The intelligibility of an act, within a hierarchy of acts, assumes an infrastructure in the background. The concept of the 'I' may be conceived, ontologically, as representing the infrastructure behind mental acts. And the 'I' must be evoked in order to explain, not only the *coordination* but also the *continuity* of, acts. For example, the artistic progression of the compositions of Mozart, from the early ones to the later ones, becomes intelligible only on the basis of assuming the continued identity of the artist. In this sense, then, the 'I' designates a person — or a "primary being"[39] — or (as I say) a *psyche*.

The integrative function of the 'I' may be depicted as follows:
(a) that the ensemble of the moments of my experience in time *belong to me*;
(b) that the 'I' serves as the *bearer* of my memories and imagery and the possibility of their persistence in time;
(c) that there are levels of integration and levels of reflection in my mental life: conceptual hierarchies and value hierarchies.

Assuming the ontological status of the 'I', the question remains as to its enduring 'identity' through time. And when we speak of the identity of the self through time, it is the 'transcendental self' (represented by the 'I'), as pure consciousness, and not the 'empirical self' of which psychology speaks. For the identity of the empirical self barely endures from day to day, much less through the course of a lifetime. But the identity of the transcendental self through time derives from the inherent dialectic of consciousness: i.e. the plurality of the moments of self-consciousness and their unification in a higher consciousness. Consider the following diagram:

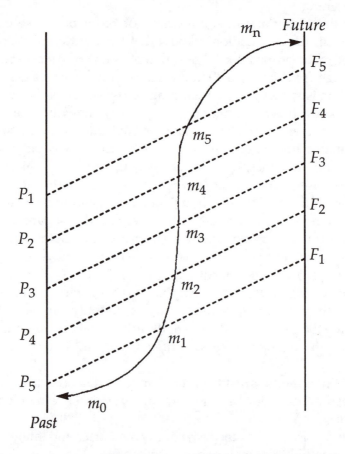

In the 'continuum of consciousness' (represented by the curve X) the moments of self-consciousness (m_1, m_2, m_3,...m_n) arrange themselves dialectically. Thus, while a given moment (m_3) may be in the "future", from the viewpoint of the relative past (P_4), it may be in the "past" from the viewpoint of a relative future (F_4); etc. Moreover, every moment of self-consciousness either recaptures or anticipates another moment, given its place and viewpoint in the continuum. Hence *each* moment of self-consciousness is compatible with the awareness of the set of *all* such moments, within its range, in the past or in the future. The self-conscious 'I', looking *backward* from the present to the past, is aware of its *actual existence* in the set of past moments; and, looking *forward* from the present to the future, it is aware of its *potential existence* in a set of future moments. Thus, if the 'I', at m_3, looking back at m_1, can say "*I was*"; then it can also, at m_2, looking ahead at m_3 say "*I will be*". And all such moments of retrospective and prospective self-consciousness are possible by the transcendental capacity of the 'I', at any moment in the continuum of consciousness, to say "*I am*". What is true of a segment of the continuum, is true of the entire line, indefinitely. Thus the identity of the self through time, according to our model, is to be proved, not through any phenomenology of the contents of consciousness, but through the dialectic of the pure moments of self-consciousness.

This is a rough sketch of the 'I' - and it must remain so: for a philosopher's elucidation of the 'I' is analogous to a primitive sculptor's carving his own image in stone.

Intentionality

It is 'intentionality' that distinguishes mental acts from bodily acts: Mental acts are directed to, and appropriate, their objects independently of their character. *Noesis* includes the *noema*: perhaps it even determines it. The 'psychological object' — we say with Brentano — precedes every 'physical object'.

I distinguish two kinds of 'intentionality' with radically different operations:

Intentionality A: a mental act directed to an object *per se* (whether concrete/abstract or actual/possible) as in perceiving, thinking, imagining, and remembering.

Intentionality B: a mental act directed to an object *as an end* (whether actual or possible) as in intending to act or willing to act: "I do X because I intended to do X."

To see the import of *Intentionality B*, consider the two kinds of human expressions:

ϕ - Expressions: automatic acts — as in a facial expression at tasting something bitter.

ψ - Expressions: willful acts expressing one's thoughts / feelings — as in the facial expression of disgust at a vulgar joke.

The difference between the two kinds of expressions is evident: the one could, and the other could not, occur *without* an intention. Hence the one could be explained physiologically, while the other must be explained psychologically. Correspondingly, we understand the one kind of expression as a natural *event*, and the other as a human *act* portending a meaning — a distinction which Anfinn Stigen has made[40] — and which I assume.

The epistemological distinction between the two kinds of expressions also has an important implication: it ascribes 'power' to the human psyche — the power to *actualize* its potential intentions and meanings — and of this power we shall speak in the following section.

That there are levels of intentionality is shown by the possibility of constructing the following types of propositions:

Intentionality A: "I know that X"
"I know that 'I know that X'"

Intentionality B: "I will do X"
"I will that my will to do X becomes a universal principle of conduct for all human beings"

Bergmann argues: Every primary mental act (A_1) has a text which refers to its object, and the name of the mental act itself could not possibly occur in its text; so we need a secondary mental act (A_2) whose text refers to (A_1) as its object; and, consequently, it is exactly in this sense of reflexive self-reference of intentionality that one mental act may refer to another in the "ideal language".[41] This shows the epistemic possibility of reflexive thinking.

Consciousness, then, may be defined in terms of internal relations (i.e. relations which are determined by the inherent properties of the relata). Let o be the object of awareness, and i the intentional act which is the awareness of o, then consciousness (C) provides the context for the possibility of the nexus between the two:

Consciousness : (i)C(o) And since consciousness is reflexive, it can take its primary intentional act as an object of its secondary intentional act:

Consciousness : (i)'C(i) (This proves the ontological status of mental acts.)

Two characteristics of mental acts emerge:

Firstly, that mental acts are *transcendental*, i.e., relatively independent of the character of objects to which they are directed.

Secondly, that mental acts are *private* in a twofold sense: (a) that one is aware of one's own mental acts as meaningful entities directly; and (b) that others cannot be aware of one's mental acts in the same way — but, perhaps, only indirectly. Thus one has a "privileged access" to one's own mental life.

Can intentionality then be directed *inward* as well as *outward*: is authentic introspection possible?

The prevailing objection to introspection derives from a pair of associated problems: ineffability and infinite regress. It is true that the character of a moment of conscious experience is altered by the process of introspection — as if its liquid form gave way to the intrusion of visual ray — and hence it remains ineffable. But it is also true that ineffability pertains to the present moment — and not to a past moment whose character is set in time as it were — and introspection is possible only after a moment of conscious experience has run its course in time. Nor is it necessary, in order to become aware of a mental act, that one must be aware of the act of awareness, and so on *ad infinitum*. For to insist that this, or something like it, must be the case, would be to confuse the two meanings of the 'mental act': the act as a 'conscious state' and the act as a 'mental state' (a useful distinction made by Reinhardt Grossmann).[42] The former is known by the latter; and the awareness of the former does not imply awareness of the latter. In becoming aware of X, through introspection, I need not also thereby become aware of my awareness of X. E.g. I may feel anger, and know that I am angry, without also knowing that I know what I know. This would require another, higher level, mental act.

In any act of introspection it is noteworthy: (a) that the immediate data of consciousness constitute self-presenting evidence; and (b) that if we grant the validity of the original data of consciousness, as self-presenting, we must also grant the validity of their recurrence on the *same* phenomenological grounds.[43]

The possibility of introspection entails the possibility of private language.

However, Wittgenstein argues against this possibility, in his well-known example of the tribe.[44] Suppose that a foreigner visits a tribe which have their own unique language; and naturally the visitor does not understand them. But, observing and correlating their sounds with their facial expressions, their actions and events, he will reconstruct their language for himself eventually. Wittgenstein insists that this is a public process. Yet, the visitor must experience, privately (at the psychological level) as it were, the correlation of the strange language to the world. He must reconstruct for himself the language, privately, before he can use it publicly (at the social level). And it is only after undergoing such an experience in private thinking that he will be able to understand, and communicate in, the public language.

Accordingly, I interpret the example of the tribe — and the example of the "beetle in the box" presented elsewhere—to illustrate the *dialectical relation* between private/public languages rather than the negation of the possibility of either. For the intelligibility of a 'public language' presupposes its prior reconstruction at the level of 'private thinking'. Indeed, the words and sentences of any 'public language' must be *verifiable* at the level of private experience *in order to be intelligible to* the person. The interiorization and exteriorization of language are dialectically complementary operations. The rejection of the possibility of private thinking/language would entail the negation of the intelligibility of public thinking/language as a consequence.

And so we must reaffirm, not only the *possibility* of introspection and "privileged access" to one's own mental life, but also its *necessity* — and reaffirm the validity of self-meditation or (to use Plato's depiction) the "conversation of the psyche with itself" — as the original source of all public expression and discourse.

§ 23

The Question of Mind/Body Relation

The question of mind/body relation arises in two contexts: (a) as the interaction of mental acts and bodily movements in the life-world, and (b) as the interaction of mental states and bodily states at the level of neuroscience. Nor are the two contexts unrelated: both levels of interaction have implications for the question of freewill in human action.

Freewill and Human Action

I am walking in the garden, and my hand reaches and plucks a flower; and, again, a bee stings me, and my hand reaches and rubs the spot. What is the difference between these two movements of my hand? The issue of freewill hangs upon this question.

Consider two dramatic cases:

A leaf flying before a gust of wind

and

A man fleeing before an angry tribe

To the question — What is the difference between the two cases? — we might answer: that the one represents an instance of mechanical action (completely explainable by the laws of physics); and the other represents an instance of human action (not entirely explainable by the laws of physics). What, then, is a 'human action'; and of what sort of explanation is it susceptible?

A 'human action', by contrast to an 'event' in the world, involves an internal 'motive': i.e. an intention or a reason. Viewed as an event, it represents a mere sequence of movements; but, as an action, it is an "expression" of the intention of the person. And the *explanation* of the action — and, correspondingly, its understanding — requires that its *motive* be revealed.

The *motive* of an action consists of the *reason* for the action (of which the person is conscious) which one would disclose in response to the question as to *why* one performed the action. When a reason for an action is given, in its justification as it were, it tells us that the action was taken *because* of it. Reasons (we may say with Von Wright) constitute the *explanation* of actions. An action determined in this way may be said to be *self-determined*, by the person, rather than externally determined. Such an action, we may say, indicates the *freewill* of the person.

To Von Wright's question: "What sorts of things count as reasons for action?"[45] — we may answer: A person's beliefs concerning actual and/or potential values — his *Weltanschauung* and *Ideals* — serve as reasons for actions.

I assume two kinds of *reasons* for actions: the *internal reasons* (which cause an action to be performed for the sake of an end within the person's belief system); and the *external reasons* (which cause an action to be performed in response to a symbolic challenge from the world). But are not 'internal reasons' really 'external reasons' which have been internalized? Some, undoubtedly, are; but when the person has appropriated them into his belief system, then they are transformed into internal reasons. In that case, one may say, again, that the action has been self-determined. This, too, is part of the dialectical scenario of the inner and the outer. Similarly, internal reasons may be externalized by the use of pragmatic signs.

Since reasons for actions often reflect the value-system of the person, it is not merely the having of reasons, but the having of "good reasons" that motivates action. E.g. my telephone rings: whether I intend to answer it or not will be determined by my belief as to the importance of its possible message. And yet, even the having of a "good reason" may not always be sufficient for action: the case of *akrasia* (weakness of the will) demonstrates the limits of rationality. However, one may say that, without "good reason", a rational person cannot act, or, act as a free agent. Indeed, the very "intelligibility" of a human action, either to the person himself or to other persons, would be impossible without the disclosure of reasons behind the action.

The basic presupposition of the concept of 'freewill' is the concept of the *person*. And the dynamic of the interplay between the inner forces (internal reasons) and outer forces (external reasons), acting upon the person, varies in each case. Hence, dialectically viewed, there are *degrees* of personal freedom:

Personal Freedom = *f* (*Inner Forces/Outer Forces*)

It is evident then, that 'freedom', as a state of the psyche as it were, must be earned by each person through the exercise of practical reason, the development of a value hierarchy, and the discipline of willpower.

The question remains however: Can I know, through introspection, that I have freewill in my actions? And the answer must be: I may know that I have freewill in my actions *only insofar as* I see/understand, through introspection, the reasons for my actions *as* the motive of my action.

It may also be true that reasons (at the psychological level) may correspond to neural events (at the physiological level). But this fact does not detract from the explanatory power of reasons. For, even after a complete inventory of neural events underlying an action has been disclosed, the question still remains to be answered: Why did the person *believe* that this particular action, *among several possible actions*, was the appropriate response to the situation? The neurological argument, philosophically interesting as it may be, remains irrelevant to the personal *understanding* of one's motives for action. And this observation will be rendered clearer in our critical examination of materialism in the following.

Mind/Body Interaction in the Light of Neuroscience

The mind is dependent upon the body, in one sense, and yet in another sense, the mind is independent of the body: the relation between the two is analogous to the relation that holds between a page of written score and a musical melody.

Some philosophers (at Oxford and elsewhere) have suggested that the apparent differences between mental and bodily phenomena are merely a matter of dual language and nothing more. If this be the case, then the two languages ought to be translatable into each other. For example, if one utters a false proposition, then one ought to be able to say that one has made a "mistake in speaking" *as accurately as* saying that one made a "mistake in thinking/believing"; or, again, if one invents a faulty gadget, one ought to be able to say "My body made a blunder" *as accurately as* saying "I made a blunder"; etc. But it is clear that the two propositions would not mean the same thing. The confusion of bodily act and mental act has an epistemological source: it assumes the reducibility of secondary intentions ("I know that I made a blunder") to primary intentions ("I made a blunder") which, we have seen already, is not possible. It is on the basis of this erroneous assumption that the 'I' is replaced with the 'it' in the physical language. But since the replacement of intentional language by physical language results in the dissolution of meaning—ironically through the abuse of language — the proposed dissolution of the mind/body problem by 'linguistic philosophers' remains a failure.

Yet, even if the bodily language cannot simulate the mental language, would it be impossible for an electronic machine to simulate the mind?

This possibility is precisely what the "artificial intelligence" theory claims to materialize. It claims that the electronic computer, not only can *simulate* human thinking, but also can *understand* the story involved in the imitation game. Thus the Turing Experiment demonstrates that, assuming a restricted definition of "thinking" in operational terms, one can attribute "thinking" to such machines on the basis of their behavior. Besides the evident circularity in this kind of argument, there is another serious problem associated with it: the problem of *understanding* versus apparent *simulation*. I believe that the root of the problem lies in the fact that the AI theorists fail to distinguish two very distinct things: *intellect* (which is capable of simulative act) and *mind* (which is capable of the act of understanding). So they attribute a "mind" to machines when they display presumably "intelligent" behavior.

An ingenious thought-experiment by J.R. Searle, presenting the "Chinese Room" paradigm, discloses this problem: It demonstrates that it is possible, for a human being, to be programmed in his native language, to correlate the symbols of a foreign language, *without* understanding their meanings or the story involved. One would not, in this case of blind symbol manipulation, attribute "thinking" or "understanding" to this human being.[46] Exactly the same may be said about computers as so called "thinking machines".

The trouble with any variant of the "artificial intelligence" theory is that it remains ontologically groundless. The new materialism seeks to provide an ontological ground. However, for reasons that will be evident presently, the new materialism fails also.

Both or either of the following propositions are held by the new materialists: (a) that there are no emergent phenomena (at the biological/psychological levels) which are not reducible to the level of physical concepts; and (b) that there exists an underlying structural identity between certain aspects of brain events and mental phenomena. From these propositions J.J.C. Smart infers that "reality" may be attributed, not to mental phenomena, but to brain processes only.[47] But (in the light of some recent developments in the philosophy of science) the first proposition of materialism appears to be patently false; and its second proposition rests upon a confusion of "continuity" and "identity". For even if it be shown that there is a one-to-one correspondence between sense-impressions and cerebral events, this does *not* imply the reducibility of the one to the other, *but only* their qualitative correlativity. And from the fact that a structural homology may exist between brain events and mental phenomena — as indeed the researches of Wolfgang Köhler, Henri Piéron, and other scientists have shown[48] — we can only infer a *continuity* of physiological/psychological strata and not their *identity*. Moreover, though the materialist theory is able to explain the unilateral causal connection (brain → mind), it is unable to explain the bilateral causal connection (brain ⇄ mind) as is evident in cases of intentional action and in psychosomatic phenomena. Here a set of psychophysical laws are needed to explain the intricate and subtle processes of mind/body interaction. That materialists denounce these laws as "nomological danglers" (the expression used by Herbert Feigl) only reveals their own dogmatic assumptions.

This recalls the old argument of Bergson concerning the *difference radicale* between mind and body: that while bodily sensations occur and recur with non-selective passivity, mental imagery has the power to selectively activate past memories and selectively evoke future anticipations. For consciousness — Bergson argues in his *Matière et mémoire* — confronts the ensemble of past images, rummages through them, selecting only those images which happen to be relevant to its present and/or future interests, and leaves the rest to recede into "*l'ombre de la mémoire*" as it were. And the criteria of the veracity of a mental image, which consciousness entertains, consist of: (a) the presentability of the image as an immediate datum of consciousness, and (b) the cognitive bond of the given image with other moments of memory. "*Il n'y aura pas plus de raison pour dire que le passé, une fois perçu, s'éfface...*" observes Bergson.[49] And modern neuroscience — with its distinction between 'semantic memory' and 'episodic memory', their interaction, and the recognition of *the reconstructive role* of the mind — seems to confirm Bergson's phenomenological description.

Where two radically different perspectives converge, there lies the truth, perhaps: compare the results of phenomenology with those of neuroscience.

Here, the work of Sir John Eccles is of special philosophical interest. Eccles poses the question as follows: "How can *willing* of a muscular movement set in train neuronal events that lead to the discharge of pyramidal cells of the motor cortex and so to activation of the neuronal pathway that leads to muscle contraction?" And, on the basis of his research in neuroscience, he answers: "It can be presumed that during the readiness potential there is a developing specificity of the patterned impulse discharges in neurones so that *eventually* there are activated the pyramidal cells in the correct motor cortical areas for bringing about the required movement. The readiness potential can be regarded as the neuronal *counterpart* of the voluntary command... at the stage of *willing* a movement, there is a very wide *influence of the self-conscious mind* on the patterns of module operation."[50] And, in a subsequent work, Eccles again writes: "The *self-conscious mind* is actively engaged in *reading out* from the multitude of liaison modules (neocortex) that are largely in the dominant cerebral hemisphere... (it) *selects* from these modules *according to attention and interest,* and from movement to movement *integrates* its selection to give unity even to the most transient experiences... (it) *acts upon* these modules modifying their dynamic spatio-temporal patterns. Thus it is proposed that the *self-conscious mind* exercises *a superior interpretative and controlling role...* (and) the *unity* of conscious experience *is provided by* the self-conscious mind *and not by* the neural machinery of the liaison areas of the cerebral hemisphere."[51]

This scientific account corresponds to the phenomenological experience of the intentional act and voluntary movement. Thus, e.g., I think that it would be nice to drink a glass of wine, and my hand reaches and takes a goblet. According to the introspective experience of my self-conscious mind, my intention was the motive (and cause) of my overt behavior: and my brain and nervous system seem to have served as an indispensable *mediator* in this behavioral scenario.

Accordingly, the schema for mind/body interaction may be reconstructed as follows:

(T_1) Intentionality ----------------------- Bodily Movement (T_4)

        ↓   ↑

(T_2) Module Patterning   →   Physiological (T_3)
      & Neuron Firings   Changes

This schema is similar to that constructed by John Searle[52]—but with the exception of one critical difference: that I have *reversed* the direction of the arrow connecting intentionality and neuron firings. And the grounds for this are: the immediate evidence of introspection *as well as* the results of neuroscience.

If the emergence (and power) of the *mind* seems extraordinary, consider the *brain* itself. For what is the chemistry of the human brain after all? The brain is composed of some amino acids, electrolytes (electrically charged atoms of some elements), some lipids (including phosphorous and other elements), some trace metals, a quantity of carbohydrates as fuel reserve, and a large amount of water (70-80%). There is nothing extraordinary about the contents of the brain; what is extraordinary is its *emergent* Gestalt quality and function.

In the relation between the *mind* and the *world*, the brain (and the body) serves as the liaison:

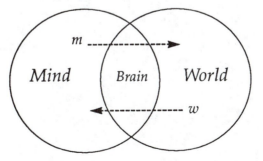

Two overlapping circles: Where the one arrow (w) signifies the inflow of experience from the external world; and the other arrow (m) signifies the interpretational matrix within which the mind receives the experience and acts in response. It is a two-way interrelation, wherein the psychophysical interaction involved precludes one-way reductionism, and the two dynamic systems retain their partial autonomy.

§ 24

Journey of the Psyche

The hypothesis of the identity and continuity of the psyche through time evokes the question of the journey of the psyche through the world.

The early natural philosophers of Hellas spoke of the "journey of the psyche"; and, for them, it was more than a metaphor. They believed that the psyche was destined to endure a cosmic journey: that it had to wander for "30,000 horae" or more, through plant, animal, and human forms, wrapped in the strange garment of the material body, until, at last, it shed this garment too at its earthly "death"... And, similarly, Meister Eckhart, blending the heathen and the mystic strains of thought, taught the doctrine of the "pilgrimage of the soul", i.e., the moral journey of the psyche in this life and beyond — until "*er sollte eine höhere Welt schauuen*" — until he enters the twilight of a 'higher world'.

But nowhere do we read a more dramatic narrative of the "journey of the psyche" than in Plato's *Phaedo* (70): here he elucidates, in the "language of probability", admittedly, the arduous course of the journey of the psyche and its moral motive. "There is an old legend..." Plato writes, "to the effect that they (psyches) do come to exist *there*, after leaving *here*, and that they may return again to this world..." and so on. But whether they return, and under what conditions, will be determined by their life and character. And the "doctrine of recollection" — that the apparent acquisition of knowledge by the person, in this world, involves in reality a deeper process of recollecting of truths known earlier — would provide (Plato thought) the metaphysical argument for the survival of the psyche.

The ancient doctrine of the "journey of the psyche", then, may be stated explicitly as follows: That this earthly life represents an intermediary phase of existence; that the human psyche has existed before and will continue to exist after this life (for birth is not creation *ex nihilo* nor death an extinction *ad nihilum*); and that the psyche retains, at some deeper level of its consciousness, the memory of its past existence.

We may interpret the metaphor of the "journey of the psyche" in a twofold way: (a) as the passage of the psyche through this earthly life, and (b) as the prospect of the passage of the psyche through cosmos (including another world). Then the one passage may be said to describe the 'worldly biography' of the person; and the other, the 'cosmic biography' of the psyche. And these, taken together, may be said to constitute the idea of 'personal destiny'. Our concern will be with the *meaning*, as well as with the *truth*, of the doctrine of the "journey of the psyche".

In what sense, then, may we speak of the "journey of the psyche" through this earthly life?

Perhaps in this sense: that, not only the psyche witnesses and endures the events of life, but it also undergoes a transfiguration, an inner self-realization, in the course of time. The practice of freewill in action assumes the self-determining power of the psyche; and the preservation of self-identity through time assumes the continuum of consciousness in the psyche. We have argued for both these assumptions already. Here we may add only: that, besides these, there may be another power, a more arcane and mysterious power, which may act upon the psyche and influence its course in life: the power of deeper intuitions and dreams emanating from the darker region of subconsciousness within the psyche. Thus the *outer* drama of the life of the psyche may be determined, in part at least, by the drama of its *inner* life.

The *inner* and the *outer*, stand in dialectical relation: we may say that ontologically the inner is prior to the outer; but that phenomenologically the outer is prior to the inner. Thus the processes of the experience of the world and the tracking of one's cosmic destiny appear to be intertwined. And this relationship is articulated in the "Theory of Eudaimonism", by my colleague David Norton, in a recent work: "Self-knowledge (self-understanding) is the precondition of the knowledge (understanding) of other things, and truth to oneself is the precondition of truthfulness to others... When an individual allows himself to be deflected from his own true course, he fails in that first responsibility from which all other genuine responsibilities follow, and whose fulfillment is the precondition of the least fulfillment of other responsibility... (with) the recognition that outside the individual's constellation of personal truths lie countless other truths belonging to other persons..."[53] The implication of this theory for the philosophy of life is clear: one's modality of self-realization and one's existential stance in life dialectically hang together.

The journey of the psyche is further complicated by the fact that the drama of present life is interwoven with the dramas of past and future lives. The persistence of the 'I' through time (as the personal designator of the psyche) we have already seen. Memory constitutes the link, *through the present*, between the past and the future. But the persistence of the 'psyche', as the bearer of memories, is presupposed by the consciousness of the connection between the past and the future. Hence the psyche retains, in a sense, an independence — or (to use an expressive German word) *unabhängigkeit* — relative to the body which remains tied to contemporary sensations. Herein lies the theoretical possibility of persistence of the psyche through time.

Can the relation of the present to past/future be compared to the relation between sleep and wakefulness? Consider an example from Aristotle: one may say of a "sleeping musician", that he *is* potentially a musician, for he *was* actually trained to be a musician in the preceding state of wakefulness, or that he *will be* an active musician in the next state of wakefulness. The "sleeping musician" (his dreams notwithstanding) does not appear to have any memory of his previous phase of life, nor any anticipation concerning his succeeding phase of life. Yet, his personal identity (in some form) remains a necessary condition for the preservation of his memory through these phases of life.

However, *memory*, owing to its transiency, is neither always accessible nor always reliable. To what extent, then, is the self-ascription of memory beliefs acceptable? Only to the extent, perhaps, that they meet the twofold criterion of phenomenal distinctness *and* contextual confirmation within one's belief system.[54] This criterion, however, applies only to *conscious memory*, which suffers from transiency. It does not apply to *subconscious memory*, which may be relatively more ineffable and more permanent. For it must be observed, that beneath the ensemble of conscious memories, lies the deep sea of subconsciousness, which harbors a reserve of 'deeper memories' and 'pan-awareness'. Herein lies our "psychic reserve", as it were, whence our conscious mind may drink from time to time. Artists and writers, in particular, are aware of the power and influence of what emanates from this darker region into their conscious life and work: their diaries and letters provide abundant illustrations.

Even if the hypothesis of the cosmic journey of the psyche, in a refined sense, were theoretically possible, the question remains as to its intelligibility. What conceivable life form could be attributed to the psyche *after* its earthly life? In an interesting essay, Professor H.H. Price has depicted the hypothetical scenario:[55] Being "alive" in such a world would mean — in contrast to the chemical/physiological life of the body — a purely psychological existence. One may conceive a world, representing a realm of mental imagery; for, in the absence of the body and sense organs, there can be no sensation and no action, but only a dreamlike participation in reality. And, since the continuum of consciousness is preserved, the sense of personal identity endures, as the psyche begins yet another phase of its cosmic existence... *etcetera*.

A similar attempt at rendering "intelligible" the continuation of man's cosmic biography, through two or more cosmic worlds, has been made by Professor J.N. Findlay, on the basis of the platonic "Cave Image", in the context of a phenomenological interpretation:

> This continued life in two media need not be thought to involve the full actuality of a memory spanning the whole period of continuance, though it does involve the real possibility of such a memory. Even in this life we all acknowledge the possibility that we may have done and undergone many things of which we now have no recollection, and that we may pass over into states in which we shall not remember what we are now doing or undergoing. Identity of self is a matter presupposed by memory and not constituted by it, and nothing is easier to conceive than that we shall be in states without remembering the state in which we now look forward to them...
>
> We may now hazard a view which applies alike to the Indo-Pythagorean and the Christian view of *the after-life*: that the after-life is in a sense parasitic upon the present one, and that its task consists mainly in an assimilation, a spiritual digestion, of the experiences and acts of this one, seeing them in wider and more fluid contexts, comparing them with ideals and values of varying sorts, consolidating their contributions into a new phase of resolution and attitude, but not advancing effectively beyond them. Whereas our this-world existence, with all its agony and blindness,

is the phase of our life where alone we confront serious problems and resistances, where alone we enter into profound personal commitments to others, and where alone we make firm resolves and perform momentous and influential acts. In the essentially yielding medium of the upper world, the events of earth-life can be relived over and over, their import seen in most varied connections, their lessons learnt and their outcome purified from whatever dross clings to them but they cannot significantly be added to: that can alone be done among the resistances and obscurities of *earth-life*, in what we have called *the cave*.[56]

Perhaps, then, arguably the idea of a possible life in another world, as another phase of cosmic existence, might be rendered "intelligible" in one of the above ways, or in some similar way.

The remaining question concerning the "journey of the psyche" pertains to the *relation* of this life to the future life.

A colleague of mine wrote to me:

"The Zen Master asked of his disciple: 'When thou leavest this world, and enterst the other world, thou willst need a candle to illuminate thy path: who then provideth the light if it be not carried within thyself?'" adding that: "The implication is clear — but *you*, who have been reared in the heritage of Socrates, *will* question the questioner..."

Indeed we may question the Zen Master:

In what sense, then, is the earthly life to be regarded as a phase — even a preparatory phase — in the cosmic journey of the psyche?

We recall the hypothetical answer of Socrates to the question: that this 'earthly life', viewed *sub specie aeterni*, might be seen as a phase in the 'cosmic life' of the psyche.

I suggest the following paradigm:

Imagine a spiral figure with a vertical line cutting across it tangentially. Then the line, which intersects the successive curves of the spiral at analogous points, may be said to depict the path of the "cosmic journey" of the psyche. The position of each point — representing the modality of self-realization of the person at a given time — would determine the position of the successive point. Tilt the intersecting line, against or toward the slope of the spiral, and you obtain a curve of the *evolution* or *devolution* of the psyche. And the recurrence of the points of intersection, at successive levels, would represent the phases of the "cosmic biography" of the person.

Schematically:

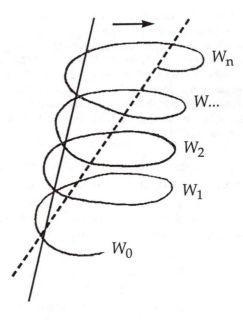

If one regards the idea of the "cosmic journey" of the psyche as a *personal ideal* — à la Kant or à la Nietzsche — then its moral significance becomes evident. The modality of self-realization at a preceding phase determines the modality of self-realization at a succeeding phase. Thus the orbit of life, assumed by the psyche in any given world, would determine its orbit of life in the succeeding world.

The theme of the "journey of the psyche" recalls — besides the ancient viewpoint of Plato as noted earlier — the discourses of Avicenna concerning the human soul. We recall that Avicenna, in his treatise on the psyche (*De Anima*), defined the "soul" as the "principle of emanation", a natural force, from which proceed human acts at will as it were. And, because the spiritual will precedes the bodily act, the person can have knowledge of the workings of his soul prior to having knowledge of the workings of his body. This indicates the ontological primacy of the soul from the human viewpoint — as distinct from the cosmic viewpoint — as well as its existential primacy. And, further, since the soul "mirrors" the actions of the body, *before* as well as *after* their occurrence, its powers of emanation transcend the material powers of the body. And yet the soul requires the body, to actualize its own mode of potential being in *this* world, as it were. Other modes of being, in *other* possible worlds, would be intelligible however. For, assuming that the soul and the body represent two distinct substances — i.e. two essences whose beings are not derivative relative to each other — their union in this world could only be contingent and not necessary. Hence, the destruction of the one does not entail the destruction of the other — but merely a destruction of the relation of the one to the other. Death is but the dissolution of a contingent union of the soul and the body in this life. The journey of the psyche, and its probable transmigration from one world to another, is therefore understandable. Understandable, too, would be the diverging lines of cosmic destiny for the body and the soul: for the body to return to earth and to dust, as the poet would say, and for the soul to return to fire and to air. But can we assume the assumptions of such a metaphysical perspective? The arguments adduced by Avicenna in favor of this perspective bear a resemblance to those of Aristotle, in their subtlety and elegance, but this is a theme for another occasion.

It is significant that recent research in psychiatry, particularly the work of Stanislav Grof, corroborates our understanding of the nature of the psyche. His depiction of the *holotropic mind* provides a paradigm for the integrative character as well as the dimensionality of human consciousness. What I have referred to as "higher consciousness", he refers to as "transpersonal consciousness"; and he elucidates the "levels of consciousness" in terms of their phenomenological irreducibility. Our very different perspectives converge in the notions of the "journey of the psyche" and the attainment of "cosmic consciousness". Thus Grof succeeds in disclosing (in the context of psychiatric research) what Freud failed to disclose: The authenticity of the spiritual dimension of human existence. And this spiritual dimension displays two distinct and interrelated aspects: the existential and the temporal.

Concerning the existential aspect of the psyche Grof writes: "In some rare instances, people experience themselves expanding into a consciousness that encompasses all life on our planet — embracing all humanity and the entire world of flora and fauna, from the viruses to the largest animals and plants. Instead of identifying with a single plant or animal species, they experience the totality of life. This experience could be described as identification with *life as a cosmic phenomenon*, as an entity or force in and of itself... Transpersonal experiences often lead to a deepened understanding of the role of primal forces in nature, an enhanced awareness of the laws that govern our lives, *and* an appreciation for the extraordinary intelligence that underlies all life processes."[57] And, concerning the temporal aspect of the psyche, he writes: "While the possibility of cellular memory from the earliest stages of our lives may stretch the boundaries of our imagination, it is by no means the greatest challenge posed by transpersonal experience. It is not unusual for people in non-ordinary states of mind to accurately portray material that precedes their conception or to explore the world of their parents, their ancestors, or of the human race. Particularly interesting are 'past life' experiences, which suggest that individual consciousness might maintain continuity from one lifetime to another."[58] An interesting insight of modern psychiatry.

The differences in our perspectives notwithstanding, this convergence of philosophical thinking and psychiatric research is significant. It brings to light the character of the human psyche: that the psyche harbors, not only the potential for cognitive transcendence in the glass-bead game of symbolic forms, but also the potential for transpersonal awareness across the boundaries of time.

The philosophical motive of our approach to the question of the "journey of the psyche" has been to explore its theoretical intelligibility and its moral prospects. There is also another body of literature pertaining to the same question.[59] But, as the arguments of this literature are anecdotal and empirical rather than philosophical, I pass them over in silence.

CHAPTER VIII

A Dialectical View of the Meaning of Life

The philosophical question concerning the meaning of life is: Is there a meaning in this earthly life — a meaning which might vindicate the *conditio humane*? We shall examine this question from the perspective of dialectical realism. This perspective, as will be seen, will overcome some of the conundrums which have plagued philosophical discussions of the question hitherto.

§ 25

Eksistence versus Existence

Our foregoing discussion of 'higher consciousness' purposely avoided its existential dimension. Now this dimension can be brought out: Man reflects upon his own being, other beings, and the man/world relation. Man is a questioning being: he questions the meaning of his own existence. Thus, while other beings remain submerged in the web of existence, as it were, man stands out vis-à-vis the world. This mode of existence, which is uniquely human, requires a special designation: *eksistence*.

The word 'eksistence' was originally used by Heidegger to refer to a modality of reflective existence which he depicted as "standing before the light of Being": i.e. seeing one's own being and other beings in relation to Being. And he observes that this way of being is proper only to man. Hence Heidegger holds that the 'essence' of man lies in his 'eksistence'; and that here *essentia* and *existentia* blend into one, as it were, in man's being in-relation-to Being.[1] My usage of the word 'eksistence', while retaining its Heideggerian root, ties it even more radically to higher consciousness.

Human eksistence is characterized, not only by its relation to Being (and other beings), but also by its relation to Time and temporality. The human psyche tends to envelope, in the warp of its higher consciousness, the memories of the past and the anticipations of the future. This imbues the present moment of human eksistence with a dialectical character.

Analytically viewed, the 'present moment' appears to be an euclidean point without dimensions in time: for, the very instant that one names a given 'present moment' as "Now!", that very instant perishes the objective reference of the naming. To attempt to fix the 'present moment' as an object of intentionality, would be like lighting a match to see the face of darkness. Yet, viewed retrospectively, the past 'present moments' are distinctly visible as precipitated congeries in the continuum of time; and, viewed prospectively, the future 'present moments' appear as ineffable moments of being in time.

Perhaps a radically reconstructed Minkowskian diagram might represent the dialectical character of human 'eksistence' in time:

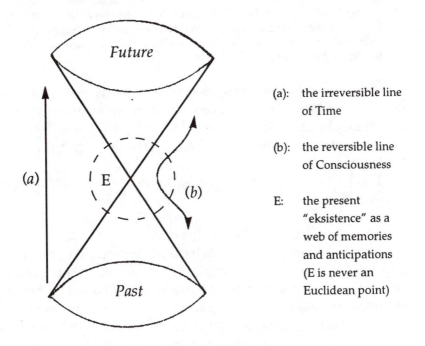

(a): the irreversible line of Time

(b): the reversible line of Consciousness

E: the present "eksistence" as a web of memories and anticipations (E is never an Euclidean point)

Thus, at no moment of the present life a real human being may be said to live in the present only. Moreover, not only does the past determine the present life through memories; but also the future determines the present through projects and anticipations. And every time one reflects critically upon one's past, one exercises the power to alter one's future.

This dialectic of the past and the future in human eksistence — this sense of temporality in relation to one's own being and to other beings — gives rise to an abiding concern in the higher consciousness of man: the question concerning the meaning of life.

We recall how a great writer, Leo Tolstoy, was haunted by the question of the meaning of life:

> At first I experienced moments of perplexity and arrest of life, as though I did not know what to do or how to live... But this passed, and I

> went on living as before. Then these moments of perplexity began to recur oftener and oftener, and always in the same form:...What is it (life) for?... At first it seemed to me that these were aimless and irrelevant questions. I thought that it was all well known... (that) just at present I had no time for it, but when I wanted to, I should be able to find the answer. The questions however began to repeat themselves frequently, and to demand replies more and more insistently; and like drops of ink always falling on one place they ran together into one black blot.[2]

This confession remains unsurpassed in its poignancy as a document of *Angst*. Similar expressions of concern over the "meaning of life" may be encountered among serious contemporary writers — Thomas Mann and Hermann Hesse especially. But we need no further examples.

The question of the meaning of life for us, however, unfolds itself in two senses:

(a) Is there a meaning in life generally?

(b) Is there a meaning in my life particularly?

And the two questions are dialectically interrelated. It would be impossible for my personal life to have any meaning, if life generally be meaningless: it would be impossible to build a lasting house of stone on a foundation of shifting sands. Yet, it would be possible for the scheme of life generally to have some meaning, while my personal life (owing to particular circumstances) might remain, and appear to be, meaningless.

The question arises, then, as to the meaning of 'meaning', when we speak of the meaningfulness or meaninglessness of life. By 'meaning' I understand (in this existential context) either intelligible 'order' and/or conscious 'purpose'. And the two concepts are not unrelated: to the question, "Why (*to what purpose*) did I do X?", one answers, "I did X so as to (*in order to*) attain Z." And by 'purpose' we mean here, not merely the pragmatic purpose (e.g. the purpose of an instrument), but rather the transcendental purpose of realizing a value or ideal in human life.

We may say, then, that insofar as there is discernible order and/or purpose in life, there is meaning; and, conversely, that disorder, formlessness, and purposelessness represent meaninglessness.

However, the contradictory evidences for order/purpose in life generally are striking:

We think of the orders of periodicity and rhythmicity in the biological realm: the life-cycle of the bee colony; the diurnal life-order of the European marine worm which, as part animal and part plant, submerges during high-tide to absorb algae, and emerges during low-tide to absorb the sunlight for photosynthesis; or, on a larger scale, the seasonal migrations of birds; and other such phenomena which, intrinsically as well as extrinsically, represent complex patterns. But we also think of the senseless existence of hordes of other species: We might ask, for example, what is the purpose in the life of *drosophila melanogaster* (the fruit-fly) hovering like a puff of cloud over a bowl of peaches, momentarily, before disappearing into the oblivion of non-existence?

There are caverns in South America, which seem to the explorer who enters them to be veritable havens of sublime silence. Surrounded by walls of stone and engulfed in darkness, a crystalline world of rock and mineral formation encloses pools of clear water. In the water one sees the reflected array of jagged russet-colored forms against the dark background, as a piece of nature's panorama in water-color. But, as one looks up at the original of the reflection, the phenomenon is revealed: the ceiling of the cavern serves as the roosting place for a colony of vampire bats which rest by hanging upside down. These creatures, whose life-span exceeds a decade, live by sucking the blood of other animals: they leave their caverns, as the rest of the world sleeps, after dusk and return before dawn. Born blind, or nearly blind, they navigate by the echoes of their own sounds (with high frequency far above the range of human hearing). And their only contribution to the earth which sustains them is the guano deposit as the historical record of their existence from generation to generation. What is the meaning of life for these parasitic creatures?

Or consider a naturalist's encounter with a spider's world: Loren Eiseley tells us how, having come across a yellow-and-black orb spider clinging in her huge web at the upper edge of an arroyo, he touched a strand with the tip of his pencil. Immediately there was a response: the web was plucked by its occupant and vibrated into a blur (as a means of entrapping the prospective prey). But as there was no prey, and no struggle, there was no further response in this case. Everything receded into their motionless silence. "As I proceeded on my way..." Eiseley remarks, "I realized that in the world of the spider I did not exist."[3] Within the spider's web of meaning *we* may not exist; but the spider (and other creatures) may exist within *our* web of meaning. Therein lies the critical difference.

Man eksists — other beings exist merely.

But, from this distinction, does it follow that the lives of other beings — even when they appear to be meaningless to *our* eyes — are either meaningless or valueless?

We must ask anew the question then: What does a 'living being' mean? And this question must not be taken in a pragmatic or utilitarian sense — the sense in which the exploiters of the natural world have taken it. Rather, it is to be taken in a phenomenological sense: i.e. what is the *character* of the living being, as it presents itself to us, and what is its *niche* in the objective picture of the natural world? Only then would we be able to see the being of other living beings — their meaning and their value in the grand design of nature as a megasystem.

(We must ask, parenthetically, a further question: Must not our entire science be restructured to include, besides questions of *fact*, also questions of *value* concerning living beings? — a question which the Swiss biologist, Adolf Portmann, has raised, but which has remained largely ignored by biologists.[4])

What are we to conclude, then, from this dialectical scenario of order/disorder and apparent manifestation of purpose/purposelessness in the realm of life?

We may conclude that 'meaning' itself is an *emergent phenomenon*: that it emerges at the level of higher consciousness — at the level of human *eksistence*. Hence, the apparent contradiction between the meaninglessness of a bat-colony and the meaningfulness of a human community dissolves itself. Yet, this dialectical conclusion needs to be qualified further.

As we recall, from a previous discussion, the perception of apparent disorder does not imply the absence of inherent order. Man must not forget the limitations of his own understanding. A striking analogy concerning the limitations of human perspective, suggested by Spinoza, is worth quoting here:

> Let us imagine... a little worm, living in the blood, able to distinguish

by sight the particles of blood, lymph, etc., and to reflect on the manner in which each particle, on meeting with another particle, either is repulsed, or communicates a portion of its own motion. This little worm would live in the blood, in the same way as we live in a part of the universe, and would consider each particle of blood, not as a part, but as a whole. It would be unable to determine, how all the parts are modified by the general nature of blood, and are compelled by it to adapt themselves, so as to stand in a fixed relation to one another... But as there exist, as a matter of fact, very many causes which modify, in a given manner, the nature of the blood, and are in turn modified thereby, it follows that other motions and other relations arise in the blood, springing not from the mutual relations of its parts only, but from relations between the blood as a whole and external causes. Thus the blood comes to be regarded as a part and not as a whole."[5]

We may look upon nature (and life generally) as a panorama in the process of being painted by a Demiurge as it were: aspects of it might appear to the *outside* view to be discrete and meaningless, but to the *inside* view to form a continuous and meaningful whole. For us to be able to see the whole, we must assume the impossible perspective of *sub specie aeternitatis* (to use Spinoza's expression). We, however, can view the world hypothetically only.

We must leave, then, the question concerning the meaning of life generally, as a hypothetical possibility, and turn to the personal question: "Whence do I derive the meaning of my life?"

And our answer must be: I derive the meaning of my life from my "philosophy of life", i.e., my philosophical self-concept and my worldview, in the light of which I am able to see (and interpret) my own being, other beings, and my relation to the world. From this, too, I derive my 'existential stance' vis-à-vis good and evil in the world.

Nor is the formation of one's "philosophy of life" an arbitrary matter: it echoes the inner calling of one's psyche. But it must meet the criteria of rational understanding. The praxis of one's "philosophy of life", whether explicit or implicit, is in a deep sense the process of one's self-realization. Then one can say (given one's philosophy of life): "I am the architect of my life" — versus saying "I am a victim of circumstances."

("Believe that life *is* worth living, and your belief *will* help create the fact — " urges William James.[6] But subjective belief is hardly sufficient, or even viable, without an objective foundation. And even if someone were to be capable of believing, without adequate ground, would not such belief properly qualify as a "religion of life" rather than a "philosophy of life"?)

The measure of our understanding of order and meaning in life is to be determined by our reigning philosophical paradigm. It is true, in a deep sense, that we ourselves are the wellsprings of meaning and purpose in our life. And we may say (with Schiller): "*Es ist in dir, du bringst es ewig hervor*" — it is in thee, thou art the harbinger. For, the range of our reigning philosophical paradigm is to be determined by our modality of the psyche. But, once formed, our reigning philosophical paradigm would determine the modality of our existential stance, in a world which represents a phenomenological mélange of good and evil.

§ 26

Dialectic of Good and Evil

The dialectic of good and evil arises from the fact that human eksistence implies personal freedom: that man has the potential power to alter the course of his life. But how one alters the course of one's life will be determined by the modality of one's higher consciousness: for the "journey of the psyche" — in the sense of which we have spoken — may be seen as an arduous process of progress/retrogress along the jagged line of good and evil over the abyss of nihilism.

Nihilism Revisited

The negation of the validity of any value hierarchy, the negation of the distinction between higher values and lower values, the negation of the very antinomy of good and evil — the rejection, as a consequence, of the meaning and value of life — is *nihilism*.

There is an ancient tale about King Midas in search of the knowledge of the "highest good". To that end, he sets out with his entourage to the forest to find the wise Silenus. And when they have captured him at last, and the King poses to him the question of what would be the "highest good" for man, the demigod utters a shrill laugh and replies: "O ephemeral children of chance and misery, why do you compel me to tell you what is best for you not to hear? The highest good is beyond your reach: not to be born, not to be, to be nothing."

Can nihilism, as the negation of everything meaningful in life, itself be negated?

To overcome nihilism — and to be able to handle the struggle between good and evil meaningfully — the ancient Greeks innovated a complex mythology: every major power, representing every aspect of good and evil, was attributed to a god or a goddess which, among themselves, had their own opposites. In this way the Greeks were able to soften the harsh dialectic of good and evil, by sharing their responsibility with their deities. From mythology to religion is but a step. The hope of redemption, which is implicit in mythology, is rendered explicit in religion. But, as religion is derived from *faith* rather than *reason*, it remains vulnerable to the challenge of nihilism.

Moreover, religion — e.g. Christianity which is presumed to be, philosophically speaking, the most enlightened religion — presents its own philosophical problems. The main proposition of religion is: that man must die to this "unreal life" before he can be born to the other "real life". But from the perspective of philosophy — i.e. dialectical realism — this very proposition is unacceptable. For this life and this world, ontologically speaking, do represent a genre of reality. However this admission does not imply the negation of the possibility of another world and another life. For it is conceivable (as we have seen already) that this life, along with another life, might constitute but a phase in the "cosmic biography" of the psyche. And life in this world might then be seen as serving as a formation phase, even a preparatory phase, in the larger context of one's personal destiny.

We moderns must confront the struggle between good and evil anew, barehanded, as it were. We must draw upon our inherent power of reason and moral sense. We must bear the torch which we have inherited from Socrates to the end of our journey in the world.

It is, for example, as a modern thinker that Nietzsche displays the intellectual courage to confront nihilism: "Nihilism stands at the door: whence comes this uncanniest of all guests?... What does nihilism mean? — That the highest values be devaluated. But its aim is missing; and there is no answer to the question 'Why?'"[7] Here, with unerring insight, Nietzsche exposes the weakness of nihilism: that nihilism, which questions the raison d'être of every value, stands before us with its own raison d'etre questionable but unquestioned. And Nietzsche's radical answer to nihilism, we recall, is to eliminate it at its source: i.e. the human nature in its present condition wherein the moribund nihilism originates — (to be followed by the "cure" of the equally moribund religion) — this human nature must be overcome by "man" *as a* "higher man" in a last struggle of spiritual transfiguration... or spiritual death.

There is, however, another genre of nihilism which haunts us: a laughing and deriding kind of nihilism born of the artistic spirit. This nihilism (given voice by Shakespeare) depicts life as a mere shadow of reality: "a tale told by an idiot, full of sound and fury, signifying nothing."[8] This is the obverse of the morbid nihilism of the "underground man" of Dostoevsky, who lives and meditates in the dark cellar of despondency, and when he finally comes out into the open, he announces his existence to the world with the opening statement: "I am a sick man..."[9] — a statement, may it be noted, not unworthy of our contemporary "existential man".

Both these forms of nihilism, the morbid and the laughing, have an essential feature in common: they *assume* alike that 'life', which presents but the illusion of reality, is merely a game. And therein, lies their error. Games can be played again. And if 'life' were merely a game, then we ought to be able to play it over again. But 'life' precipitates into 'history' and history can never be played again. Even the games which we play *in* life precipitate in time, as it were, forming a history of life which can never be repeated. This fact, this irretrievability of the course of life in time, gives life its unique historicity and significance. It also imbues life with a subtle sense of tragedy...

The root of nihilism lies in the heightened consciousness of evil at a predialectical level of understanding. Then the encounter with evil is heightened into existential anxiety. Nihilism, then, emerges as a panacea to anxiety: it masks the face of evil with feigned indifference.

Higher Values

The recognition and reification of 'higher values' — i.e. moral values and aesthetic values — is the dialectical answer to nihilism.

Higher values are intrinsically good: they are to be acquired for their own sake, and it is for their sake that other things acquire value. E.g. even 'health', which is often taken to be a higher value, would be valueless without moral character; for it is questionable that the health of a "bad person", serving an evil end, is a good thing. The same may be said of other goods. Higher values confer worth, as it were, upon lower values. Things of lower value are regarded to be of value *because* they provide the means for the attainment of higher values. E.g. the 'health' of a "good person" is valuable, for it enables him to live a good life, and to contribute to the good life of mankind; etc.

My basic proposition is therefore: *If* there are no higher values, *then* there are also no lower values; *for* without higher values (ideals), nothing in this world would be of any value.

(The paradox of ordinary pragmatism — John Dewey and others — is that: while negating 'ideals' as intrinsic values, it affirms extrinsic values; but without intrinsic values, extrinsic values also lose their value.)

The question arises then: Is there a 'moral ideal', and a 'moral point of view', above the subjective interests of human beings?

The very meaning and justifiability of the moral point of view have been challenged in our time. Writes a contemporary moral philosopher: "A note of *urgency* can sometimes be heard, even in otherwise unhurried writers, when they ask for a justification of morality. Unless the ethical life... can be justified by philosophy, we shall be open to relativism, amoralism, and disorder... When an amoralist calls ethical considerations in doubt, and suggests that there is no reason to follow the requirements of morality, *what can we say to him?*"[10] The question concerns, clearly, not only the *criteria* of moral judgments but also their very raison d'être.

I argue that there is a 'moral ideal', and a 'moral point of view'; and that they provide the highest level of 'existential stance' available to man.

The 'moral ideal', as I conceive it, is the acquisition of 'moral character'. A person may be said to have a 'moral character', whose behavior in relation to himself and to others, represents the 'moral point of view'. And by this I understand:

(a) that one acts *from* the motive of goodwill *and according to* the sense of moral obligation;

(b) that one acts on moral principles *and regardless of* subjective interest or personal suffering.

'Moral value' pertains to human acts. By a 'moral act' I understand an act, motivated by goodwill, and showing due regard for the integrity/wellbeing of oneself and other persons. By an 'immoral act' I understand an act, motivated by ill-will, and showing disregard for the integrity/wellbeing of oneself or other persons. And the pragmatic results of immoral actions constitute what we may call 'moral evil' which is the antithesis of 'moral good'. It is understood that the practice of 'good-will' assumes that the persons involved are 'good'; and, consequently, that 'ill-will' toward a 'bad' person is morally acceptable. For, the "good" which contributes to moral evil, is bad; and the "bad" which works against moral evil, is good.

Whence do we derive our 'moral point of view' then?

That the moral sense, the sensibility to good and evil, is inherent in man — in some modality of his being at least — is evident. We *experience* the feeling of revulsion in the face of inhuman acts; and we *experience* the feeling of elation in the face of supererogatory acts. We do not need to be taught — (the doctrines of social scientists notwithstanding) — that human cruelty is repugnant and that human courage is admirable *any more than* we have to be taught that a rose is beautiful and that a viper is dreadful. And there is abundant phenomenological evidence — as described by Richard Taylor[11] — to support this conception of human nature.

We derive our 'moral point of view' from our inner 'moral sense' *and* from our 'rational understanding' of its meaning and import. The role of culture, in the formation of moral character and moral point of view, is secondary: culture may strengthen or retard the moral development of the young person.

Nevertheless, it is clear that 'moral character' and the 'moral point of view', thus depicted, remain but an idealization. The actuality of human life presents a somewhat different picture. There is a wide range of moral life in which human beings partake in varying degrees: the moral person, the amoral person, the morally blind (*agnosia*), the morally crippled (*akrasia*), and the immoral person. Moreover, there is a natural history of moral development — as Lawrence Kohlberg and other psychologists have explored[12] — in the early phases of the life of normal human beings.

Hence, there is a marked variation in the quality of life among human beings. While some human lives are above animal existence, other human lives remain below animal existence. And should the reader be startled by such seemingly "undemocratic" assertion, I beg him/her to compare the biography of a child murderer and the case of an ordinary dog:[13] A household dog in a small town in West Virginia saved the life of a four-year old girl, when her house caught fire, by dragging her out onto the porch, and then himself lay down and died owing to smoke inhalation. Is not, *from the moral point of view*, the value of the life of that lowly dog infinitely higher than the value of the life of that supposed "human being"? Numerous other cases could be cited to make the point.

As to the issue of the *criteria* of value judgments, it may be observed that this will depend upon the *kind of value* under consideration. This implies the complementarity of values — a point which has been demonstrated by Professor G. H. Von Wright in his elegant treatise[14] — in the context of the "phenomenology of values". Hence, the various kinds of value — moral, aesthetic, utilitarian, hedonic, or other — would require different operational criteria. Thus, for example, one judges the "goodness" of a pocket knife by technical criteria which are different from the aesthetic criteria by which one may judge the "goodness" of a painting or the hedonic criteria for the "goodness" of a glass of wine. And the judgment of the moral value of a human action, as we have seen already, requires an altogether different kind of criterion: i.e. the intent behind the act of the person. Accordingly, the skeptic, who insists upon a single answer to his own ambiguous question ("What is *the* criterion of value judgments?") poses the question wrongly. Nor does the hypothesis of the complementarity of values preclude the *priority* of moral values and the overriding character of moral principles.

The transcendental character of moral values may be expressed in this way: that, while all other kinds of goodness are relative to persons and contexts, moral goodness is independent of the personalities involved but belongs to us *qua* human beings.

We may answer, then, the "last question" of modern man: "Why should I be moral?" by saying: To strive to acquire a moral character (and to act morally) *is requisite to* your being true to your own nature, *as a human being*, and *is requisite* for being able to *assume* a viable 'existential stance', vis-à-vis the problems of life: vis-à-vis the ongoing struggle between good and evil in our existential world.

(I agree, too, with the formalist answer to the above question given by Kurt Baier: that being a rational person means acting on the basis of "best reasons"; and that, since moral reasons are overriding reasons for action, they represent the "best reasons" for action[15] — yet I prefer, in view of the quasi-rational character of human beings, the dialectical answer above.)

So the ancient call of Socrates, that the "care of the psyche" must take precedence over everything else, acquires a renewed meaning and urgency in our time: a time when our *conditio humane*, as we tread on the edge of light and darkness, remains questionable more than ever.

Conditio Humane:
Edge of Light and Darkness

Antinomies are inherent in the structure of life. Man assumes an 'existential stance' vis-à-vis the conflict between good and evil. Man treads on the edge of light and darkness...

But we must make a stark distinction between good/evil as natural phenomena on the one hand and good/evil as moral phenomena on the other. Compare, for example, the case of the heart-worm in the body of a healthy dog and the case of the betrayal of friendship by a human being. In the one case, the cause of the evil may be said to be natural; and, in the other case, the cause of the evil may be said to lie in the ill-will of man toward man. By 'natural good' I understand a positive gestalt representing a harmonious whole; and by 'natural evil' I understand a negative gestalt where some element contributes to the disequilibrium of the whole.

The question of evil, then, is twofold:

(a) Why is there evil in the natural world?

(b) Why is there evil in the human world?

I shall evoke a pair of hypotheses, in response to these questions, placing the burden of the proof upon their ranges of explanation.

The first hypothesis says: that the realm of order is limited by the realm of disorder. As an illustration we may evoke the analogy of the Sun: while the rays of the Sun illuminate the world, and sustain the forms of life, they nevertheless remain limited in their range, as there

are caverns and crevices in the Earth where the sunrays never reach...
The same thing may be said about the natural world as a whole: that,
while 'natural good' prevails in the world, its range is limited (from
the human perspective) by 'natural evil'. This, then, represents a
natural antinomy.

And the second hypothesis says: that man — through his
ignorance and/or ill-will — is responsible for the existence of moral
evil in human life. But, we may ask, why is the nature of man such
that he must harbor this defect? And the sympathetic answer would
be: that the spiritual development of man is still in the process of
maturation; and that, perhaps, the encounter with moral good/evil
(and the experience of tragedy in life) may be requisite for the
spiritual development of man. We may say, by analogy, that as the
experience of illness heightens one's understanding and appreciation
of healthy life, so the encounter with evil may heighten the moral
sense and the understanding of the morally good life...

From this pair of hypothetical answers to the question of evil we
may draw a dialectical conclusion: that man (through his freedom)
may define his 'existential stance' vis-à-vis good and evil in the
world; and that, thereby, man may determine the direction of his
moral evolution or his *moral devolution*. Thus the immature existence
of man, in the context of a mixed and unfinished universe, acquires
a deep significance: man treads on the very edge of light and
darkness. That is the primordial *conditio humane* — the cosmic
condition of man as it were.

"Character is man's destiny" — observed Heraclitus more than
two thousand years ago — and I interpret this pregnant proposition
to mean: that the inner calling of man, to assume this rather than that
'existential stance' in the world, also determines his cosmic biography.
But there are levels of 'existential stance', ranging between the
polarities of good and evil in human life. Thus, for example, it is the
'existential stance' of Wilhelm Tell that distinguishes him from
Hermann Gessler; or Hamlet from Polonius; or Monseigneur Myriel
from Monsieur Thénardier; and so on. It is not a question of the
variation of *Lebensformen* only — in the sense which Eduard Spranger
has elucidated — but, primarily, it is a question of the modalities of
character. For the 'character' of a person, as the harbinger of his
daimon, determines his 'existential stance' and his lifestyle.

However, assuming an 'existential stance', in accord with one's character, does not mean that every future decision and action be premeditated. One cannot expect to prescribe all one's prospects *for* oneself beforehand; one must allow one's character the prerogative to proceed *from* its inner resources as the occasion might challenge. To deny this would be to negate the dynamism of human character and the essence of human creativity.

Not to take an 'existential stance' vis-à-vis the challenge of good and evil, would be a sign of the atrophy of conscience. It would be the state of the psyche, suspended between either/or, without vision and/or without willpower. It would be a sign of the "sickness" of the psyche. The "sick soul" is characterized by: (a) emotional apathy or the loss of zest for life's values; and (b) intellectual nihilism or loss of belief in any meaning in life.

The existential condition of the "sick soul" was depicted by William James as follows: "Conceive yourself, if possible, suddenly stripped of all the emotion with which your world now inspires you, and try to imagine it as it exists, purely by itself, without your favorable or unfavorable, hopeful or apprehensive comment (i.e. thought or feeling). It will be almost impossible for you to realize such a condition of negativity and deadness. No one portion of the universe would then have importance beyond another; and the whole collection of its things and series of its events would be without significance..."[16]

The "sick soul", subsisting on amoralism and indifference, faces a dialectical choice: either to slide gradually into moral parasitism, and therewith, to learn to savour "*les fleurs du mal*" eventually; or to struggle but one last time to overcome its moribund condition by the willpower to transcend its existing level of consciousness. And, on this point, William James and Simone Weil seem to agree: here the courage of existential pragmatism and the hope of refined existentialism converge.[17] Man is then seen at once as fallen and as arisen. The human predicament is heightened, through man's responsible/irresponsible role vis-à-vis good and evil, into a "divine experiment" — or, should one say, into a droll *tragedie humaine*?

The *conditio humane* involves, not only moral values, but also aesthetic values. For the 'aesthetic sense', no less than the 'moral sense', is an essential quality of the human being. So the question arises:

Would not art prove to be *as* effective a "healer" as morality for the existential condition of man?

In a rare moment of hope, Feodor Dostoevsky remarked: "Beauty will save the world." As a writer of deep vision, by 'beauty' he meant, not the phenomenon that is merely pleasing to the eye, but the reality of the 'sublime': the sublime as the beauty of nature, and the sublime as the beauty of human character, which transcends our immediate vision. And, as art and literature are the harbingers of the 'sublime', he hoped that they would "save" the world from evil and ugliness and decadence.

Can art and literature save the world then?

Once I had the occasion to walk through the ghetto of a large city. As I strolled, like a maladapted alien, I surveyed the ugly scene: the ravaged buildings, the squalid alleys shrouded by the odor of human waste, and the haphazard piles of debris everywhere. The atmosphere gave one the vague feeling that all this represented a state of affairs "after" — after some event of disastrous proportions which had left its mark in material and human terms. Was the disastrous event but the *shadow* of civilization inadvertently cast upon this humble region? Then a little window, on the side of a ramshackle house, caught my eye: it had affixed to one of its panels a small plate of stained glass, framed in blackened lead came, and chipped in one corner. It hung there — as if this tiny symbol of beauty would bring happiness and wellbeing to the poor family who dwelled there. And then I wondered whether there be any home, where normal human beings dwelled, that would not contain some objects of beauty, however modest it might be. It occurred to me, then, that the 'aesthetic sense' in man, like the 'moral sense', cannot be eliminated by the adverse conditions of environment.

Art and literature, through their form-giving and meaning-making powers, bring us "intuitive truths" — truths without proofs, as it were, but not truths with consequence. They depict "special moments" of reality from the aesthetic perspective: scenes of extraordinary beauty and ugliness, of good and evil. For example, *Der Ring des Nibelungen* of Wagner may be seen, philosophically, as representing the *conditio humane*: ranging from hubris and pathos, struggle and conflict, to purification and salvation. Is not this dialectic that we see in the music of Mozart, Beethoven, or Stravinsky; or the paintings of Rembrandt, Van Gogh, Picasso; or the literature of high realism and the science fiction of the philosophical genre? Art holds the aesthetic mirror to the human psyche.

However, that not all art and literature is enlightened or enlightening, is also evident. The crisis of contemporary art and literature is disquieting: while they yearn to "save" the world, they themselves are "drowning" in the existential whirlpool of the world. An abstract artist, Wassily Kandinsky, depicts the crisis in these words: "The (benighted) artist uses his strength to flatter his lower needs; in an ostensibly artistic form he presents that which is impure, draws the weaker elements to him, mixes them with evil, betrays men and helps them betray themselves, while they convince themselves and others that they are spiritually thirsty, and that from this pure spring they may quench their thirst...(Then) art has lost her soul."[18] And then — Kandinsky adds metaphorically — the "black, death-giving, hand" takes over the process of uglification and decadence which "art without a soul" has procured.

The diagnosis of decadence in modern art and literature is articulated by Georg Lukács, in a philosophical critique, some lines of which are worth quoting:

"The process begins in literature with the substitution of pure psychologism for the representation of the real, social, human being — and slowly transforms the individual into a shapeless bundle or uncontrolled torrent of free, undisciplined, associations...(Then) deformities arise with grim inevitability. The man of decadent bourgeois society who stunts himself spiritually and morally not only has to go on living and acting in his crippled state; in this human self-deformity, he must even seek a psychological and moral 'cosmic' justification for his condition... no longer basing his conception of the world on how the world is objectively constituted...instead he adapts his conception of the world to fit his own deformity and to provide an appropriate environment for his own crippled state..." concluding that: "The deformity is not restricted to artistic practice; it extends to the entire conception of art and of the artist. The abnormal attitude toward life is canonized by decadent aesthetics. While the philosophy of art in healthier periods viewed the artist as a normal and even exemplary human being, today artistic creativity and artistic greatness are associated with disease... The ultimate consequence is the inhumanity and antihumanism of modern decadent art, sometimes explicit... and sometimes only implicit in artistic practice."[19]

Perspective and conscience, then, are of overriding importance in art and literature — for they enable the artist and the writer to provide an exposé of the phenomena of life in the context of the good/evil antinomy. Without a perspective and a conscience the artist or the writer would "drown" in the world he aspires to "save". Art would then be incapable of representing life, but only revomiting it, as it were. It would then become a "sick art" (to use Lukács' expression) where "more and more the bowels dominate the head". Such "art" could not save itself from its own malaise, let alone saving the world.

Neither *art bourgeois*, without perspective or conscience; nor *art engagé*, enslaved by some alien ideology; but the *art of higher humanism* alone may save the world from nihilism: art that expresses the conflict of good and evil and of beauty and ugliness; art that depicts the dreams and the nightmares of humanity with equal poignancy; art that holds the mirror to the human psyche. Only true art may have the "healing power" to save the human psyche from the disease of nihilism — only it may succeed in dragging humanity out of their existential cave — only it may give man the symbols of meaning and hope in life.

The demigod character of man is perhaps nowhere more evident than here: man *creates* his art and science; and then he hopes that they will *save* him. But what if his art and science have themselves been demoralized by human malaise? Then man must "heal" *them* before they can "save" *him*. Thus man holds in his hands the means of his own self-realization or his own self-destruction.

That, then, appears to be the *conditio humane*: to strive to create the values that would reign over human life, or to invert and warp those values, or to strive and fail, and lapse miserably into the void of valueless existence — nay the abyss of nihilism even — and therefore modern man has reason to tread with trepidation, along the edge of light and darkness, in the journey he calls "life".

§ 27

Philosophical Significance of the Mountain Image

Man's journey in life, along the edge of light and darkness, may be illustrated by the "Mountain Image" as a philosophical paradigm.

Hitherto — ever since Plato — the "Cave Image" has dominated the debate concerning the philosophy of life. Here, man's progress is depicted, through the purgation of the senses and meditation, from the darkness of the phenomenal world into the light of the ideal world. And the assumption — underlying any version of the Cave Image[20] — is a special metaphysics.

The Mountain Image presents a starkly different alternative: it depicts man's progress, in the real world of antinomies, toward the levels of personal enlightenment; it relates the experience of 'truth' to the experience of 'self-transcendence'; and it displays the dialectic of meaning/meaninglessness in life. It would seem, then, that everything essential and significant, as well as odd and absurd, would find a place in this dialectical setting. And for these reasons — given my 'dialectical realism' — I favor this paradigm concerning the philosophy of life over others.[21]

Metaphorically speaking: Is not our 'philosophy of life' but an attempt, in thought, at scaling the mountain of reality?

Our initial vision of the Mountain remains only an image: an image which harbors, but does not reveal, the rugged terrain and the dangers lurking therein. However, the possession of the Image (as an ideal) is essential: without the image we would have no objective nor the motive to strive toward an objective.

Similarly, without an ideal in life, we would not be able to give a direction to our daily existence; we would fail to *avoid* the *void* of meaningless existence. Thus our first step toward the Mountain already involves moral courage: we turn our back on the valley below — and to its inveterate hedonism and nihilism — as it remains shrouded in the fog which darkens the vision.

As we approach the Mountain, the foothills magnify, the ruggedness of the terrain manifests itself, and the lofty peak disappears from the view altogether. Then the obstacles crowd us as our image remains eclipsed: there is even the danger that we might lose our way. For a long time we must struggle upward, against rocky obstacle, without seeing our objective. So, in early youth, we strive in life, stumbling and rising, toward the realization of a dream which we carry inside our head only.

After having attained a moderate height in the mountain of life — above the hills and the valleys below — we become aware of the real dangers which haunt us:

The *inner danger* derives from the forces of inertia which challenge our willpower. No one understood this struggle within the individual better than Nietzsche: "It is not the height, but the declivity that is terrible: the declivity where the gaze shooteth *downwards*, and the hand graspeth *upwards*."[22] So in life, one strives forward and upward, to realize one's ideals and higher values, as the forces of culture and Zeitgeist seek to drag one down.

The *outer dangers* harbor the possibility of falling, and therewith, failing to attain one's ideal objective. It would be a mistake to assume, however, that the fall could be precipitated only by the ruggedness of the mountainside or by an unexpected avalanche. The fall could also be caused by the climber's own misstep. And the higher one climbs the greater the danger and the extent of the possible fall — and this too is part of the dialectic of good and evil on the Mountain.

The fall, on the Mountain, is from the heights to the lower depths; in life, it is from authentic existence to inauthentic existence.

However, the 'fall' does not always mean 'failure'; nor is the 'fall' altogether valueless. Owing to the jagged structure of the mountainside, one never falls at the same spot again. One only falls higher or lower. Thus, not all falling is of equal value, dialectically speaking.

Analogously, the recurrence of negative experiences in daily life, owing to the dynamics of consciousness and the change of one's existential position, never again carry the same meaning in the course of one's life-journey: they carry a lesser or a greater meaning.

Mountain climbing is a form-discovering activity. As the hills and ridges gradually move, by a parallax effect, in relation to the moving observer, they *disclose* partial views of the landscape which remained hidden hitherto: hills behind hills, ravines, valleys. "The most primordial phenomenon of truth," we come to agree with Heidegger, "is first shown by the existential-ontological ground of *uncovering.*"[23] We begin to prehend, then, the meaning of the Greek word for 'truth': *aletheia* (α'λη'θεια) - *unhiddenness.* For we experience 'truth' through encountering the unexpected moments of reality.

Can anyone see what I see? Only if they stand where I stand — and this shows the objectivity of phenomenological truths. But not everyone stands where I stand; and even if they did, they might have arrived at it by a path different from mine. And this demonstrates the emptiness of the democratic insistence upon "public verification".

The two primordial experiences in mountain climbing — as in life — are: the experience of 'truth' as a form-discovering activity *and* the experience of the endurance of the psyche.

The experience of the endurance of the psyche, throughout the journey, is the experience of living-through, and remaining true to, one's ideals. Here the identity of the psyche and the reality of character are to be verified. Only the *true* becomes the *enduring.*

As one staggers along the range of the Mountain, one harbors an awareness of the I/World relation. The past, with its congeries of memories, hangs in the background of the psyche; the present challenges and captivates the psyche; and the future, with its ideals and anticipations, beckons and directs the psyche. The journey on the Mountain represents an abridged life-history as it were: and here also the confession, "I have remained true", becomes a meaningful moment of self-cognition as a final encounter with the 'truth' of one's struggle in life.

My fundamental proposition is that: the higher we ascend, the angle of vision being constant, the farther we see into the horizon of existence. And, in the light of our amplified vision of the horizon, we see the limitations of our previous horizons of existence.

Sight leads to *insight.*

This, then, is the meaning of *self-transcendence* in our paradigm: that our consciousness, which encompasses our past life, is directed *beyond* it. And here we come to agree with the psychiatrist Viktor Frankl: "It is a severe and grave misunderstanding of man to deal with him as if he were a closed system... being human profoundly means to be open to the world... this self-transcending quality of human existence is ignored and neglected by those motivation theories which are based on the homeostasis principle."[24] Self-transcendence involves self-negation. Yet, while the "denial *in* self" (e.g. self-criticism) is requisite for a dynamic and healthy psyche, the "denial *of* self" (i.e. self-rejection) is a sign of the illness of the psyche. For the negation of 'actuality' cannot be taken to mean the negation of 'potentiality'.

In mountain climbing, as in life, the relation of 'actuality' to 'potentiality' acquires a two-fold character: on the one side, there is the failure/success dimension; on the other, there is the meaning/void dimension. The dotted curve indicates the wavering line of progress:

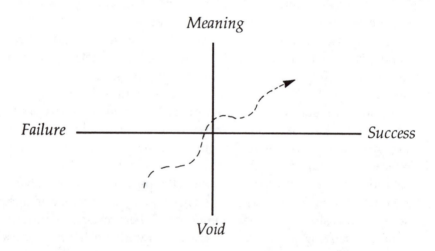

'Meaning' in life emerges as a gestalt-quality of experience indicating the purposive movement of the psyche from actual order to potential order. This movement of the psyche occurs as a form-giving and/or form-discovering activity. A "successful life", no less than a "failing life", may be meaningless; and a "failing life" may sometimes be more meaningful than a "successful life". The interaction between the two dimensions underlies the dialectical character of life.

Looking down aside the lofty peak we see space, void, and farther on the abyss of death. We have avoided the void; but the dread of death haunts us. We see what Nietzsche saw: "When, however, the path again curved around a rock, all at once the landscape altered, and Zarathustra entered into a realm of death. Here bristled black and red cliffs: no grass, no trees, no bird sounds. It was a valley which all animals avoided, even the beasts of prey, except that a species of ugly, thick, green serpent came here, when they were old, to die..."[25] It is then that Zarathustra meets the "Ugliest Man" — the murderer of the godly in man — and defies him. And Nietzsche, instead of the counsel of despair, gives us the counsel of the "will-to-power": "Man is something that has to be surpassed."

However, the momentary encounter with nonbeing is sufficient to hurl existentialists (those who place *existence* before *essence*) into spells of dizziness and nausea. It is instructive to read these lines in the confession of one contemporary existentialist following his encounter with 'nonbeing': "I recognize the formlessness, the aimlessness, and the disunity implicit in my own insignificance, my mortality, my ultimate dissolution: I peer into madness, chaos, and death."[26] Thus the pre-dialectical propensity of ordinary existentialism generates a blindspot: it fails to see that 'nonbeing' sets 'being' in relief — even as the valleys set the Mountain in relief.

Recall the predicament of the aged ephemera — depicted by Benjamin Franklin in one of his *parva scripta* — a tiny being, having witnessed the slight declension of the Sun and the corresponding shifting of the shadows on earth — in his brief lifetime of a few hours — predicts the eventual doom of the Sun into the sea, and therewith, the inevitable ending of the world. It is easy to imagine that the eagle, soaring high above the ridges and valleys, might have a very different picture of the world: with the anticipation of the succession of starry nights and golden dawns. It is perspective that defines the contour of the world for us.

In the realm of the Mountain men are not equal: they neither have the same perspective nor hold the same existential stance. Here 'brotherhood' must replace 'equality' as the ideal relation between human beings. 'Equality' is a concept applicable to flatland dwellers.

For example, a brilliant psychiatrist once wrote to this author: that he has seen, again and again, that his patients have been shattered by problems in life, which he himself had encountered, suffered, and overcome in the course of his own personal life.[27] What accounts for the difference? Evidently, one's philosophy of life and character, and hence, one's 'existential stance' in life and the mode of one's struggle in life.

On the way up the Mountain, we encounter people who have resolved not to proceed, or who are unresolved to proceed, any farther. They have settled by the wayside near the warm caverns: these are the cave-dwellers. They are the 'fallen people' without ever having experienced a fall. When one meets them, one must beware of lingering: they would fain detain you; and then, like the inhabitants of the "Country of the Blind", say with complacency:
"You are one of us now."

The analogy between the Mountain Image and real life can be discerned, in its varying modalities, in the markedly varied biographies of creative men and women. Their converging point remains constant: on the Mountain we strive to arrive at the highest peak; in life we strive to attain a higher level of consciousness in the evolution of mankind. But the great truth must not be lost among the crowds: that all great work in this world must be done by individual hands — *Der Starke ist am mächtigsten allein.*

CHAPTER IX

The Role of Philosophy as Cultural Healer

In one of his lesser dream-compositions the gifted poet, Rainer Maria Rilke, tells us of his visit to Apollo: when he posed a question before the "god of reason", concerning the prospects of humanity, the latter replied simply: "Mend thy ways."

But how can mankind mend their ways?

It is in response to this question that I evoke the theme of "philosophical enlightenment" — and the concurrent role of philosophy as a "cultural healer" — as the only true means of altering our culture (and civilization) toward the attainment of a possible utopia.

Philosophy serves as the *critical conscience* of our culture and civilization. It alone provides the mediation between our actual existence and our ideal aspirations. It alone articulates a critique of the import of scientific/technological discoveries for the quality of life. For philosophy — rightly pursued and rightly understood — may harbor ideas which will bring about a *cultural reconstruction*: by extending to mankind generally the level of higher enlightenment attained by individual thinkers occasionally. Thus philosophy provides a road to freedom, freedom from human bondage to the existing conditions, and freedom from the presumed "tyranny of culture" (as social scientists use the expression).

Consider the existential condition of modern man in the context of his "bourgeois culture" and civilization: a culture which offers him a choice — discounting the pathos of religion — between two hollow lifestyles: the ideology of material gadgetry and the ideology of existential nihilism. The two alternatives appear at first view to be anathema to each other. But they both originate in the same non-reflective and non-philosophical state of consciousness which characterizes the spiritual disinheritance of modern man.

And what is the prospect of the "younger generation" entering a world dominated by such a culture? To experience only crude materialism or sick nihilism — to suffer (borrowing Heidegger's expression) the "darkening of the world" — to live in a world beset by moral pollution and by environmental destruction.

Modern man, then, must face his existential challenge: he must envision the great project of reconstructing his culture, and transforming his civilization as a consequence, or else he must be prepared to take the dire consequences of persisting in his present ways. For, if man be the *maker* of his culture, and not its product merely, then he has to assume the responsibility to *remake* his culture.

'Culture' consists of the *inner* value system of a person or of a society as a community of persons; and 'civilization' consists of the *outer* effects and results of culture in the realm of pragmata. Therefore, the philosophical project of culture reconstruction must *precede* the pragmatic project of the transformation of our civilization.

The role of philosophy as the conscience of the age — when mankind face the great value-laden problems of culture and civilization — is becoming increasingly evident. To this attest the programs of three recent World Congresses of Philosophy (Varna 1973/Düsseldorf 1978/Montréal 1983) especially. In the last of these congresses — following a dramatic debate between philosophical purists and philosophical pragmatists — this author raised a critical question: "Is not philosophy, after all, the only true cultural healer?" There was scarcely any disagreement as to the end of philosophy as a cultural healer — or (as a German colleague expressed it)...*dass die Philosophie eine höhere Heilkunde sei...* — the disagreement was only as to the mode of attaining that objective.

Philosophy, as I see it, may serve as a "cultural healer" in three senses: (a) it will elucidate the self-image of man in the light of the ideal of 'higher humanism' dawning in our time; (b) it will provide a critique of culture/nature relation at the niveau of higher consciousness; and lastly (c) it will articulate the 'philosophical ideology' which will determine the shape of things to come, i.e., the conditions requisite for the attainment of utopia *versus* dystopia. Nor are these issues dialectically unrelated: the ideal of 'higher humanism' contributes to the reshaping of the self-image of modern man; and this enlightened self-image will enable modern man to envision his authentic place in the natural world; resulting in the reconstruction of his philosophical ideology. These last themes, themes with lasting import for the future, we shall handle in the following.

§ 28

The Ideal of Higher Humanism

The all-important question of what it means to be an authentic human being — and the related issue of the ideal of higher humanism — may be posed by a critical analogy:

Imagine a group of children from a civilized country, orphaned too early to remember anything of their family history or their cultural heritage, abandoned on a primitive island. The islanders, a genial tribe, adopts them, giving them shelter in their island. As the children come of age, they are so well adapted to the culture of the island that their way of life conforms to that of the natives. Like the natives, they work, play, and make "moral decisions", according to the "mores" of the natives; and not according to any "rational principles" or "ideals" of which they remain unaware in any case. To a visitor from outside, they would appear to share a common cultural heritage with the natives. But there remains one crucial difference between the two: that the natives can explain *who* they are and *why* they believe what they do; but the settlers can explain neither of these...

I suggest that a similar state of philosophical amnesia darkens the world of modern man: that modern man has forgotten *who* he really is, *whence* he derives the values and norms of his present behavior, and *why* his present-day culture *is* what it happens to be, much less what it *ought* to be. What we now seem to represent are but "fragments of a conceptual scheme" — to use the apt depiction of Alasdair MacIntyre — the philosophical roots of which have been lost in the dross of material progress. Let us focus on the *conditio humane* of our time more closely.

The Failure of Bourgeois Humanism

Modern man seems to have a conception of 'man', as he once had, no longer. Indeed, the conception of 'man', which originated in the age of *historical enlightenment*, and endured through the ideological strifes of the next century, remains something of an anathema to the mentality of our bourgeois age. And yet this very conception — the finest illustration of which we have seen in the philosophy of Kant earlier (§20) — represented a "miracle of insight" (to borrow Ernst Cassirer's expression) into the potential harmony of the reflective, the aesthetic, and the moral dimensions of the human psyche. Writes Cassirer: "It is one of the imperishable titles to distinction of the epoch of the Enlightenment that it accomplished that task, that it joined, to a degree scarcely ever achieved before, the *critical* with the *productive* function, and converted the one directly into the other."[1] And we could not disagree.

However, the "miracle" evaporated, in the heat of the coming industrial civilization, which also occasioned the transformation of 'man' from *homo sapiens* to *homo faber*. Then the 'ideal of man', as it had been conceived earlier, appeared as an "unreal image" in the distance. It was inevitable, then, that it would be denounced as such by pragmatism and then by existentialism. And both these philosophies, which claim to represent 'humanism' themselves, are to be credited with the rise of "bourgeois humanism". Thus writes John Dewey, the pragmatist, as an apology for materialism as a condition for this genre of humanism:

> No one can possibly estimate how much of the obnoxious materialism and brutality of our economic life is due to the fact that economic ends have been regarded as *merely* instrumental. When they are recognized to be *as intrinsic and final* in their place as any others, then it will be seen that *they are capable of idealization*, and that if life is to be worth-while, they *must* acquire ideal and intrinsic value. Esthetic, religious and other 'ideal' ends *are now thin and meager* or else *idle and luxurious* because of the separation from 'instrumental' or economic ends. Only in connection with the latter can they be woven into the texture of daily life and made substantial and pervasive... The latter then loses its peculiar flavor of the didactic and the pedantic; its ultra-moralistic and hortatory tone... *etcetera*.[2]

And, on this point, the viewpoint of J-P. Sartre (his antipathy to pragmatism notwithstanding) converges with that of John Dewey: he too idolizes the *existentia* at the expense of the *essentia*. For the systematic negation of 'ideal values' constitutes the primary motive, and the ultimate end, of "bourgeois humanism". And this is true of Sartre no less than of Dewey.

But the 'ideal values' of man — his aesthetic and moral values — are not unreal: they are not "thin and meager" notions, nor are they mere mental luxuries. They are the ultimate realities of human life. This is shown by the fact that ideal values *are presupposed by* utilitarian and pragmatic values: the latter, as extrinsic goods, *derive* their value from the former as intrinsic goods. In the absence of "higher values", the "lower values" would also lose their value. And to say that we can live by the latter, without the former, would be a paradox. And this paradox — that everything is for the sake of nothing — lies in the heart of bourgeois humanism. It is also the source of the inferiority complex which is camouflaged by intellectual assertiveness.

Existentially speaking — but in a sense deeper than Sartrean existentialism — the 'ideal values' provide still the only true fiber in human character: the only wellspring of power to handle the problems of life. And it is of this deeper reality of human life that the greatest and the best literary writers of our time speak to us, again and again, in their ever changing modes of art. They uphold it, against the sound and the fury of a runaway world, so that the rest of mankind may re-experience their own potentiality for the struggle of life. In the writings of such realist writers as Anatole France, Fyodor Dostoevsky, Henrik Ibsen, Thomas Wolfe, Thomas Mann, Hermann Hesse, we see the drama of human ideals set on the living stage with undeniable reality. It is no mere accident, therefore, that the literature of high realism is so deeply satisfying to readers from all walks of life. These writers represent, in a profound sense, a true humanism despite — nay because of — the way of the world to the contrary.

But, in contrast, the literature which is inspired by "bourgeois humanism" frustrates the reader's sense of humanity; for it depicts the superficial aspects of the human psyche and leaves its deeper reality untouched and unfathomed.

Take a modern writer like Ernest Hemingway (who, evidently, has been nurtured by the philosophy of John Dewey) and in whom "bourgeois humanism" bubbles to the surface. He writes in the name of "life" as it were. He depicts the struggle of an "old man" against a great fish at sea; and his imagery is as vivid as life-experience itself.

He makes us feel the ebb and tide of events as if we were there: he makes us privy to the old man's cunning scheme, to the hit-and-miss game with truth that goes on inside his head, and to the recurrence of memories from his dubious past. The author makes us feel and relive all these — for what purpose? — so that we may witness how his alter-ego may kill, for "sport" as it were, a great marlin at sea. But when it comes to the heart of the matter, when it comes to the all-important question (a question which even arises in the feeble head of the "old man" himself) — as to *why* a man must go through so much trouble in order to destroy a harmless and beautiful creature of the sea? — the man fails miserably to give us any answer. Nor, evidently, can the writer help his protagonist answer the question. And since the question arises in the context of life, his claim to write in the name of "life" becomes a shallow pretense. For, in this case, the failure of the hero, who lives and dies by hedonic values merely, represents really the failure of the writer — a bourgeois writer who himself remains utterly blind to aesthetic and moral issues.

But, we may ask, why do bourgeois writers remain blind to aesthetic and moral issues? Georg Lukács, who has given us an expose of the neglect and/or repression of 'higher values' in bourgeois literature, explains: "They reject without compromise all ideals of beauty and harmony as 'out-of-date'; they take people and society 'as they are', or rather as they usually appear in ordinary life... And these writers set out to represent a world destroyed, and *not* the battle against the destruction, not a dynamic process but a lifeless result. The consequence is that they reject beauty and harmony and produce a mere chronicle of the 'iron age'."[3]   And yet (as Lukács observes) there is scarcely a "true writer" — no matter what his ideology may be — who would reject 'beauty' or 'goodness' altogether.

The dialectical relations between the writer and the world are too complex to be reduced to any paradigm. For different writers approach reality, or "aspects of reality", in their own terms. And the manner and style in which something is said also says something. It is hardly a question at issue, *whether* a writer should depict the "lower depths" of life, or *whether* he should confine himself to its "higher moments" only. The question at issue is rather: that for a writer to be able to depict any moment of human life *significantly* he must overcome "bourgeois humanism" in his own soul before he can overcome it in his art.

The ideology of "bourgeois humanism" reflects the contemporary human condition — embedded in contemporary culture[4] — and not the essence of man.

The onetime bullying self-proclamation, "I am a pragmatist!" — or its glamourous counterpart, "*Mais je suis un existentialiste!*" — becomes, in the perspective of dialectical realism, a self-derogatory confession to the effect that: "I am but a quasi-human being."

What is 'Higher Humanism'?

The ideal of 'higher humanism' — an ideal that has been in the making from Socrates and Erasmus to Kant and Heidegger — answers to the question: *What is it to be an authentic 'human being'?* The focus on the essentia of man, however, need not detract from the phenomenology of human types and characters. Life harbors the dialectic of self- realization. And the human phenomenology is to be seen as representing the modalities of *human personality* in everyday life.

I conceive the essentia of man to comprise:

(a) *higher consciousness*: i.e. reflection about oneself (including one's personal identity through time — the sense of temporality — as illustrated by memories of the past and images of the future) *and* reflection about one's relation to the world.

(b) *moral conscience*: i.e. the sensibility to the phenomena of good and evil in human life, a sensibility without which a human being would remain "morally dead", and unworthy of being called a "human being" in a true sense.

c) *aesthetic sense*: i.e. the sensibility to the phenomena of the beautiful/sublime and the ugly/vile, without which a human being would remain "aesthetically blind", and assume an unappreciative attitude vis-à-vis the world and other living beings.

It follows that the entire world of values are contingent upon the essence and character of man. For man is the seeker of truth, about himself and about the world, and the creator of values in his life. And man derives his purpose in life from his special relation with 'Truth' and 'Value'. Were man to deny himself his relation to 'Truth' and 'Value' — or were he to be denied his freedom to pursue them and live according to them — then he would also lose his "dignity".[5] For then the personality of man would diminish, as it were, and therewith diminish also his humanity.

We recall Schiller's desperate call to humanity when he feared lest modern man's image of himself would be in danger of becoming blurred: "*Die Kunst, O Mensch, du hast allein*" — *You alone, O man, have art.* And we may repeat Schiller's call a second time: *You alone, O man, have moral conscience.* Nor are the two, beauty and goodness, unrelated: Is not "morality", in a sense, but the "beauty" of intention and action? And does not "immorality", in a sense, involve the destruction, in part or in whole, of some beautiful being and/or relationship? But it is higher consciousness which provides the infrastructure for both the aesthetic and the moral sensibilities, and therewith, provides the basis for the highest mode of human existence.

The essential dimensions of human nature, however, constitute dynamic realities which no static categorization could adequately represent. For the essence of man — the meaning of what it is to be a human being — would be falsified by any set of static categories proposed by any reductive analysis. The continuum of potentiality/actuality alone represents the reality of life. It is only on the basis of the dialectic of potentiality/actuality that we can understand, and interpret, the modalities of 'personality' and 'human character': These represent but forms of self-actualization and, as it were, degrees of humanization.

On this point a passage from D.L. Norton is worth quoting:

Every person is both his empirical actuality and his ideal possibility, or daimon. Connecting the two is a path of implications, whose progressive explication constitutes what the Greeks termed the person's "destiny" (*eimarmene*, deriving from the archaic *moira*, or "fate," and representing the interiorization within man of what had earlier been thought to be imposed upon him from the heavens). According to self-actualization ethics it is every person's primary responsibility first to discover the daimon within him and thereafter to live in accordance with it. Because perfection is incompatible with the conditions of existence, one's daimon can never be fully actualized in the world, but by living in truth to it one's unique perfection can be progressively approached, and such endeavor manifests in the world one's excellence or *areté* — an objective value.[6]

Granting, then, that essential dimensions of human nature involve *modalities*, owing to the dynamism of the potential/actual continuum, the question remains: Is there a dialectic of the self which depicts its transition from a 'lower state' to a 'higher state' of being?

It is in response to this question that we recall the nigh-forgotten idea of Hegel concerning the "unhappy consciousness" which haunts modern man like a shadow nevertheless: an inwardly disparate state of being *in the absence of* any higher vision which would make self-integration possible. And the resulting oscillation and wavering of the psyche, between the existential polarities of the "base spirit" and the "noble spirit" (to use Hegel's expressions), represent the modalities of "unhappy consciousness". The psychological novels of Dostoevsky and Hesse, for example, provide us vivid illustrations of "unhappy consciousness" in various realms of human existence.

Hermann Hesse, in whose literary works the theme of the transfiguration of the human personality recurs, depicts the transition of the "lower self" to the "higher self" as follows:

> Hard is the road that leads man to his conscience. Almost all the people all the time live counter to their conscience, they resist it, they are weighed down more and more heavily until they are destroyed by a suffocated conscience. But for everyone, at every moment, beyond suffering and despair lies open the calm road that makes life meaningful and death easy. Yet some people have to rage and sin against conscience until they have experienced all the hells and soiled themselves with all the horrors in order finally, sighing with relief, to recognize their error and experience the hour of transformation.[7]

The possibility of the transfiguration of man, and therewith, the prospect of the realization of a 'higher humanism' have been envisioned by two philosophers especially: The one is Nietzsche whose struggle to overcome the "unhappy consciousness" of his age is well known: and the other is Heidegger whose call for a return to the "thought of Being" is also well known. But neither philosopher is well understood by the modern advocates of 'humanism' for reasons which deserve to be explored on another occasion.

By one incisive stroke, Nietzsche averted the threat of pessimism (and nihilism) directed at life: "Modern pessimism is an expression of the uselessness of *modern* world — not of the world of *existence*...

In sum this constitutes the tragic age."[8] And he reminds us, lest we have forgotten this simple truth also, that the "reduction to nothing" in thought is inevitably followed by the "reduction to nothing" in action. Hence nihilism is to be seen as a symptom of our cultural malaise: "Nihilism is no cause but merely the result of decadence" — he observes — and catalogues for us the "consequences" of decadence: "... vice — addiction to vice; sickness — sickliness; crime — criminality ... hystericism — weakness of the will; alcoholism; pessimism; anarchism; libertinism (also of the spirit)..."[9] Thus the decadence-nihilism link leads, further on, to the nihilism-decadence link and completes the tragic cycle of our cultural demise.

Even man's relation to 'Truth' has been untruthful. In his "untimely meditations" on the meaning of history, for us moderns, Nietzsche criticizes the bourgeois attitude of acquisitiveness extended to the realm of pure knowledge itself: "Knowledge, taken in excess without hunger, even contrary to need, no longer acts as a transforming motive impelling to action and remains hidden in a certain chaotic inner world... and so the world of modern culture is essentially internal... a 'Handbook of Inner Culture for External Barbarians'."[10] And in his notebooks he writes: "The *unselective* knowledge-drive resembles the indiscriminate sexual-drive — signs of vulgarity!"[11] We may amass our "scientific truths", and build our scientific pyramids, but the human psyche will still yearn for truth of a deeper genre.

A heartless demigod, Nietzsche tells us, would see our "truths" of science in a different light than we may be accustomed to see them:

> Once upon a time, in some out of the way corner of that universe which is dispersed into numberless twinkling solar systems, there was a star upon which clever beasts invented 'knowing'. It was the most arrogant and mendacious minute of world history, but nevertheless only a minute. After nature had drawn a few breaths the star cooled and solidified, and the clever beasts had to die. The time had come too, for although they boasted of how much they had understood, in the end they discovered to their great annoyance that they had understood everything falsely. They died, and in dying they cursed truth.[12]

The implication of this thought-experiment is evident: that the half-truths of our sciences give the lie to human vision, and in the end, are themselves given the lie by the inevitable demise of life on earth; and so, in dying, man shall "curse truth" — as a "lie" in humanity's last hour.

It was not by accident that Nietzsche regarded Dostoevsky — the master diagnostician of human phenomenology — as his mentor. But, unlike Dostoevsky whose remedy to our cultural malaise was to evoke the ethos of Christianity, Nietzsche evokes the ideal of a 'higher man', who must inevitably be the "last man" as it were. "Man is something to be surpassed" — he tells us — and urges that man must exercise his *willpower* to attain self-transcendence. Man must answer, beyond the Socratic call to *know* himself, to a new call to *remake* himself...

So Zarathustra, the dream-image of Nietzsche as a 'higher man', descends from his mountain abode to the valley of the world, and, like a mad grave-robber who seems to be convinced that he can blow the breath of new life into the desiccated human bodies of yestertime, hopes to restore the *humanitas* of man to mankind in whom it is deplorably lacking. To the dwellers of the "Land of the Sleepers" he says: "I teach you the *Overman*. Man is something to be surpassed. What have you done to surpass him?" — and again — "I love the great despisers, because they are the great adorers, and arrows longing for the other shore." And later, when a performing artist of the village of Piedmont falls from his trapeze and dies, he speaks to the dead man: "Thou hast made danger thy calling... therefore I will bury thee with mine own hands."[13]

However, there is little assurance that man might be able to attain self-transcendence in a single lifetime. And it becomes imperative for Nietzsche to evoke the hypothesis of "eternal recurrence." And he adduces an ingenious argument in its favor: If we assume the quantity of energy in the cosmos to be finite, and assume a finite number of its possible combinations and recombinations in the matrix of infinite space, then the recurrence of the world becomes a necessary consequence of the infinite flow of time. And the Nietzschean project of human utopia — like the successive and overlapping waves of rhythm in the musical art-epics of Wagner which Nietzsche admired — is to be extended beyond one life cycle and beyond one world. Philosophy alone constitutes an Ariadne's thread — "*als eine Kunst des Lebens*" — as an art *of* life and as an art *for* life. But, alas, the courage to *live* a philosophy has broken down —

Nietzsche observes — and modern man drifts in life without a "mythology".

That man could not live without a "mythology" — a mythology which *originates* in philosophical reflection and *ends* in philosophical vision — was the call of Nietzsche. And to this call Heidegger was to answer. Seeing this hidden connection — and affinity — between these two thinkers is requisite for understanding the dialectic of the debate concerning 'higher humanism' in recent philosophy.

"Who is Nietzsche's Zarathustra?" asks Heidegger; and answers: "Zarathustra speaks on behalf of life, suffering, the circle — and this is what he advocates... The 'overman' surpasses previous and contemporary man, and is therefore a passage, a bridge. If we, the learners, are to follow the teacher who teaches the 'overman', we must, to retain the metaphor, get onto the bridge... The person crossing over and even the teacher who shows him the way is ... on the way to his authentic nature."[14] The crossing over the "bridge", however, for Heidegger means: that man will go beyond 'beings' toward 'Being'.

"Does not the essence of man, does not his belonging to Being, remain yet and evermore the concern of thinking?"[15] — asks Heidegger. And, in his *Letter on Humanism*, he defines the *essence* of man in terms of his *eksistence*: i.e. man's reflective relation to other beings in the light of Being. For it is only through thinking and reflection that man comes to see himself as a unique being, as *Dasein*, in relation to Being and, in that light, in relation to other beings. Man is the "neighbor" of Being: he is a near-dweller to Being, for he harbors the thought of Being, and assumes a sense of responsibility toward Being.

Concerning the ontic character of man, Heidegger narrates an ancient myth: that originally the goddess of Care formed man from clay; that subsequently there was a strife between Earth (who had given it its body) and Jupiter (who had given it its soul) over claiming its name and its destiny; and that Saturn had finally intervened and appointed Care to remain the guardian and the companion of man as long as he shall live on earth.[16]

"Conscience," writes Heidegger, "manifests itself as the call of care."[17] 'Care' is associated with the being of man and his mode of existence: Care for Being, as the ground of man's own being, and care for Earth as the natural abode of beings. Without such primordial propensity to care, man would lose his ontic bearing. Heidegger writes therefore:

> The essence of the homeland, however, is also (to be) mentioned with the intention of thinking the homelessness of contemporary man from the essence of Being's history... Homelessness so understood consists in the abandonment of Being by beings. Homelessness is the symptom of oblivion of Being; because of it the truth of Being remains unthought. The oblivion of Being makes itself known indirectly through the fact that man always observes and handles only beings.[18]

Modern man, living under the canopy of 'bourgeois culture', remains in this sense a homeless man. He is an orphan, philosophically speaking, an estranged man in his own homeland. For he remains preoccupied with utilitarian things and values; and his consciousness is confined to these. He fails to ask himself the primordial question: "What is it to be a human being — to live on this earth?" Therefore his existence (even by his own admission) hovers over the abyss of meaninglessness. And his philosophies of pragmatism and existentialism cannot help him; on the contrary, by urging him to attend to his *existence* rather than to human *essence*, they reinforce his feeble condition and hopelessness.

And the popular ideologies which are peddled in the name of "humanism" today — e.g. the "macho ideology" and the "feminist ideology" — are but variants of bourgeois humanism. Their persistent appeal is to human *existence* rather than to human *essence*. They fail to see that, to have failed as 'man' or as a 'woman', one must have first failed as a 'human being'. They remain, as such, at a pre-dialectical niveau of thinking.

The way to overcome the alienation of the individual person from society, and the homelessness of man in the world, involves something other than joining a social/political movement. It involves the effort to reconcile one's *existence* with one's *essence*: by taking a step inward, as it were, from the level of *ordinary consciousness* to the level of *higher consciousness*. Only then, in the light of higher consciousness, would man be able to reflect on himself *qua* 'human being': i.e. as the harbinger of 'ideal values'. Only then will he come to see his place in the cosmos: as the representation of the highest mode of existence. For man is a being who is endowed with freewill; and, in the light of his 'moral conscience', he can order his relations to other beings and the world he shares with them. The existential choice: whether to see the world from the narrow view of utilitarian/hedonic interest *or* from the higher aesthetic/moral view of appreciation — this existential choice too remains open to man. But it is only through the realization of his 'ideal values', and the exercise of freewill in the light of them, that man attains a due measure of 'human dignity'.

The ideal of 'higher humanism' has implications for the relations between human societies. A new principle of tolerance, which recognizes the essence of humanity and cultural pluralism at the same time, emerges: *variety in cultures — unity in humanity*. The world cannot pretend to be democratic without due respect for national identities and their cultures. Indeed, the wellbeing of the 'world' depends upon the wellbeing of 'nations'. "A true world culture will evolve only by various cultures understanding and preserving their own respective viewpoints," observes Nishida-Kitaró the eminent philosopher of Japan, "but simultaneously developing themselves through the mediation of (universal elements in) the world."[19]

However, the principle of tolerance does not mean that cultural relativism implies ethical relativism. Evidently, anthropologists and sociologists become moral relativists by mistake as it were: i.e. by confusing 'mores' with 'morality'. That the two are not identical is shown by the fact that, in every case of *mores*, the question *whether* it is *morally* right or wrong arises. For it is quite possible for an act to be according to the accepted mores of a given society and yet be morally wrong: e.g. infanticide or promise-breaking. And though there is a diversity of mores and manners, there is only one possible ethics susceptible of rational justification. Thus, e.g., the ethical principle — "Never treat other persons as means merely but always as ends in themselves" — would hold good in all societies and cultures because its justification appeals to formal concepts intelligible by all reasonable human beings. Thus the "moral point of view" — as a dimension of the ideal of higher humanism — underlies cultural diversity as it underscores the *humanity* of man in relation to man.

The ideal of 'higher humanism' — as elucidated in the foregoing

— harbors a pragmatic meaning for human existence: whether man, by actualizing his higher essence, will follow the line of *evolution*; or by failing to actualize his higher essence, will descend further in the vertigo of *devolution*. For the dogma of a fixed future is but a delusion; and to approach an 'open future' requires that we have enlightened vision.

A Commentary on the Ideology of Postmodernity

The ideal of 'higher humanism' which we have elucidated assumes, as the background of its discourse, the heritage of historical enlightenment. Yet, this very heritage and therewith the context of any discourse concerning this theme, has been challenged recently. Moreover, the contemporary disenchantment with *historical enlightenment* has been generalized into a skepticism and pessimism with regard to any programme of *philosophical enlightenment*: including the ideal of higher humanism as well as the prospect of progress for humanity.

I argue — the prevalent view of some contemporary scholars notwithstanding — that the worldview of *historical enlightenment* did not *fail*, owing to some irremediable flaw inherent therein, as it were. Rather, that modern man, whose head was turned by the material and utilitarian prospects of the applied arts and sciences, fell victim to his own forgetfulness: *forgetfulness* of his philosophical lineage and his philosophical heritage. For the transfiguration of man from *homo sapiens* to *homo faber* occurred imperceptibly and gradually as it were. As man harvested the material fruits of the "tree of knowledge" — the very tree which had been planted during the Renaissance and had been nurtured during the Enlightenment — he ceased to attend to the philosophical nurturing of the "tree of knowledge".

Hence man, the creator of arts and sciences, ceased to understand either the *raison d'être* of his creation — beyond their material utility — or to envision its long-range problems and prospects. And, in this state of philosophical ignorance, modern man no longer reflected over his own nature, or on the nature of his motive in doing the things he was about to do, but carried on the "business of living" merely.

Man in the age of historical enlightenment still heeded the call of Socrates — *Gnothi sauton*: Know thyself! — and defined his relation to the cosmos on that basis. But modern man has long since ceased to hear that call. It is understandable, then, that contemporary man, living in the midst of his materially comfortable civilization, should question, not only the *meaning* but also the very *worth* of his own existence.

(I disagree, accordingly, with the opinion of Theodor Adorno and Max Horkheimer which, motivated by a mixture of political ideology and nostalgia for mythology, blames historical enlightenment for the evils of contemporary civilization (repressive-alienating aspects of social order) but credits it for none of its virtues (emancipatory-reconciling aspects of social order), which renders their alleged exposition of the "dialectic" of the historical enlightenment invalid.[20])

The entry of modern man into the self-styled age of "postmodernity", as a culture of antimodernity, is understandable then. But not understandable, nor justifiable altogether, is to place the onus of the turning-point — as some scholars do — upon Nietzsche and Heidegger. It must be remembered, above all, that these two thinkers shared a profound dread of nihilism. And this dread was so profound, indeed, that one might argue that it (and the aspiration to overcome it) constituted a main philosophical motive of much of their endeavors. That Heidegger was to write eventually a one-thousand page commentary on the thought of Nietzsche — of which one-third was devoted to the theme of nihilism and its overcoming — was not mere coincidence.[21] The urge and the aspiration to overcome nihilism, however, they inherited from the historical enlightenment. The ideologists of "postmodernity" do not display any dread of nihilism or of its aura of meaninglessness; on the contrary, it is easy to see, they *thrive* in its vacuous realm. This is not to say, however, that there are no ideas in Nietzsche and in Heidegger, which do not lend themselves to being used, by these ideologists, in other contexts and for other purposes.

The ideology of "postmodernity", which presents itself as a critique of historical enlightenment, also implies a rejection of praxis philosophy and the project of modernity. For all their differences, its leaders — Jacques Derrida, Michel Foucault, Richard Rorty — are unanimous in decrying the role of reason in theory and in practice. We have seen already — in Section § 14 above — the potential responses of these "marginal philosophers" when confronted with the question of truth: they create for themselves epistemological problems which, on their own ground and from their own perspective, they cannot resolve. They also present — as Jürgen Habermas has remarked — "the aporias of self-referential critique of reason which is bound to undermine its own foundations" *if* they were to be taken earnestly. For, in rejecting the autonomy and/or power of reason, they must nevertheless assume a framework of rational discourse, *if* they are not to render themselves unintelligible to themselves, not to mention others. Nevertheless, the various modes of their socalled "critical theory" — (as if epistemology were not the primary critical theory already!) — proceed with reckless disregard of their own assumptions, camouflaged comfortably each in its own genre of *rhétorique*.

What were the basic assumptions of historical enlightenment, then, which have been called into question? These: *firstly*, that human reason and imagination would be able to comprehend the structure of reality; and, *secondly*, that the arts and sciences (as the fruits of human reason and imagination) would contribute to the betterment of human life on earth. The twofold humanistic concern was evident in this fundamental belief system: namely, the appropriateness of the use of reason in all realms of human inquiry; and, correspondingly, the appropriation of the results of human inquiry for the building of human culture and progress of human civilization. These concerns — in the realm of *theoria* and in the realm of *praxis* — made possible the great project of modernity, which has provided European culture its motive and its momentum, but which remains as yet an unfinished project for mankind.

When, for example, the great thinker of historical enlightenment Kant posed the question, "What is enlightenment?", his answer could only be: it is to have the courage to use one's reason and critical thinking in handling the problems of life.[22] That was the 'call' of historical enlightenment. It was a call away from the dark tradition of collective mythology; a call which represented a counterforce to the oppressive structures of sociopolitical tradition; a call which called for thinking and rethinking — and for cultural revolution.

It is this historical enlightenment, and its project of modernity, which the ideology of postmodernity challenges and wishes to reject altogether.

Why?

In attempting to answer this simple question, one finds that it is easier to give a negative answer than a positive one. For evidently "postmodernity" means different things to different authors — (nor is it an accident that the art of 'hermeneutics' is now in vogue) — and it is easier to say what it stands *against* than to say what it stands *for*. Nor need we care about the internal problems of the ideology of "postmodernity".[23] We care only to understand its "rationale" — even if the use of the very word be paradoxical in this context — for abandoning the worldview of historical enlightenment and its project of modernity.

The radical abandonment of that worldview must involve a rejection of its philosophical assumptions — namely: (a) the abandonment of the belief in the possibility of attaining true knowledge by means of theoretical and/or experimental reason; (b) the abandonment of the hope for reappropriating our acquired knowledge for the amelioration of the quality of human life; and, consequently, (c) the abandonment of the ideal of 'higher humanism' based upon the conception of a thinking being who can shape his life on earth on the basis of his access to 'truth' and to 'ideal values'.

In view of the radical pronouncements of the ideologists of "postmodernity", it is significant that the social philosopher, Jürgen Habermas, should reopen the debate concerning modernity/ postmodernity with the critical question: "Should we try to hold on to the *intentions* of (historical) enlightenment... or should we declare the entire project of modernity a lost cause?"[24]

Not quite.

The epistemological dilemma of the ideology of "postmodernity" manifests itself in its ambivalent attitude toward 'reason' and 'rationality'. It claims to represent the 'other of reason', rejecting the autonomy and power of 'reason', and yet it tacitly assumes the 'framework of rationality' as the matrix of intelligibility for its own discourse. But such an assumption is precluded by the very credo of "postmodernity". This presents a dilemma: that either the advocates of the 'other of reason' must also reject the 'framework of rationality', in which case their own discourses become unintelligible, or they must recognize the 'framework of rationality' as indispensable, and therewith retract their uncritical and rhetorical assault against 'reason' and 'rationality'. Such a transcendental counter-argument is admittedly called for here, given the radical character of the challenge itself, where ground-assumptions are called into question.

The predicament of the postmodern intellectual is depicted by Jürgen Habermas as follows:

> Anyone who abides in a paradox on the very spot once occupied by philosophy with its ultimate groundings is not just taking up an uncomfortable position; one can only hold that place if one makes it at least minimally plausible that there is *no way out*. Even the retreat from an aporetic situation has to be barred, for otherwise there is a way — *the way back*. But I believe this is precisely the case.[25]

Speaking from the perspective of praxis philosophy, Habermas argues, we must earnestly continue the project of modernity which is as yet an "unfinished project" as it were; and our proper response to the limitations of historical enlightenment ought to be, *not* to abandon the cause of enlightenment, but to seek *more* enlightenment. For the main motif of historical enlightenment, i.e. to link the *theoria* of knowledge with the *praxis* of society, remains as valid as ever. And, so long as the rational integration of theory and practice remains an unfulfilled desideratum, the continuation of the project of modernity remains an imperative.

To ignore this imperative, Habermas observes, would exact its price in terms of human wellbeing and social progress:

> As soon as we give up praxis philosophy's understanding of society as a self-referential subject-writ-large, encompassing all individual subjects, the corresponding models for the diagnosis and mastery of crisis — division and revolution — are no longer applicable. Because the successive releasing of the rational potential inherent in communicative action is no longer thought of as self-reflection writ large, this specification of the normative content of modernity can prejudge neither the conceptual tools for diagnosing crises nor the way of overcoming them... With the differentiation of the structures of the lifeworld, the forms in which social pathologies appear are multiplied according to which aspects of (these) structural factors are insufficiently taken care of: Loss of meaning, conditions of anomie, and psychopathologies are the most obvious kinds of symptoms,

but not the only ones... The marginalized lifeworld could survive only if it were to be transformed in turn into a media-steered subsystem and if it were to shed everyday communicative practice like a snakeskin.[26]

What then is the intent (not to say the meaning) of the ideology of "postmodernity", behind its inflated designation, and beyond its tedious modes of cognitive confusion?

This complex question perhaps should not be asked. For the philosophical motives of the ideologists of "postmodernity" may not be even known to themselves — in the same way, e.g., that the philosophical motives of neopositivists or of the phenomenologists were known to themselves — and hence their motives may remain unknowable to others. And this state of unphilosophical motivelessness, too, may be taken as their mode of rationality-crisis-ridden existence.

That the ideology of "postmodernity" harbors ugly consequences for the future of mankind and culture is evident: the abandonment of reflective inquiry and rational dialogue and their replacement by rhetorical discourse; the destruction of *pure reason*, and in consequence, the destruction of *practical reason*; and, therefore (through the erosion of its ground) the withering of the ideal of 'higher humanism'. Eventually, the entire realm of praxis philosophy with its applications to the actual problems of our culture and civilization, social as well as ecological, would have to be abandoned.

It would be naive to suppose that the lowest ebb of our modern culture lies safely behind us — buried under the debris of the last world war as it were. It lies, on the contrary, before us — if the programme of the ideology of "postmodernity" were to replace the project of modernity and the philosophy of enlightenment altogether. For the programme of the "destruction of reason", under the sophisticated label of the "deconstruction of philosophy", would give rise to an era of pervasive intellectual and moral chaos, resulting in unprecedented intellectual and cultural decadence. Then the way would be open to the spiritual peddlers of irrational mythologies and cults — waiting with their baggage of bad literature just outside the gates as it were — to enter the barren "house of culture" and present anew their bizarre worldviews...

In the perspective of dialectical realism, the countermove to the ideology of "postmodernity" is, not the abandonment of enlightenment and its project of modernity, but a renewed search for *philosophical enlightenment.* For, if our earlier programme of *historical enlightenment* suffered from limitations and/or was forgotten, then the remedy is not to decry 'enlightenment' but to seek a *higher form* of 'enlightenment'. This, however, is a task for 'philosophy', whose alleged "end" would also mean the "end" of our hope for 'cultural reconstruction' and for the progress of mankind.

§ 29

Paradigm of the Island
(A Thought-Experiment about Utopia/Dystopia)

The question of culture/nature predicament may be stated as follows: *What kind of relation ought to exist between man and earth?*

I suggest a thought-experiment, which involves the "paradigm of the island". Here, two opposing models for man/earth relation are envisioned, each harboring its own genre of philosophical worldview. And the two models would illustrate the conditions for utopia/dystopia.

Imagine, then, two islands separated by a great distance. The two islands display starkly different cultures: Their philosophies of life and their value hierarchies appear to be the inversion of each other. Call the one Alpha Island, and the other Omega Island.

The people of Alpha Island perceive their relation to their natural habitat in terms of possession and exploitation. Accordingly, material/utilitarian values represent the top priorities, while aesthetic/moral values are relegated to the arbitrariness of personal and/or social tastes merely. A negative concept of freedom — freedom *from* material want, political control, etc.— constitutes the basis of their philosophy of life. And the ultimate motivation for their actions and policies is the pleasure principle. Their motto reads: *To be in order to have.*

The people of Omega Island perceive their relation to their natural habitat in terms of symbiosis and harmony. Accordingly, they assign the highest priority to aesthetic/moral values, while material/utilitarian values are handled as instrumental goods only. And a positive concept of freedom — freedom *for* the actualization of their personal/social ideals—constitutes the basis of their philosophy of life. And the ultimate motivation for their actions and policies is the harmony principle: harmony with earth and harmony with themselves. Their motto reads: *To have in order to be.*

Now suppose that the people of Alpha Island, during one of their seasons of discontent, think enviously about the pleasant conditions of life on Omega Island. And suppose that they decide—suppressing their desire to attack and occupy the other island (an idea which to them is conceivable though not practical for various reasons) — to send over one of their young citizens to visit the other island and learn the secret of their apparent wellbeing and happiness. The visitor remains on the host island for a long time—owing to his own spirit of inquiry—during which time he acquires an understanding of their way of life before he returns to his home island.

We can imagine that his return, after acclimatization in a foreign culture and after re-education in an alien philosophy of life, would occasion a dramatic scenario: a traumatic re-encounter with his own culture and an eristic dialogue with his own people.

The visitor is appalled to find his home island devastated: air and water pollution, a land poisoned by runaway toxics and pesticides, and where once stood virgin forests now remained dust valleys. Within the city he sees crowds of listless youths roaming aimlessly in alleys reeking with drugs, violence, and heinous crimes. And, where there were a healthy people before, now the demoralized population is suffering an epidemic of venereal diseases. He asks the officials responsible for the affairs of the island for an explanation; and they tell him that these negative phenomena are the inevitable byproducts of the road to "progress". And, when he asks them for a definition of "progress", they answer in terms of the "standard of living" materially interpreted. It is evident to him, then, that the amelioration of their "standard of living" (so interpreted) has been all along at the expense of their "quality of life". But this distinction they themselves, given their philosophical blinders of materialism, cannot and would not make.

The visitor then realizes that his people have abandoned their calling of being the "gardeners of the island" and instead have become the "despoilers of the island". And, in the absence of an enlightened philosophy of life — or under the aegis of a warped philosophy of life—their government is run by a band of opportunists practicing an oddball mix of reckless and feckless policies of which the long-range consequences are unknown even to themselves. He sees, too, that behind their mask of "democracy" lies a conspiracy of hidden special interests. In this society political corruption seems to feed upon moral corruption.

We can imagine that the visitor, having had the perspective of time, has a clearer vision of the ills of his home island than its own inhabitants do. Also, given his exposure to and understanding of, the philosophy of life and culture of the other island, he can be more critical of conditions on his own island. Naturally, then, he would want to reform the conditions of his own island. To that end he prepares a report — a manual for praxis as it were —adopting and adapting the policies of the other island for his home island. And his own people, naturally, reject his report after examination.

Why?

Because, insofar as practical policies are *the consequence of* philosophical worldview, one cannot accept (or appreciate) the former without *understanding* the latter. The visitor, unless he has the means to teach the new philosophical worldview to his people, will remain ineffective as a reformer. Indeed, he may even be treated as an alien, culturally speaking, and expelled from the island.

The allegory embodied in this thought-experiment need not be taken literally.[27] Yet, insofar as it represents a paradigm, it holds a philosophical lesson: that man's relation to nature is determined by the level of man's philosophical enlightenment.

If the cultures of the two imaginary islands represent but inversions of each other, if the ideology of the one is anathema to the other, it is undoubtedly because their inhabitants entertain starkly different philosophies of life — and (therefore) different value hierarchies. The one philosophy is enlightened by the consciousness of man's place in the cosmos; the other is not. The one philosophy places *being* (and wellbeing) before *having* (and exploiting); the other conversely. It is understandable, then, why the visitor, who returns from Omega Island after a long time, no longer "recognizes" his homeland and its people; while the people of Alpha Island, ironically, do not find his proffered ideas for reform to be "useful" to them.

The culture of the one island involves a pragmatic self-contradiction: in its herculean effort to raise its "standard of living" (materially interpreted) it detracts from its "quality of life" writ large, defeating its own purpose in the long-run. The culture of the other island involves a harmonious relation between human society and its natural environment, which minimizes entropy and destruction, and assures its survival in the long-run. Their destinies will be ruled by the goddess of cosmic equilibrium — Nemesis — doling out to each what is their just due.

Nor does the paradigm of the island, depicting utopia and dystopia in their stark forms by two models, preclude the idea of the historical development of human society and culture. It illustrates, on the contrary, the possibility of *cultural evolution* and *cultural devolution*. For, between the polarities of utopia and dystopia, lies the entire range of historical change: progress as well as regress. The critical issue, I argue, is the character of the *philosophical worldview* of a people, reflecting their niveau of spiritual enlightenment, and determining the course of their living history.

§ 30

Diseases of Culture in Philosophical Perspective

In the epilogue to the anthology of essays addressing the question, "Where do we stand today?", its thoughtful editor Walter Bähr observes: "Before our eyes the peril of Man through Man accelerates — and finally in its web the regions of Nature are being cunningly drawn."[28] That was the apprehension about our cultural dream in 1960. Now, in 1990, that apprehension is acquiring the proportions of a cultural nightmare. Our very Zeitgeist has altered.

The maladies of our culture are susceptible of a philosophical diagnosis:

(a) Existential vacuum: the absence of higher values and ideals (including the ideal of 'higher humanism') in the belief system of the ordinary man.

(b) Value inversion: the predominance of material/utilitarian values over aesthetic/moral values.

(c) Disharmony in the relation between man and nature — both his own nature and his natural homeland — as a consequence.

These maladies of culture are not caused by any lack of scientific knowledge or by an inherent defect in human nature. They are caused, rather, by an underdeveloped and/or warped philosophy of life: a philosophy of life that does not have the nerve or the vision to face up to the "tyranny of culture". One may say, then, that the diseases of culture are to be seen as the symptoms of an *ailing culture*.

Nor did the transfiguration of our cultural dream into a cultural nightmare materialize suddenly as it were. The harsher Baconian strain of ideology was always there, alongside the gentler Spinozistic strain, and eventually it acquired predominance. Consider one example:

A painting hangs in the National Gallery (London); a disturbing painting by Joseph Wright titled "Experiment with the Air Pump" and done in late 1700s. It depicts a cockatoo inside a glass globe, from

240

which the scientist is extracting the air, and presumably the bird's eventual death would demonstrate the efficacy of the invention — while the faces of people surrounding him display mixed feelings of curiosity and dismay. The painting symbolizes the advent of technology, its potential power over nature, *as well as* the early response of human conscience. In our time, more than two hundred years later, it would be accurate to say that the bird of the early experiment has been replaced by whole ecological regions which are trapped by the encroachment of technology and by the gathering dome of the greenhouse effect. Thus, man the earth-dweller has become, through the rise of industrial civilization, man the earth-exploiter.

The philosophical question before mankind is: *Does man know how big a niche is right for mankind to occupy in the total scheme of things?*

Consider the recent phase of man's relation to nature: World population will have nearly doubled (from 2.5 to 5.0 billion) — but, correspondingly, world energy consumption will have increased tenfold (from 2500 to 25,000 mtce) — between the years 1950 and 2000. Yet, the human concern for conservation, for organic methods in agriculture, or for research directed toward nuclear fusion rather than nuclear fission, remains minimal at the present time. Nor does man seem to know how to separate his *needs* (that which is requisite for human wellbeing) from his *luxuries* (that which is not requisite for human wellbeing) in the context of his world.

Meanwhile, the damage to the natural environment continues apace on several fronts: the advancing deforestation of land continents (in 1950 one-fourth of the Earth was forested — but by 1990 only one-fifth of the Earth remained forested); the increasing pollution of land and waters (in USA alone one billion pounds of pesticide are used annually); the damage to the ozone layer owing to the emission of high density chloro-fluoro-carbons; and, lastly, the gradual creation of the "greenhouse effect" which, unless checked, would result in the rise of overall temperature, causing the thaw of the lower icebergs in the antarctica, raising the sea-level, and resulting in the universal inundation of the lower regions of land continents.[29]

The ecological impact of human civilization may be summarily depicted as follows:

Ecological Impact = f   *(Resource Depletion*
                          X Environmental Pollution
                          X Landscape Deterioration)

As an appeal to humanity in anticipation of the Year 2000, the "Geneva Statement" was drawn by the representatives of the Christian Churches of USA and USSR even when a political "iron curtain" separated the two continents, containing these words: "Even now, only twenty years separate us from the moment when we will be called upon to mark the bimillenary anniversary of the coming to the world of our Savior. How shall we meet that day? In what state shall we present our planet to the Creator: shall it be a blooming garden or a lifeless, burnt out, devastated land?"[30] This question becomes modern man to ask himself — unless the human hubris has passed the point of self-reflection and self-examination.

Nature, as we know it, is a megasystem of order, comprising an infinitely complex network of interrelated systems and subsystems, which it has taken millions of years to evolve. But now man, wittingly or unwittingly, is engaged in introducing into the natural world irreversible changes with long-range consequences. Eventually, in the remote long-run, these irreversible changes would backfire, causing the destruction of the niche of the destroyer.

The inexorable dialectic of man's relation to nature is that the damage done to nature turns out to be also damage done to man. This is evident in the "health crisis" of our age. The three major kinds of diseases — cardiovascular diseases, cancer, respiratory diseases — are (as specialists in the health sciences tell us) "diseases of civilization". They are caused by the threefold condition of bad nutrition, environmental toxics, and emotional stress. The nice hypothesis, that man in the state of nature would be healthy and happy, may still be true. But the same civilization, which boasts of "miracle drugs", has also transformed the ideal of hygeia into a "mirage of health".

The "mirage of health" extends to the psychological realm as well and pervades human society and sociality. The attitude of "healthy-mindedness" (of which William James spoke) gives way to the attitude of "sick-mindedness". The healthy motivation for self-actualization and work with fellow man gives way to mercenary motivation and egoistic relationships with others. And this too reflects an underlying value inversion which materialism represents. The diagnosis of Karl Marx was unerring on this point: The emergence of money, not merely as a means of living, but eventually as the end of life for the bourgeois man; and money as the paradoxical cause of both alienation and appropriation in the web of human relations which is modern society.[31] Indeed, if modern man were to continue worshiping the goddess of materialism, there is the danger that he might lose his gifts as a human being altogether.

However unwelcome the impact of modern civilization upon human health may be, its impact upon the human psyche involves an even greater tragedy. For the epidemic of 'moral decadence' — the atrophy of moral conscience and exaggerated hedonism — is the result of our nihilistic civilization: its value inversion, its existential vacuum, and its negative idea of freedom. It was Jean-Jacques Rousseau who early anticipated the moral troubles of civilization. But it remained for Nietzsche to depict the psychology of decadence, and its connection with nihilism, with bold strokes: "The destruction of ideals — the new desert; new arts by means of which we can endure it, we amphibians."[32] But the arts have had to express ugly truths, because they have had the courage to be truthful, and thereby themselves have become ugly and uglified in the process.

The same existential vacuum, the same absence of ideals in life, which engenders decadence also engenders neurosis. A significant number of young persons in industrial countries turn to drugs or to suicide. The psychiatrist Viktor Frankl calls this psychological malady "noogenic neurosis", i.e., a sustained anxiety about the meaning and/or direction of life. "When a neurosis is noogenic, that is, when it has its roots, not in psychological complexes and traumata, but in spiritual problems, moral conflicts, and existential crises, then such a spiritually rooted neurosis requires a psychotherapy focusing on the spirit..."[33] He calls this kind of psychotherapy "logotherapy" — with its emphasis on conscious meanings and and dialogue concerning meanings and ideals in life, in order to help modern man define his "purpose in life" (for which Frankl uses the witty acronym PIL).

And what role are the human sciences playing in restoring man's understanding of himself and of his life? The recent work in humanistic disciplines themselves have been infected, as it were, by the infusion of ideas from the social sciences, which contribute to the obliteration of the 'human image' rather than to its restoration. The lone voice of a woman-philosopher, Jeanne Hersch of Geneva, in the recent World Congress of Philosophy (Montréal/1983) called upon 'philosophy' to resume the task of "restoring" the meaning of the 'human being' against the camouflages effected upon it by the technological and social sciences in our culture. But, until recently, the human sciences seemed to have lost their moral nerve, as they waited at the doors of the social sciences in order to borrow "data" for understanding 'man'. And when their human-product would look at the mirror of his self-image he would see only the droll figure of a homunculist man — little removed from the ape.

244

§ 31

Philosophical Ideology and the Shape of Things to Come:
The Argument of Praxis Philosophy

The 'philosophical ideology' of a person and of a society represents the totality of their beliefs, at a certain level of abstraction, concerning life and the world. It may be argued that our philosophical ideology determines the shape of things to come in our world: the kind of culture we shall have and the kind of world we shall live in.

To understand this is to embark upon the path of practical reason — i.e. the path that leads from *theoria* to *praxis* — and to acknowledge *praxis philosophy* as the basis of cultural reconstruction and cultural healing.

The argument of praxis philosophy — from the perspective of dialectical realism — may be stated as follows: That a philosophical ideology implies a certain value hierarchy; that the system of value hierarchy functions in directing praxis (the system of practical principles); and that the latter determines the 'quality of life'. It follows that, in order to reform our culture and our civilization, we must alter or radically reconstruct, our philosophical ideology.[34] Schematically:

(Philosophical Ideology) $\longrightarrow$ (Value Hierarchy)

(Praxis) $\longrightarrow$ (Quality of Life)

This argument derives its validity from the fact that, given the interdependence of its categories, one cannot negate the link between its theoretical categories without rendering its practical categories groundless. Moreover, accepting the argument would entail some significant consequences: (a) that a change in one's ideology entails a change in one's value hierarchy, and eventually, in one's quality of life; and (b) that the connection between philosophical ideology and the quality of life holds good for individual persons as well as for society at large.

The question remains however: Given the possibility of rival ideologies for cultural reform, each with its own rationale, how to decide which is best for one? The criterion of rational choice, in this case, is twofold: (a) that, given two ideologies, the one which promises to serve the 'wellbeing of man' to a greater degree is the better one; and (b) that, if ideology A, translating the language of ideology B in the context of its own language, is able to restate its crucial problems and suggest intelligible solutions, but not conversely, then ideology A may be said to be superior to ideology B. The two criteria, representing a telic requirement and a formal requirement, may be regarded as complementary.[35]

Granting the relevance of philosophical ideology to social change, the issue is: How does philosophy in fact bring about a cultural reconstruction?

The definition of 'culture' by Nelli Motrošilova — i.e. the inner integration of values and ideals by human society—sets it in contrast to 'civilization' as the corresponding external institutions and activities. Further, she argues, a society at any given epoch represents a veritable "arena of struggle" between cultures: between the old and the new forms of spiritual movements and their attending sets of ideals and values. And she suggests that the proper task of praxis philosophy would be, not only to visualize and anticipate new ideals (in the context of a new *Weltanschauung*) but also to propose ways of employing these ideals toward the renovation of culture and civilization.[36]

Moreover, a distinction needs to be made — as has been made by Fernand Dumont — between "culture as milieu" and "culture as horizon": i.e. the distinction between the existential state of a culture and the potential/ideal state of a culture. Philosophy as praxis plays the role of mediation between the two. For philosophy represents, Dumont argues, the "conscience of crisis" in the context of human culture. It intervenes in the social scene when, due to an emerging cultural crisis, the ground truths are shaken and the horizon values appear to be blurred. Then philosophy, as a critic of culture-in-crisis and as the harbinger of new values, anticipates a cultural renovation and motivates a "cultural mutation" as it were. It is this critical role of philosophy which sets it apart from the social sciences and their approach to the problems of culture. Sociology examines the patterns of culture; philosophy examines the crisis of culture. The one operates within the matrix of culture; the other operates outside it. Therefore (observes Dumont) *la philosophie trouve son départ dans la dénégation de la culture où elle travaille.*[37]

Too, praxis philosophy serves as the mediator between the arts and sciences on the one hand and society and the lifeworld on the other. My colleague, W. Ch. Zimmerli, goes so far as to define the very task of philosophy in terms of the critical assessment and evaluation of the discoveries and innovations in the sciences and technologies with respect to their effects upon the quality of human life.[38] It is understandable, then, that in the debates of the recent World Congress of Philosophy (Montréal/1983) the following radical question should have been raised: "Can modern society afford to leave in the hands of politicians alone the task of defining the social/cultural goals for our world?" The thoughtful discussion which followed underlined the unanimity of conviction as to the role of praxis philosophy.

In a significant essay, Josef Seifert articulates the case for the "healing role" of philosophy in a "broken world". He argues on the basis of a distinction between the two senses of 'use' and 'usefulness' — the utilitarian sense (i.e. the potential of an activity for yielding material goods) and the humanistic sense (i.e. the raison d'être of the activity in itself and in its relation to human wellbeing) — that philosophy is relevant to society and to life as a "practical science" writ large. And he depicts the responsibility of philosophy to the *conditio humane* in these words:

> As the answer to the contemporary situation of the loss of meaning... various forms of the renewal of spirit and of heart must take place... Philosophy, which countenances this very crisis, which in its foundation is a crisis of and for philosophy, to which it is called, a great task with all its modesty, ever mindful that its contributions to the wellbeing and deliverance of mankind are not carried out by itself alone, but it is to be fulfilled with full commitment and consciousness of itself as the wellspring of the very project which involves Society.[39]

Philosophy has always had a reluctance to intervene in the life of society — despite the examples set by Plato and Aristotle. But when philosophy has intervened — as in the case of Thomas Jefferson or Karl Marx — it has resulted in ideological revolution. And now, perhaps, the time has come for philosophy to intervene in the affairs of the world again.

The inauguration of a new philosophical ideology in the context of a culture will generate a cultural reconstruction (or revolution) sooner or later. And of all revolutions — technological, economic, political — the revolution caused by a philosophical ideology is the most fundamental and enduring. For it sets the philosophical framework for other genres of revolutions. It is also the slowest in brewing — and harbors the most radical and wide-ranging consequences.

Yet the long history of the intellectual attack upon philosophy and philosophical inquiry is well known. To what may we attribute it? To the latent fear of the potential power of philosophy. Unlikely parties with varied motives — materialist scientists, orthodox theologians, existential literati, and recently the self-styled postmodern intellectuals — have aligned themselves against 'philosophy' generally and against 'philosophical enlightenment' especially. They dread still the dream of Plato, and the anticipation of his proposed utopia, after two thousand years. And, lastly, the social scientists challenge the very autonomy of philosophy: "But is not philosophy itself a product of culture?" they ask. And they themselves could hardly provide any adequate definition of 'culture' beyond an unreconstructed empirical rapportage. What they call 'culture' is but an umbrella paradigm, sustained and nourished by the contributions of the arts, the sciences, and philosophy — however primitive or advanced — without which it would collapse as a meaningless notion. That is the irony of their "critique".

The very relation between 'philosophy' and the 'world' is to be reversed therefore: *hitherto the world, and the men of the world, questioned the meaning and value of philosophy; now the time has come for philosophy to question the condition of the men of the world and the prospect of their world.*

§ 32

Recent Ideas Toward a Cultural Reconstruction

Since the philosophy of materialism/hedonism has proven to be pragmatically self-defeating in the long-run, we must seek a new philosophy of life as a basis for a cultural reconstruction. We need a new praxis philosophy, which assumes some form of a critical and/or dialectical realism, and which might provide an answer to the crisis of our culture and civilization. I shall review some recent ideas, proposed by creative philosophers working on the cutting-edge of inquiry today, in the following pages.

Writing from the perspective of a general systems theory — which views nature as a megasystem wherein natural systems of different orders have taken millions of years to evolve and to find their place in relation to each other — Ervin Laszlo argues that man is not a being apart from nature but belongs in the natural scheme of things. Whether human institutions enter into an antagonistic or a symbiotic relationship with other natural systems would determine the future fate of human civilization. So far man has assumed a materialist and hedonist philosophy of life which shows little sensitivity to the aesthetic and moral aspects of his relation to his natural environment. "The use of nature for our egoistic ends has had far-reaching consequences in altering the relationships which form the preconditions of our very being. These relationships took millions of years to evolve, and they could only evolve in balance, for any imbalance would have had to either be rectified, or result in disorganization... Only man has upset the balance of his environment by favoring his own species over others."[40] We are at the cross-roads, and we either must reassess mankind's place within the natural order of things or prepare to face eventual extinction. It is time to leave the arrogance of our tradition behind us; and abandon the exploitative relationship with our natural homeland. Laszlo observes:

It is our misfortune to live at a time when the accumulated effects of man's arbitrary use of nature to his own ends begin to tell, and to cut into the survival potential of the species itself. Our 'natural sins' are not new — new only is their acceleration through our egoistical use of technology and the feedback of effects in the form of a survival threat... But it is not too late now to undo (the damage done by) the work of the past hundred years... We must try to recognize the effects of having overstepped the limits, and transgressed on the checks and balances of nature, and correct our future activities to reduce the margin between human survival and technological-social development.[41]

As a step toward the reassessment of man's relationship to nature, Laszlo suggests the assumption of a "new ethos" comprising two essential imperatives: (a) that we must begin to see our human world in the context of an "ecological hierarchy" and not apart from it; and (b) that we must begin to practice the ethics of "reverence for natural systems" in contrast to the nonethics of exploitation. A revision of our worldview, then, is called for; an abandonment of the materialist/mechanist view of nature in favor of a realist/dynamic view of nature; and an abandonment of our self-image as an egoist/hedonist being in favor of a morally/ecologically conscious being. We must return, in other words, to the nobler instincts still inherent in us as the highest form of living beings — despite, nay because of, the currents of our present culture to the contrary.

Indeed, a radical revision in our very ethics is called for: the range of our 'moral point of view' must be enlarged to include, beyond its formal aspect, an explicit teleological aspect as well. Hans Jonas proposes such a revision in ethics on the basis of the concept of 'responsibility'.[42] Jonas suggests that the Kantian categorical imperative — "Act such that you can will that the principle of your action must become a principle of action for everyone" — though valid is no longer sufficient. For, in our time, the emergence of technological power involves not only persons but also other living beings and natural things; and, consequently, we need a new categorical imperative which is asymmetrical and refers to moral desiderata. The new moral imperative would read: "Act in such a way that the effect of your action is compatible with the permanence of authentic human life on earth;" or negatively stated, "Act so that the effects of your action do not destroy the future possibility of such life."[43] The burden of proof of the new imperative, as that of the old imperative, lies upon the criterion of the avoidance of pragmatically self-defeating acts. And it may be noted — as Hans Lenk has noted already — that the "new imperative" is not only not incompatible with the Kantian imperative but also it evokes the very same ground of proof. What is significant, however, is that Jonas derives, from the asymmetry of the "new imperative", the concept of *extended responsibility* for human acts. "My power over something at the same time includes obligation with respect to it... the exercise of power without observation of duty is then irresponsible..." writes Jonas, defining 'responsibility' as "the obligation to acknowledge care for another being."[44] It is clear that this extension of the concept of responsibility — as distinct from the traditional concept of responsibility based upon retroactive causality (i.e. I am responsible for the facticity of X which I have caused) — *projects* the ethical burden to the future where the present power is directed: it is a responsibility for the shape of things, which are not, but are yet to come.

However, the issue is more profound. Professor Hans Lenk argues that behind the inadequacy of the ethics of man with respect *to* nature lies the inadequacy of man's philosophy *of* nature. So far anti-realism and anti-naturalism has characterized our culture resulting from, and contributing to, technological hubris. For modern man, under the spell of an antiquated picture of the world — mechanism or neopositivism — and under the euphoria of newly acquired technological power, has come to believe that man is the "maker of nature", or its remaker. However, Lenk observes, this belief is belied by the autonomy and constancy of natural order — even granting the interpretative character of our knowledge of nature and granting the variation of the models by which we represent nature to ourselves — as a precondition of the possibility of scientific knowledge.

Implicit in the discourse of the "new ethics" is the assumption of a revised conception of 'pragmatic reason'. Hans Lenk has rendered this assumption explicit in the context of praxis philosophy.[45] Here the adjective 'pragmatic' is to mean, no longer 'workable' in the human world alone (as traditional pragmatism took it to mean) but 'workable' in the context of the natural world order (which is inclusive of the human world). Pragmatic reason, thus interpreted, must involve — if it is to avoid the paradoxes of pragmatically self-defeating acts — a consideration of the multidimensional aspects of praxis and their anticipatory consequences for the quality of life generally. And Lenk advances a new 'social philosophy' of technology[46] — on the basis of the revised conception of 'pragmatic reason' — most worthy of study and consideration.

(It may be noted that the epistemological investigation of the nature of 'practical reasoning' and its interpretation in the light of the larger concept of 'rationality' — as is presented in the work of Robert Audi especially — provides a corroboration for the proposed revision of the idea of 'pragmatic reason'.[47])

The new social philosophy involves a new ethics. "In the past, ethics was essentially anthropocentrically oriented around actions, interactions, and their consequences among men; however, ethics must now gain an ecological relevance, giving significance to other forms of life..."[48] This, the positive interest of the new ethics of responsibility, is to be complemented by a negative interest: namely, the averting of the encroaching harm of the technological civilization to the quality of life and to the future of mankind.

One would hope that modern society would give as much attention to its ethics as it does to its budget; but modern man appears to be content in being "practical" without using his 'pragmatic reason'. Yet — "The ecological crisis may teach man a bit of unpretentiousness, moderation, or even modesty..." Lenk observes, "We have to learn to retreat from our technological hubris, to overcome the conception of total technicalization, technocracy, the myth of unlimited feasibility, if catastrophic consequences are to be avoided."[49] Perhaps — if there still be time.

The cause of much of the malaise of our civilization is traceable to the fact that we have, wittingly or unwittingly, engaged in an "Antiplatonic Experiment": that is the opening theme of a series of critical studies by Walther Zimmerli. The fragmentation of culture, and the disorientation of the person in society, are but the results of our antiplatonic experiment. We have already begun to talk of an ideology (and technology) of "postmodernity" — as if the "modern age", with its platonic dream of the 'good life', were already behind us in time. What does "postmodernity" mean? "That which we call 'postmodern' represents the experiment to break with the two-and-half thousand years tradition of philosophical thinking, which retained a certain interrelation of unity and plurality..." writes Zimmerli, "For it is not unity merely, but the unity of the forms of rationality, of value norms and culture, which in the postmodern situation are abandoned."[50] Yet, dialectically speaking the two ideas, plurality and unity, are bound together: beyond the plurality of the modes of scientific inquiry lies the unity of the forms of rationality; beyond the plurality of the art forms lies the unity of aesthetic truth; and beyond the plurality of technological projects lies the unity of moral responsibility. The demise of reflective thinking about the dialectic of the self/world issue is responsible for the predicament of "postmodernity": "that man might be the being who, with every step forwards in cadence with technological knowledge, also takes a further step in the direction of non-understanding."[51] Thus the competence and the ignorance of *homo faber* complement each other. And, it is an irony of the ideologists of "postmodernity" that, while they may protest against the scientific/technological culture (as their literati indeed do) their own advocacy of the ethic of "anything goes" would also invite the untrammeled advancement of the very scientific/technological hegemony over human life which they pretend to dread.

The main theme in the discourses of Zimmerli concerns the need for an enlargement of our concept of the 'philosophy of science'. Hitherto the philosophy of science concerned itself with the *presuppositions* of scientific theories; now it must also concern itself with the *consequences* of the innovations and projects of sciences/technologies for the quality of human life on earth. It is in the context of such a realistic enlargement of the scope of the philosophy of science that Zimmerli sees, and articulates, the ethical issues involved in the practice of modern science and technology. The "new ethics" —toward which Jonas and Lenk have already contributed—provides a perspective which involves but transcends traditional ethical concerns. The overriding concern here becomes the 'wellbeing' of the person and the society — and the conditions of the relationship between mankind and nature. The *formalist principles* of ethics are not sufficient to answer to this concern; and a set of *teleological principles* must be evoked.

Concerning the dialectical relations between man, technology, and nature — not as static essences but as dynamic essences — a pair of theses by Zimmerli are especially noteworthy here: Firstly, that the ethical principles underlying scientific inquiry (i.e. the respect for truth and concern for the consequences) are also true of, and applicable to, the practice of technology.[52] Secondly, that the new concept of 'responsibility' — ranging from the narrow domain of *technical responsibility* (as the individual craftsman has for the quality of his work) to the wider domain of *social responsibility* (as the scientist/ technologist must have for the impact of their innovations upon the quality of human life) — converts what was regarded to be "external factors" in relation to the subject into what may now be regarded to be "internal factors" in the context of the new ethics.[53]

Even if the burden of decision-making and operations in modern society is shifting from individual persons to organizations, the moral responsibility remains ultimately with the individual persons who make up the teams, groups, and corporations: they are answerable for what they contribute to bringing into our world directly or indirectly.

The closing theme of the discourses of Zimmerli — or what I take to be their closing theme — consists of the concern about the process of the 'decentering' of man, in the context of his own civilization, by the technological culture he himself has created. Decentering represents a subtle degradation of man's place and dignity in his world. It may also signify, tragically, his demise:

> From the crisis of civilization, depicted in the critique of civilization, the vision of the catastrophe of civilization is born, which derives its import and pathos from the state of consciousness, that not only development but also knowledge, and not only knowledge but also practice, and not only practice but also the time, which is allotted to homo sapiens on the Earth, could come to an end.[54]

We must have the "courage to fear", Zimmerli urges, what the future might hold for mankind; the courage to look the present in its face as it were; and the courage to renounce antiquated ways of thinking (materialism and neopositivism) which remain blind to the larger picture.

An episode from *The Shape of Things to Come* by H.G. Wells, depicting technological civilization sometime beyond the year 2000, may be recalled: When the artists and poets of the postmodern megapolis gather in protest before a gigantic tower, where the architects of high technology and social engineers have their offices, an invisible megaphone asks them: "What is your complaint?" The protesters at the base of the tower—decentered, bedwarfed, degraded —answer in unison: "That you make great things to appear small..." By "great things" they mean, of course, great persons and their works representing human ideals. For these rare citizens of the futurist city still cling to the classical ideal of a 'human being' as the miracle of existence. This human degradation, then, will be the last "sin" of the antiplatonic experiment of our age.

The process of the "recovery" of man, i.e. the restoration of his role and dignity as the author of his own culture and civilization, requires the "humanization" of science and technology through the identification of our ideal values — the task of the new philosophy of science.

In the context of the new philosophy of science, the relationship between man and nature must also be redefined. And such a redefinition — proposed by P.W. Taylor in a recent treatise[55] — would involve: (a) the recognition that, owing to man's greater intelligence and power, he must assume the main responsibility for the preservation and wellbeing of the natural world which he inhabits; and (b) the recognition that other living beings have an intrinsic goodness apart from their serving human needs and the human good. And, consequently, even when man must use animals and plants, for the continuation of his own existence, it should be according to the ethical principles of 'proportionality' and 'coexistence' as far as possible. On the basis of these principles, the "anthropocentric viewpoint" is to be replaced by a "biocentric viewpoint". Only in this way may we attain a world-order, Taylor observes, "where human civilization is brought in harmony with nature."[56] For an attitude of "respect for nature" becomes man—as a higher being who ought to harbor a consciousness of, and appreciation for, the natural world which he is destined to share with other living beings.

Toward this new vision of man/nature relationship other authors have contributed: notably Arne Naess who argues for a human commitment to a "deep ecology" (in contrast to the shallow interest in ecology motivated by human egoism); and Van Melsen who argues, beyond the myth of "value neutrality" in science, for the compatibility of scientific objectivity and moral responsibility in the realm of inquiry. These and other worthy contributions are noted in the bibliography of this work; and, instead of dwelling upon them, I turn to another related issue of critical importance.

It would seem improbable that man might attain any measure of utopia in the society without attaining some measure of utopia in its members: for is not the *external utopia* of society determined by the *inner utopia* of individual persons?

This question introduces the issue of the moral development of modern man; and this issue has been addressed by my colleague David Norton recently.[57] He presents the dialectic of the issue as follows: that, while society represents a congerie of individuals who contribute to its culture, the development of the individuals themselves is conditioned by their social milieu. For society is a "sociality of true individuals"; accordingly, the true objective of society is the development of individuals to their highest level of potentiality. And, conversely, the wellbeing and progress of society is determined by the character and the phase of development of its individual members.

Though the individual needs a social milieu for his development, Norton argues, it would be an error to define man as a "political animal" merely (as that Aristotelian designation has been corrupted by contemporary social scientists). Man is essentially a "moral being" whose acts are value-laden. The "apolitical dimension" of man is represented by the dialectic of *eudaimonia* and *dysdaimonia* in the life of the psyche. And the character of man attains concretion through the process of self-actualization of potential virtues — whether pertaining to *techné* or to *areté*. The individual, because he retains an irreducible ontic reality and autonomy, can serve as a resource for the cultural development of society. Self-actualization on the part of the individual becomes both a personal and a social obligation. The obligation, in both cases, is ethical primarily and political secondarily. Thus the ethical dimension transcends the political dimension: as the motive and as the end of activity. The social-entailment of the personal self-actualization is evident:

> We may observe that the division of labor in values-actualization entails, in particular, two cardinal virtues... One of them is the developed

256

capacity in individuals to recognize and appreciate values other than those
with which they as individuals are personally identified... The other is the
readiness to respect others' responsibilities for the values with which they
are identified, as against the impulse to arrogate those responsibilities for
ourselves.[58]

Nor is true 'individualism' to be confused with 'narcissism': for
narcissism — which Norton defines as "a particularly egregious
form of arrested development" in the individual's personal history
— represents but a possible modality, and not the essence, of
individualism.

Writing in the finer tradition of Anglo-American philosophy —
in that tradition which represents a blending of conceptual analysis
and humanistic concern — Norton poses a twofold question before
us (assuming throughout the democratic context of discourse):

"What is good government?" and, insofar as the motive of 'good
government' is the attainment of 'good life' for the society as a whole,
"What is the good life for a human being?"

Norton believes (arguably) that the answer to the primary political
question (What is good government?) is dependent upon the answer
to the primary moral question (What is good life for a human being?).
The latter, in turn, evokes an understanding of what it means to be a
'human being' essentially and not merely existentially. Thus Norton,
by posing these questions, comes to knock at the door of 'higher
humanism'.

Classical liberalism—with its misplaced emphasis upon *realpolitik*
instead of *character and responsibility* — was doomed to fail. Its sociopolitical superstructure lacked ethical underpinnings. Its failure was
guaranteed by its own "moral minimalism": it required of individual
members of society much by way of social cooperation, while requiring
of them little by way of moral development. It is a *philosophy of
eudaimonism* which provides us the perspective from which to
articulate a moral critique of modern society: our democratic society
with its unreconstructed ideology and "ethics of utilitarianism".
"We can capture the eudaimonist perspective," writes Norton, "by
recognizing the moral situation *as* the life of each individual, within
which nothing that appears is devoid of moral meaning."[59] If we
assume the perspective of eudaimonism, then we also recognize that
the moral development of persons is requisite for their constructive

and meaningful roles in society. And this recognition mandates an utopian programme of "moral education" writ large—a programme which would be ameliorative and corrective relative to the "egoistic ethics" of contemporary society.

There has been a "sea-change" in the realm of Anglo-American moral philosophy lately, Norton tells us, as the focus of debates has been shifting *from* the analysis of concepts pertaining to "right conduct" and "moral rules" *to* the elucidation of ideas pertaining to "moral character" and the meaning of "good life". Nor are the two modes of ethical inquiry entirely exclusive of each other: the one mode cannot wholly ignore the relevance of the other mode. For, how could it be expected that a social morality based upon rules/rights be voluntarily and/or earnestly adhered to by members of society who are themselves wanting in moral motivation and/or lacking in some measure of moral aspiration? Ethics, unlike politics, can only be imposed from *within* and not from *without*.

The creative ideas toward cultural reconstruction — which we have reviewed above — are at the cutting edge of praxis philosophy. They represent the call of philosophy to modern man. If modern man does not awaken to the call of philosophy, i.e. the call of his own higher consciousness, then we may envision the eventual and inevitable demise of culture and civilization — *der Untergang des Abenlandes* but in a sense even more tragic than Spengler envisioned it — and therewith the death of the project of modernity entire.

§ 33

Prospect for Utopia

The last question which philosophy poses to mankind is: *Does modern man have an authentic self-image, and ideals, to guide his praxis in the world?* Upon the answer to this question depends the prospect for utopia and the destiny of mankind. Moreover, the kind of ideals that modern man entertains shall determine the kind of world which will transpire in the future.

For 'progress' means going forward, from an actual moment of existence to an ideal moment of existence; and therefore any talk about "progress *without* ideals" would be senseless.

Hence the empirical predictions of the shape of things to come, by the social sciences, cannot serve as a guide to cultural change: for they tell us only what the future *will* be on the basis of past trends; but they do not tell us whether it *ought* to be or not to be. Nor may we blame the natural sciences for the shape of things to come. Natural sciences alone are neither the cause, nor the solution, to the problems of our culture and civilization. Science provides us a map to reality, as it were, and philosophy must provide the compass. Only through the coordination of the two together can we hope to progress toward our utopia.

On the basis of the assumption that philosophical ideology determines the shape of things to come — and on the basis of related arguments in the preceding sections in this chapter — I present some propositions concerning the conditions requisite for a prospective utopia:

(1) *That the education of the "younger generation" have a dual objective: the intellectual development as well as the moral development of the person.*

The education of the younger generation, through their several stages, must involve: (a) the learning of the techniques of some art or science; and (b) the encounter with the dialectic of 'higher values' through literature and philosophy: i.e. the ideal of 'higher humanism' and the ideal of 'reverence for nature' — and, correspondingly a sense of moral responsibility.

As soon as we have stated the purposes of education in these stark terms, the skeptic will protest: "But what is to prevent the schools and the universities, then, from becoming centers of ideological indoctrination?" One may answer—an answer articulated by Bruce Wilshire especially — that all ostensibly "neutral inquiry" is at base an "interested inquiry". I urge the recognition of the dialectical character of education: That, assuming that 'moral conscience' is inherent in the young person (an assumption which earlier we have arguably maintained), then it can be argued that it can be awakened and sharpened by good education or dampened and deadened by poor education. The critical role of education in the moral development of the youth — as demonstrated by the studies of M.J. Langeveld and Lawrence Kohlberg — can no longer be denied. And if the motive of moral education be to cause students to encounter the dialectic of values, then there is no danger of indoctrination. The critics of moral education confuse the development of moral attitude (representing 'moral conscience' and an understanding of the 'moral point of view') with the teaching of moral codes. The former can, and must, be pursued without the latter. Only in this way we may remedy the "moral flabbiness" of contemporary man — of which the humane philosopher William James complained[60] — which is generated by an absence of moral education.

The university (and the high school), above all else, must cause the students to encounter the ideal of 'higher humanism'.

When the university (or the high school) abandons the responsibility for the essentially dialectical character of education — when it turns out mere technicians in the arts and sciences without causing them to encounter the dialectic of higher values (and the ideal of higher humanism) — then it has failed to provide an "education" worthy of the name.

(2) *That the attainment of a measure of 'inner utopia' by individual persons is requisite for the attainment of an 'outer utopia' in society at large.*

Assuming the premise that society consists of a congregation of individual persons, it follows that its level of enlightenment depends upon that of its members. For persons are dynamic centers of social forces — as studies in Gestalt Psychology demonstrate — and, consequently, their level of self-actualization determines the character of their society and its culture. It would be paradoxical to imagine an enlightened society (and culture) with unenlightened individual members. Moreover, since all great contributions to society and its culture are made by the hands of individual men and women, this fundamental truth needs to be underlined in our "democracy" especially.

The *inner* determines the *outer* in this case: therefore the enlightenment of individual persons must precede everything else.

And when we plan to build our utopian city and civilization, let us remember what Heidegger reminded us at the dawn of the contemporary debate concerning human civilization: "Only if we are capable of dwelling, only then can we build."[61]

(3) *That we assume a new system of 'value hierarchy' representing an authentic equilibrium of values: wherein aesthetic/moral values predominate over material/hedonic values.*

The realm of values is wide-ranging admittedly: it comprises aesthetic, moral, hygienic, hedonic, technical, and utilitarian values. But of these some represent *intrinsic values* (e.g. aesthetic/moral values) and others represent *extrinsic values* (e.g. hedonic/utilitarian values). To reverse the order, by placing the latter above or on a par with the former, would generate a paradox: that the lower values would lose their value, for they derive their value from the higher values, resulting in nihilism. But we have discussed the dialectic of values earlier and need not dwell on it here.

The critic of the proposed reconstruction of our 'value system' would ask: "What if the two higher values, the aesthetic and the moral, conflict with each other?" And I answer: There is nothing in the two values to render them *epistemologically* incompatible; and when they appear to conflict with each other *existentially*, then the one or the other has been *warped* already.

Is there, then, an objective *criterion* for value judgment? The criterion of judgment here depends upon the *kind* of value under consideration. Thus — as G.H. Von Wright has argued[62] — there are different criteria of judgment corresponding to the "varieties of goodness": for example, one may judge the goodness of a pocket-knife by a criterion other than that of a glass of wine; or the goodness of a painting by a criterion other than that of a human act; etc. as discussed earlier.

(4) *That the ideal of 'freedom' be complemented, at the personal as well as the societal levels, by the ideal of 'responsibility'.*

Freedom and responsibility are complementary concepts. For freedom without responsibility would be a 'negative freedom': freedom *from* material want or political dominance. But 'positive freedom', which represents the power of the person for purposive behavior and for the actualization of values, involves responsibility.

(And I interpret the concept of 'responsibility' — as Hans Lenk and Walther Zimmerli have earlier — in its extended sense.)

"What is wrong with negative liberty?" Charles Taylor asks — and argues: If the idea of personal freedom derives its importance from the purposive nature of man, then it cannot be defined negatively (i.e. without reference to any purpose) without losing its essential significance.[63]

However, within a given value system, not all purposes are of equal value; and, correspondingly, some kinds of freedom are more important than others. The concept of 'justice', then, may be redefined as the equilibrium of freedoms/responsibilities — and (by implication) as the equilibrium of rights — at any level of social organization.

Too, the very concept of 'democracy' would be ill-conceived if it were to be defined, as it is ordinarily defined, merely in terms of freedom rather than in terms of responsibility as well.

A complete state of freedom (in its negative sense) is 'anarchy': Anarchy is the appropriate lifestyle either in the jungle — or in an ideal state of utopia where negative freedom and positive freedom converge in the conscience of higher beings.

(5) *That the relationship between man and earth — and correspondingly the relationship between culture and nature generally — be not one of antagonism/exploitation but one of symbiosis/harmony.*

We have seen that the *ethical issue* of the limits of the natural rights of man *versus* the natural rights of other living beings (animals and plants) has been introduced by philosophers into the center of contemporary debates. However, for modern man to restore a harmonious relation with the natural world, he must first attain a state of inner enlightenment: he must reform his "philosophy of life". For here "inner utopia" is the key to "outer utopia". And this insight — which has become the theme of a new agenda by Dr. Peter Russell at the Institute of Noetics in London and by Ervin Laszlo at the Vienna Academy for the Study of the Future — is implied by our conception of the role of philosophy as the "cultural healer".

For 'nature' represents a megasystem of order; and any particular system (including human society), whose sustained pattern of behavior runs counter to the natural order, will erode its own niche of survival in the long-run: The last cry of a single disappearing bird, whose special niche is jeopardized by a devastated environment, rings the knell for man's own eventual extinction.

We need to return to the ethos of "reverence" for nature and for life (of which Albert Schweitzer spoke) as the ethos which becomes us as higher beings — and which our intelligence and our knowledge today brings us back to.

Those who hold the reigns of power for making policy, at the regional as well as national levels, can no longer ignore this authentic concern of humanity for their natural environment — they can no longer afford to cater to the mercenary demands of private interest groups — unless they are prepared to face an eventual revolution: they will be overthrown by the "younger generation" which harbors a heightened consciousness of themselves as 'human beings' and their responsibility to their natural homeland.

(6) *That we must redefine our concept of the 'quality of life' to represent the authentic equilibrium of values, and hence, the wellbeing of man writ large.*

Since the authentic equilibrium of values represents the predominance of aesthetic/moral values over material/hedonic values, the "quality of life" varies in direct proportion to it; and, correspondingly, the "misery index" too reflects, not merely economic deprivation, but also the psychological needs of the human being.

I define therefore:

Quality of Life = f (Equilibrium of Values/Misery Index)

The quality of life is a function of the equilibrium of values; and the wellbeing of man, in the context of his natural environment, depends upon his quality of life.

(It may be noted that Kurt Baier defines the 'quality of life' in terms of "optimal-life-advancement" which may be susceptible of "empirical indicators" in some measure;[64] but in order for life-advancement to be "optimal" it must represent an 'equilibrium of values'; therefore, I prefer the definition of the 'quality of life' in terms of the 'equilibrium of values' which is phenomenologically verifiable as a pattern in the life of the individual person.)

To attain an equilibrium of values, in the context of a given culture, requires more than practical intelligence: it requires wisdom. Practical *intelligence* is the capacity to coordinate means and ends; but *wisdom* is the capacity to coordinate praxis and ideals, to envision the "large picture" from a vital perspective, as it were.

To render the realization of the 'equilibrium of values' in human society possible—and therewith to render the prospect for a relatively high 'quality of life' realizable—I make a practical proposition: That "Special Councils" be formed at the national and regional levels — composed of enlightened artists, scientists, economists, physicians, philosophers, and writers—which would have overriding advisory powers and whose recommendations would be honored by the respective governing bodies. Such councils would assure that an equilibrium of values would be maintained and implemented in social policies; and they would assure public policy against the intrusion of private interest groups. In this way a high level of 'quality of life' may be attained; and, correspondingly, the 'misery index' for both man and his natural environment may be reduced. Then, and only then, we moderns may come to experience, what Socrates called — in those passages of rare beauty in the dialogues of Plato in which he presents the dream of reason for the human future — the "good life".

(The above idea appears to me to be more practical than Plato's idea for the formation of "philosopher guardians" as the ruling body in an ideal society: that idea might have been workable in a simpler society in ancient time — or workable in a highly utopian society in a future time — but it would be hardly workable in the middling condition in which our modern societies are.)

Can we evaluate then the relative merits of the states of utopia: that one state of utopia is better or worse than another?

The concept of the 'quality of life' may be taken as the criterion of evaluation for progress toward utopia—or regress toward dystopia. We may say of two societies, when the quality of life in the one appears to be better than that in the other, that its state of utopia is also superior to that of the other. But the 'quality of life', as a multidimensional concept, represents a certain equilibrium of values. And the states of equilibria, in the contexts of different cultures, represent different gestalt-patterns as it were. The quality of life then — and, correspondingly the state of utopia in a society — may be judged and appreciated as a gestalt phenomenon and not by quantitative standards merely.

Concluding Remarks

The philosophical ideas toward the attainment of a possible utopia — articulated in this and in the preceding sections — may contribute to the enlightenment of modern man: they may cause him to reflect over the foundational issues and the horizon issues — and redefine his relation to the world.

"Will the spirit of European man finally understand itself, before its historical hour is gone?" — that is the call of philosophy — by which Hermann Wein hoped to awaken modern man to the challenges of our time.[65]

For, in the aftermath of the forgetfulness of our philosophical roots — and loss of philosophical consciousness — modern man has entered into a new dark age in the twentieth century: the darkening of the world by the spectre of knowledge *without* wisdom. Already, at the dawn of modern science, Leonardo da Vinci had had a nightmare about such a spectre — but our nightmares may be even more immense. And, in the most sophisticated works of science-fiction, we read about the nightmares of mankind concerning the possible shape of things to come. "We are making the future ... and hardly any of us troubled to think what future we were making" — says a character of H.G. Wells in *When the Sleeper Wakes*. And other writers — Huxley, LeGuin, Lessing, Lem, and Zamiatin — have other telling lines, other bitter truths, to tell about our culture and civilization and about the genuine possibility of dystopia.[66] For, philosophically viewed, the imaginary world of authentic science-fiction often acquires a reality which transcends the reality of the lifeworld — and reveals its truths in a more lucid light.

It is not too late to mend our ways: to reconstruct our culture and to redirect the course of our civilization. The ideas presented here —

under the paradigm of "philosophy as higher enlightenment" — may contribute to the awakening of modern man and to the healing of our culture. They would be also intelligible and emotionally acceptable to the "younger generation" who matter in shaping the future.

An author is but a harbinger of truth: not the whole truth is borne by any single author; yet every author derives a special insight from the particular perspective he assumes. My perspective — the philosophy of dialectical realism — envisions philosophy as a 'higher enlightenment'. And even if (as Hegel observed) the Owl of Minerva takes flight in the darkening of the evening — the evening prepares the way for the dawn of another morning. I hope, therefore, that we moderns will attain our enlightenment and make our utopia on earth, ere we arrive inevitably at our Götterdämmerung and pass the point of no return.

NOTES

CHAPTER I

1. For the background of the author's understanding of *philosophical inquiry*, as conceptual elucidation and dialectical reasoning, see my "Critical Reviews" of two World Congresses of Philosophy (1973/1987), *Philosophy Today*, 1976, v. 20, no. 4, and 1982, v. 26, no. 3.

2. Ludwig Wittgenstein, *Tractatus Logico–Philosophicus* (Bilingual Edition), London: Routledge Ltd., 1961, prop. 4.111. But Wittgenstein concludes (paradoxically) that philosophical inquiry does *not* result in "philosophical propositions"—even as the *Tractatus* itself presents a set of philosophical propositions! See, on this point, especially: Gustav Bergmann, "The Glory and the Misery of Ludwig Wittgenstein", in *Logic and Reality*, Madison: University of Wisconsin Press, 1964, pp. 225ff.

3. See Ernst Cassirer, *The Philosophy of the Enlightenment* (translated by F. Koelln & J. Pettegrove), Princeton University Press, 1951, for an exposition of the assumptions of 'historical enlightenment'.

4. Some of the writings of the representatives of the recent realist movements in philosophy are included in the Bibliography of the present work.

5. Immanuel Kant, *Kritik der reinen Vernunft* (hg. R. Schmidt), Hamburg: Meiner Verlag, 1956, B833.

6. Plato, *Phaedo*: 61a and *Republic*: vi/490e, in *Collected Dialogues* (eds. E. Hamilton & H. Cairns), Princeton: Princeton University Press, 1961.

7. Friedrich Nietzsche, *Philosophy and Truth: Selections from the Notebooks (1872–1876)*, edited by D. Braezeale, New York: Humanities Press, 1979, p. 19.

8. Martin Heidegger, *Was ist das—die Philosophie?*, Tübingen: Neske Verlag, 1960 (2 Auflage), pp. 17–18, 29–31, *et passim*.

9. Hermann Wein, *Philosophie als Erfahrungswissenschaft* (hg. Jan M. Broekman), Den Haag: M. Nijhoff, 1965.

10. Anfinn Stigen, "Philosophy as Worldview and Philosophy as Discipline", in *Contemporary Philosophy in Scandinavia* (eds. R.E. Olson & A.M. Paul), Baltimore: Johns Hopkins Press, 1972, pp. 313 and 315.

11. J.N. Findlay, *The Discipline of the Cave*, London: Allen & Unwin Ltd., 1966, pp. 35, 53, 76–77.

268

12. Ervin Laszlo, *Introduction to Systems Philosophy*, New York/ London/Paris: Gordon & Breach Publishers, 1972, p. 6.

13. See Viktor Frankl, "Collective Neurosis of Present Day" in *Psychotherapy and Existentialism*, New York: Simon & Schuster, 1967; and his other publications.

14. For other instances of dilemmas see: C.W.K. Mundle, *A Critique of Linguistic Philosophy*, Oxford: Clarendon Press, 1970; and I.S. Narskii, *Positivismus in Vergangenheit und Gegenwart*, Berlin: Aufbau Verlag, 1967.

15. Immanuel Kant, *Philosophical Correspondence (1759–99)*, edited and translated by Arnulf Zweig, Chicago: University of Chicago Press, 1967, pp. 47–49.

16. Karl Jaspers, "Philosophical Autobiography", in *Philosophy of Karl Jaspers* (edited by P.A. Schilpp), New York: Tudor Publishing Co., 1957, pp. 7–9.

17. Wolfgang Stegmüller, *Hauptströmungen der Gegenwartsphilosophie*, Stuttgart: Kröner Verlag, 1969 (4 Auflage), p. 43 (my translation).

18. Anfinn Stigen, in *Contemporary Philosophy in Scandinavia* (eds. R.E. Olson & A.M. Paul), Baltimore: Johns Hopkins Press, 1972, p. 324.

19. Gustav Bergmann, *Logic and Reality*, Madison: University of Wisconsin Press, 1964, pp. 6, 334–335, *et passim*.

20. See the author's essay, "Conceptual Turn in Recent Philosophy", *Critica*, 1985, v. 17, no. 49, wherein the dialectic of the turn is explained; and the Bibliography of the present work, wherein the writings of the philosophers who have taken the turn are represented.

CHAPTER II

1. See Georg Klaus, *Moderne Logik*, Berlin: Verlag der Wissenschaften, 1973 (7 Auflage), ch. 11; and Maria Kokoszynska, "Definitionen im engeren und weiteren Sinne", *Deutsche Zeitschrift für Philosophie*, 1976, v. 24, no. 12.

2. See Ludwig Wittgenstein, *Tractatus Logico–Philosophicus* (Bilingual Edition), London: Routledge Ltd., 1961, prop. 401–4063, concerning the "picture theory"—and its interpretation by Erik Stenius, *Wittgenstein's Tractatus: A Critical Exposition of its Main Lines of Thought*, Oxford: Blackwell Co., 1960, ch. 6, 7, 10.

3. W.V.O. Quine, *Ways of Paradox and Other Essays*, New York: Random House, 1966, pp. 17, 72, *et passim*, where he presents the case for "truth by convention"—about which we shall say something later.

4. Both Mario Bunge (*Semantics*, Dordrecht/Boston: Reidel Co., 1974, I: ch. 4) and Georg Klaus (*Moderne Logik*, Berlin, 1973, ch. 6) present realistic interpretations of 'concepts'.

5. In this dialectical analysis of meaning the author is indebted to Mikhail Markovič, *Dialectical Theory of Meaning*, Dordrecht/ Boston: Reidel Co., 1984.

6. J.L. Austin, *Philosophical Papers*, Oxford, 1961, p. 55f.

7. Until recently, attacks on 'transcendental arguments' were hardly challenged in the English–language literature: e.g. S. Körner ("Transcendental

Tendencies in Recent Philosophy", *Journal of Philosophy*, 1966, v. 63, no. 19) attempted to reject the *assumption* that "there is only one logic" *in order to* refute the objectivity of transcendental arguments, while his own counter–argument rested upon the *very same assumption* for its *intelligibility*; but see D.C. Berggren, "Transcendental and Dialectical Thinking", in *Principles of Philosophical Reasoning* (ed. J.H. Fetzer), Totowa: R & A Publishers, 1984, pp. 190–226.

8. See I.S. Narskii, "Über die Kategorie des Widerspruchs in der dialektischen Logik", *Deutsche Zeitschrift für Philosophie*, 1967, Nr. 11.

9. The term '*Paradigma*' was introduced into modern philosophy by the German natural philosopher, G.Ch. Lichtenberg (1749–1799); and (as the researches of G.H. Von Wright have revealed) he exerted a decisive influence on Ludwig Wittgenstein: *Philosophical Investigations* (trans. G.E.M. Anscombe), London, 1958 (3rd edition), ¶ 50 *et passim*.

10. Immanuel Kant, *Kritik der reinen Vernunft* (hg. R. Schmidt), Hamburg: Meiner Verlag, 1956, B 103. (my translation)

11. T. Kisiel, "Paradigms", in *Contemporary Philosophy* (ed. G. Flöistad), The Hague: M. Nijhoff, 1982, v. II, p. 95.

12. It is now evident that the 'linguistic philosophers" (at Oxford and else–where) misunderstood, and misrepresented, the character and the role of *concepts* in philosophical inquiry: see C.W.K. Mundle, *A Critique of Linguistic Philosophy*, Oxford: Clarendon Press, 1970: § 8 and § 9 especially; and H. Wein, "Über die Grenzen der Sprachphilosophie", *Zeitschrift für philosophische Forschung*, 1961, vo. 15, no. 1.

CHAPTER III

1. See the redefinition of the concept of 'existence', in the writings of Gustav Bergmann: *Meaning and Existence*, Madison: University of Wisconsin Press, 1959, pp. 91–105; and *Logic and Reality*, Madison: University of Wisconsin Press, 1964, pp. 114f.

2. Reinhardt Grossmann, *The Categorial Structure of the World*, Bloomington: Indiana University Press, 1983, ¶186.

3. See S. Avaliani, *Absoliutnoe i Otnositel'noe*, Tbilisi: Mecniereba, 1980, § 58–61.

4. See Nicolai Hartmann, *Der Aufbau der realen Welt*, Berlin: W. de Gruyter, 1964 (3 Auflage), § 50–54 especially; cf. a recent version of this hypothesis in Mario Bunge, *Method, Model, Matter*, Dordrecht/Boston: Reidel Co., 1973, pp. 160–168.

5. The recent Theory of PRP (which presents properties/relations/ propositions as irreducible entities) proposed by G. Bealer, *Quality and Concept*, Oxford: Clarendon Press, 1982, § 1–5 and 40–44 especially, develops this concept of the 'object'.

6. See M. Bunge, *Semantics: I/II*, Dordrecht/Boston: Reidel Co., 1974, I: ch. 1–3 especially.

7. L. Wittgenstein, *Tractatus Logico–Philosophicus* (Bilingual Edition), Lon–

270

don: Routledge Ltd., 1961, prop. 4021 and 4011–4014.

8. Wittgenstein, *ibidem*, prop. 2161–218
9. Wittgenstein, *ibidem*, prop. 4121–4122
10. Erik Stenius, *Wittgenstein's Tractatus: A Critical Exposition of its Main Lines of Thought*, Oxford: Blackwell, 1960, p. 99.
11. See M. Bunge (*Semantics: I/II/1974*), D. Føllesdal ("Reference and Sense" / *Actes du XVIIe Congrès Mondial de Philosophie*, Montréal / 1983), and E. Stenius ("Linguistic Structure and the Structure of Experience" in *Critical Essays /1972*) especially.
12. Y. Gauthier, *Théorétiques*, Montréal: Le Préambule, 1982, p. 242.

CHAPTER IV

1. Aristotle, *Metaphysics* (translated w. commentaries by H.G. Apostle), Bloomington: Indiana University Press, 1966, E: 1026a–b.
2. See especially Franz Brentano, *On the Several Senses of Being in Aristotle* (edited and translated from the German by Rolf George), Berkeley: University of California Press, 1975.
3. Martin Heidegger, *Being and Time* (trans. JM & ER), London: SCM Press, 1962, p. H 1.
4. Heidegger, *ibidem*, p. H7.
5. See Augustin Basave, *Tratado de Metafísica*, Mexico: Editorial Limusa, 1982, ch. 1–3, 7–9, 12–14, and 26 especially. (The quotation is from pages 40–41, translated for the author by Dr. Barbara Gaddy of Transylvania University.)
6. See Josef Seifert, *Back to Things in Themselves: A Phenomenological Foundation for Classical Realism*, London: Routledge Ltd, 1987.
7. Seifert, *ibidem*, p. 2.
8. Seifert, *ibidem*, p. 13.
9. See Ash Gobár, "*Erklärung* and *Begründung* in Kantian Epistemology", *Journal of Philosophical Research*, 1989, XIV, April Issue; cf. Erik Stenius, "On Kant's Distinction between Phenomena and Noumena", in *Critical Studies*, Amsterdam: North Holland Publishing Co., 1972.
10. "Correspondence with Professor Josef Seifert", Internationale Adademie für Philosophie, dated 29 Oktober 1992.
11. Reinhardt Grossmann, *Categorial Structure of the World*, Bloomington: Indiana University Press, 1983, pp. 9–10.
12. Jeanne Hersch, "Karl Jaspers en quête de l'être", *Philosophie et Culture* (edited by FISP), Montréal: Editions Montmorency, 1986, p. 380.
13. B.C. Van Fraassen, *Scientific Image*, Oxford: Clarendon Press, 1980, pp. 4, 202, *et passim*.
14. L. Bonjour, *Structure of Empirical Knowledge*, Cambridge: Harvard University Press, 1985, pp. 3, 79, 81, *et passim*.
15. This reconstruction of the Kantian argument is based upon an earlier study: see A. Gobár, "*Erklärung* and *Begründung* in Kantian Epistemology", *Journal of Philosophical Research*, 1989, XIV, April Issue; but compare

E. Stenius, "On Kant's Distinction between Phenomena and Noumena", in *Critical Essays*, Amsterdam: North Holland Publishing Co., 1972.

16. See Immanuel Kant, *Kritik der reinen Vernunft* (hg. R. Schmidt), Hamburg: Meiner Verlag, 1956, B20, wherein the question of the "synthetic propositions a priori" is posed as the "proper task" of pure reason.

17. See Gustav Bergmann, "Synthetic A Priori", in *Logic and Reality*, Madison: University of Wisconsin Press, 1964, pp. 272ff.

18. Kant, *Kritik der reinen Vernunft*, A253/B307.

19. N. Hartmann, *Der Aufbau der realen Welt: Grundriss der allgemeinen Kategorienlehre*, Berlin: W. de Gruyter Co., 1964 (3 Auflage), § 24.

20. Hartmann, *ibidem*, § 42 (my translation).

21. E.-W. Platzeck, "Das Reden vom 'Sein'", *Zeitschrift für philosophische Forschung*, 1970, v. 24, no. 3, p. 317.

22. The epistemological significance of this case is discussed by H. Heidelberger, "Professor Chisholm's Epistemic Principles", Noûs, 1969, v. 3, pp. 73–82.

23. A. Gobár, *Philosophic Foundations of Genetic/Gestalt Psychology*, The Hague: Martinus Nijhoff, 1968, p. 244 (my editing).

24. See G. Bergmann, "General Ontology", in *Realism: A Critique of Brentano and Meinong*, Madison: University of Wisconsin Press, 1967, pp. 3–124.

25. G. Bergmann, "Generality and Existence", *Theoria*, 1962, v. 28, no. 1, p. 9–10.

26. G. Bergmann, "Ineffability, Ontology, and Method", in *Logic and Reality*, Madison: University of Wisconsin Press, 1964, pp. 57–58.

27. G.W. Leibniz, "Letter to Burcher de Volder" (1704), in *Philosophical Papers and Letters* (translated & edited by L.E. Loemker), Dordrecht: Reidel Co., 1969, p. 536.

28. Leibniz, "Letter to John Bernoulli" (1699), *ibidem*, p. 513.

29. In distinguishing 'ideal possibility' and 'empirical possibility' I have followed Nicolai Hartmann, *Möglichkeit und Wirklichkeit*, Berlin: W. de Gruyter Co., 1965 (3 Auflage).

30. David Weissman, *Eternal Possibilities: A Neutral Ground for Meaning and Existence*, Carbondale: Southern Illinois University Press, 1977, p. 156.

CHAPTER V

1. In a pair of essays I have discussed the *question of truth* and sketched the 'hypothesis of the types of truth': see "A Critique of Current Theories of Truth", *Philosophical Inquiry*, 1982, vo. 4, no. 1; and "Are There Types of Truth?", *International Philosophical Quarterly*, 1987, v. 27, no. 3. I thank the editor of *IPQ* for permission to recast portions of the latter here.

2. See A.J. Ayer, *Language, Truth and Logic*, Oxford, 1946 (2nd edition), pp. 88–89; supported by P.F. Strawson, "Truth", in *Philosophy and Analysis* (ed. Margaret MacDonald), Oxford, 1955; and J.L. Austin's (*Philosophical Papers*, Oxford, 1961, pp. 132 ff) lukewarm reservations.

3. Among modern philosophers it was Franz Brentano who first envisioned 'truth' as a multifaceted concept: see his brief but telling discussion of the

"relation between truth and reality" in *The True and the Evident* (edited by Oskar Kraus and translated by R.M. Chisholm), New York: Humanities Press, 1966, pp. 22–25 and 126–132 especially. But, more recently, Mario Bunge has discussed the question of the 'kinds of truth' in *Semantics II*, Dordrecht/Boston: Reidel Co., 1974, pp. 82–105, more thoroughly than anyone excepting this author.

4. Ludwig Wittgenstein, *Philosophische Bemerkungen* (hg. R. Rhees), Frankfurt a.M.: Suhrkamp Verlag, 1964, ¶ 228 (my translation).

5. An adequate formalization of the hypothesis of the "degrees of truth" is presented by Mario Bunge, *Semantics II*, Dordrecht/Boston: Reidel Co., 1974, pp. 105–123.

6. We owe the definition of 'logico–mathematical truth' to Alfred Tarski: "The Concept of Truth in Formalized Languages", in *Logic, Semantics, Metamathematics*, Oxford, 1956, § 8.

7. For an elaboration of these points the reader is referred to: Henri Poincaré, *La science et l'hypothèse*, Paris: Flammarion & Cie, 1943, ch. 1–4; L.E.J. Brouwer, "Consciousness, Philosophy, and Mathematics", in *Akten des X Internationalen Kongresses für Philosophie*, Amsterdam, 1948; and Johannes Witt–Hansen, *On Generalization in the Mathematical and the Historical Sciences*, Copenhagen: University of Copenhagen, 1963.

8. See Walter Watson, *The Architectonics of Meaning: Foundations of the New Pluralism*, Albany: SUNY Press, 1985.

9. My coining of the designation "marginal philosophy" was inspired by the self–ascription of Jacques Derrida, in *Margins of Philosophy* (University of Chicago Press, 1982, p. xxiii): "Gnawing away at the border . . . (these writings) are to blur the line which separates a text from its controlled margin." An earlier version of the present discussion appeared in the *Zeitschrift für philosophische Forschung* (1991/Band 45/H3). I thank the *Zeitschrift* for permission to make extensive use of the material here.

10. Ludwig Wittgenstein, *Tractatus Logico–Philosophicus* (Bilingual Edition), London: Routledge Ltd., 1961, prop. 406 and 653; and *Philosophical Investigations* (trans. B.E.M. Anscombe), London: Macmillan Co., 1958, ¶ 373.

11. See John Wisdom, "Philosophical Perplexity", in *Linguistic Turn* (ed. R. Rorty), Chicago: University of Chicago Press, 1964, p. 101; J.L. Austin, *Philosophical Papers*, Oxford, 1961, p. 101; A.J. Ayer, *Philosophy and Language* (Inaugural Lecture), Oxford, 1960, p. 30 *et passim*.

12. Hermann Wein, "Über die Grenzen der Sprachphilosophie", *Zeitschrift für philosophische Forschung*, 1861, XV, no. 1.

13. C.W.K. Mundle, *A Critique of Linguistic Philosophy*, Oxford: Clarendon Press, 1970, pp. 91–109 and 110–119 especially.

14. See N. Goodman, *Structure of Appearance*, Indianapolis: Bobbs–Merrill Co., 1966 (2nd edition); and the critical commentary by Jules Vuillemin, *La Logique et le monde sensible*, Paris: Flammarion & Cie, 1971, § 59–65.

15. N. Goodman, *Problems and Projects*, Indianapolis: Bobbs–Merrill Co., 1972, p. 31.

16. W.V.O. Quine, *Ontological Relativity and Other Essays*, New York: Columbia University Press, 1969, p. 57.

17. This point is forcefully argued by Dagfinn Føllesdal, "Reference and Sense", *Actes du XVIIe Congrès Mondial de Philosophie*, Montréal: Editions Montmorency, 1986, pp. 229–239.

18. R. Rorty, *Philosophy and the Mirror of Nature*, Princeton: Princeton University Press, 1980, p. 315.

19. Rorty, *ibidem*, pp. 372, 373, 377, *et passim*.

20. See Kai Nielsen, "Philosophy as Critical Theory", *Proceedings of the American Philosophical Association*, 1987, v. 61, no. 1; and Peter Unger, *Philosophical Relativity*, Minneapolis: University of Minnesota Press, 1984.

21. In a recent essay, "Erklärung and Begründung in Kantian Epistemology", *Journal of Philosophical Research*, 1989, XIV, April Issue, I have articulated (with the valuable work of Wolfgang Stegmüller as the background) a modern interpretation of foundational theory by reconstructing the Kantian transcendental argument.

22. Jacques Derrida, *Margins of Philosophy* (translation of *Marges de la philosophie* by A. Bass), Chicago: University of Chicago Press, 1982, p. x.

23. Karl Jaspers, *Von der Wahrheit*, München: Piper Verlag, 1958, p. 1054; cf. Martin Heidegger, *Was ist das—die Philosophie?*, Pfullingen: Neske Verlag, 1960 (wherein he depicts the role of 'philosophy' as leading the psyche along the path toward the 'truth' concerning the 'being of beings').

24. In three World Congresses of Philosophy recently—in Vienna (1968), in Varna (1973), in Montréal (1983)—the 'realist philosophers' challenged the 'linguistic philosophers' with the question: "Do the actual problems of the world and of life disappear by merely changing our ways of talking about them?"—and there was no answer (see my reviews: "The Big Question and the XV World Congress of Philosophy", and its sequel, "Some Big Questions Revisited", in *Philosophy Today*, 1976, v. 20, no. 4, and *ibidem*, 1982, v. 26, no. 3). Too, in the recent Inter–American Congress of Philosophy (Guadalajara/ Mexico 1985) Professor L. Zea, articulating the sentiment of critical South American philosophers, denounced the trivialization of 'philosophical inquiry' on the grounds that it implied the trivialization of the "social responsibility" of philosophers in the face of the problems of contemporary civilization (see the "Special Report" in the *Proceedings of the APA*, 1986, v. 59, no. 5). More recently, the larger question of the role and future of 'philosophy'—against the challenge of the marginal philosophers in the English–speaking world—became the object of debate in the American Philosophical Association: and therein Professor Alasdair MacIntyre raised the supercritical question " . . . whether (under the circumstances) it was worth going on doing philosophy . . . " (see *Proceedings of the APA*: "Symposium on the Future of Philosophy", 1987, v. 61, no. 1).

25. René Descartes, *Philosophical Works* (trans. Elizabeth Haldane), New York: Dover Publications, 1955, I: pp. 145–146.

26. Albert Einstein, *Mein Weltbild* (hg. C. Seelig), Frankfurt a.Main: Ullstein Verlag, 1982 (revised edition), p. 159 (my translation).

27. G.E. Moore, "Proof of an External World", in *Studies in Philosophy* (British Academy Lectures), London: Oxford University Press, 1966.

28. Bertrand Russell, *Our Knowledge of the External World*, London: Allen & Unwin Ltd., 1926, pp. 80, 71—105, 115, *et passim*.

29. Albert Einstein, "Remarks on Bertrand Russell's Theory of Knowledge", in *Philosophy of Bertrand Russell* (ed. P.A. Schilpp), LaSalle: Open Court, 1944, pp. 277–291.

30. Albert Einstein, "Physics and Reality", in *Ideas and Opinions* (edited & translated by Sonja Bargmann), New York: Crown Publishers, 1954, p. 291.

31. E. Schrödinger, *Mind and Matter*, London: Cambridge University Press, 1964: "Mystery of Sensual Qualities", pp. 176–177.

CHAPTER VI

1. I am indebted, in my interpretation of Heraclitus, to M. Heidegger and E. Fink, *Seminar on Heraclitus* (1966–67), translated by C.H. Seibert, Montgomery: University of Alabama Press, 1959.

2. Leibniz expressed these ideas in his letters to Arnauld and to Clarke: see *Philosophical Papers and Letters* (ed. L.E. Loemker), Dordrecht: Reidel Publishing Co., pp. 337, 677, 691, *et passim*.

3. Albert Einsten, *Mein Weltbild* (hg. Carl Seelig), Frankfurt am Main: Ullstein Verlag, 1982, p. 116 (my translation).

4. Henry Margenau, "Some Integrative Principles of Modern Physics", in *Integrative Principles of Modern Thought* (ed. H. Margenau), New York/London/Paris: Gordon & Breach Publishers, 1972, pp. 45–68.

5. I. Velikovsky, *Worlds in Collision*, New York: Macmillan Co., 1950, p. 379.

6. Camille Flammarion, *Astronomy* (edited by Gabrielle Flammarion and André Danjon for the Societé Française d'Astronomie), American Edition: Simon & Schuster, 1964, p. 153.

7. See J.P. Crutchfield a.o., "Chaos", *Scientific American*, December 1986, pp. 46–57; and James Gleick, *Chaos*, New York: Viking Press, 1987, pp. 291, 294, *et passim*.

8. Henri Poincaré, "Chance", in *Science and Method* (trans. F. Maitland), New York: Dover Publications, 1952, pp. 81f.

9. In my exposition of these points in the Theory of Relativity, I have relied, besides the *essays* of Albert Einstein referred to below, upon Max Born's treatise, *Einstein's Theory of Relativity*, New York: Dover Publications, 1965 (revised edition), and upon S. Weinberg, *Gravitation and Cosmology: Principles and Applications of the General Theory of Relativity*, New York: Wiley Press, 1972.

10. A. Einstein, "Zur Method der theoretischen Physik", in *Mein Weltbilt*, p. 117 (my translation).

11. A. Einstein, "Geometrie and Erfahrung", in *Mein Weltbild*, pp. 119–124.

12. Henry Margenau, "Einstein's Conception of Reality", in *Albert Einstein: Philosopher–Scientist* (ed. P.A. Schilpp), LaSalle: Open Court, 1970.

13. A. Einstein, "Reply to Criticisms", *ibidem*, pp. 666, 671–673 (my emphasis).

14. See Niels Bohr, "Discussions with Einstein on Epistemological Problems in Atomic Physics", in *Albert Einstein: Philosopher–Scientist*, pp. 201–241 and

666–676; and Einstein's article, "Quanten–Mechanik und Wirklichkeit", *Dialectica*, 1948, v. 2, pp. 320–324.

15. Georges Lemaître, *Primeval Atom: An Essay on Cosmogony* (with "Preface" by Professor F. Gonseth), New York: Van Nostrand Co., 1950, pp. 161–163.

16. The "cosmological constant" was introduced by Einstein (in a paper titled "Kosmologische Betrachtungen zur allgemeinen Relativitatstheorie"/ Preussische Akademie der Wissenschaften/1917), but it was subsequently dropped as being redundant, on the assumption of a "static universe". But that assumption has now been challenged, and Lemaître has reintroduced the "cosmological constant". Writes Lemaître: "Even if the introduction of the cosmological constant (according to Einstein) 'has lost its sole original justification' it remains true that Einstein has shown that the structure of his equations quite naturally allows for the presence of a second constant besides the gravitational one . . . The history of science provides many instances of discoveries which have been made for reasons which are no longer considered satisfactory . . . the discovery of the *cosmological constant* is such a case." See Georges Lemaître, "Cosmological Constant", in *Albert Einstein: Scientist–Philosopher* (ed. P.A. Schilpp), p. 443; and *Primeval Atom: An Essay on Cosmogony*, pp. 64f and 96f.

17. Albert Szent–Gyorgyi, *Bioenergetics*, New York: Academic Press, 1963.

18. See E.N. Parker, "Magnetic Fields in the Cosmos", *Science*, 1983, August Issue.

19. Gerard de Vaucouleurs, "The Case for a Hierarchical Cosmology", *Science*, 1970, February Issue, p. 1207.

20. See Ervin Laszlo, *Introduction to Systems Philosophy*, New York/London/ Paris: Gordon & Breach Co., 1972, Chapter 4, for an elaboration of the theory of natural systems.

21. Compare Immanuel Kant, *Der einzig mögliche Beweisgrund zu einer Demonstration des Daseins Gottes: The One Possible Basis for a Demonstration of the Existence of God* (Bilingual Edition), edited by G. Treash, New York: Abaris Books, 1979, Part I especially.

CHAPTER VII

1. Two other contemporary thinkers speak of the 'psyche' in similar ways: J.C. Eccles, *The Human Psyche*, Berlin: Springer Verlag, 1980; and Stanislav Grof, *The Holotropic Mind*, San Francisco: Harper Collins Inc., 1992.

2. See Carl Sagan, "Cosmic Calendar", in *Dragons of Eden*, New York: Random House, 1977, pp. 13–17.

3. E.S. Ayensu & P. Whitfield (eds.) *Rhythms of Life*, New York: Crown Publishers, 1982, p. 15.

4. Pierre Teilhard de Chardin, *The Phenomenon of Man* (with "Introduction" by Julian Huxley), New York: Harper & Row Publishers, 1961, p. 137.

5. A.I. Oparin, *Life: Its Nature, Origin, and Development* (translated from the Russian by Ann Synge), New York: Academic Press, 1964, pp. 6, 7–8, 202, and 1–37.

6. Oparin, *ibidem*, p. 8.

7. Erwin Schrödinger, *What is Life? (and Mind and Matter)*, London: Cambridge University Press, 1967 (3rd edition), pp. 73 and 72–91.

8. See the idealist hypothesis of J.B.S. Haldane, *Causes of Evolution*, Ithaca: Cornell University Press, 1966; and the materialist hypothesis of J.J.C. Smart, "Materialism", *Journal of Philosophy*, 1963, v. 22, October Issue.

9. Bjorn Kurtén, *Not From the Apes: A History of Man's Origins and Evolution*, New York: Columbia University Press, 1984, pp. 121, 129, *et passim*; cf. B. Rensch, *HomoSapiens: From Man to Demigod*, New York: Columbia University Press, 1972.

10. Konrad Lorenz, *Behind the Mirror*, New York: Harcourt–Brace–Jovanovich, 1977, p. 170.

11. Julian Huxley, *Essays of a Humanist*, New York: Harper & Row Publishers, 1964, pp. 35f and 53f.

12. Herbert Hörz, *Materie und Bewusstsein*, Berlin: Dietz Verlag, 1965, pp. 126, 128, *et passim*. (My translation)

13. See our exposition of the *hypothesis of ontological strata* in sections § 7 and § 18 of the present work.

14. Nicolai Hartmann, *New Ways of Ontology* (trans. R.C. Kuhn), Westport: Greenwood Press, 1975, pp. 120–121 (My emphases); cf. *Das Problem des geistigen Seins*, Berlin: W. de Gruyter, 1962 (3 Auflage).

15. See A. Gobár,, "*Erklärung* and *Begründung* in Kantian Epistemology", *Journal of Philosophical Research, XIV*, 1989, April Issue.

16. It is noteworthy that Kant himself was careful to distinguish the "positive sense" and the "negative sense" of the *noumenon*: see *Kritik der reinen Vernunft* (hg. R. Schmidt) Hamburg: Verlag Felix Meiner, 1956, B307–B309; and Erik Stenius, "On Kant's Distinction between Phenomena and Noumena", in *Critical Essays*, Amsterdam: North Holland Publishing Co., 1972.

17. Kant, *Kritik der reinen Vernunft*, A155/B194.

18. See the recently discovered fragment of Kant: "*Vom Inneren Sinne*" (On Inner Sense), edited by R. Brandt and W. Stark, and published with parallel English translation in *International Philosophical Quarterly*, 1989, v. 29, no. 3, p. 253.

19. Kant, *Critique of Practical Reason* (translated by L.W. Beck), Chicago: University of Chicago Press, 1949, p. 258, *et passim*.

20. The theme of the moral education of the individual person, and the moral evolution of mankind, is discussed by Kant in *Anthropology from a Pragmatic Point of View* (translated by Mary Gregor), The Hague: Martinus Nijhoff, 1974.

21. Some arguments can be adduced in support of this hypothetical answer: see J.R. Silber, "The Moral Good and the Natural Good in Kant's Ethics", *Review of Metaphysics*, 1982, v. 36, no. 2.

22. Immanuel Kant, "What is Enlightenment?", in *Selections* (edited by L.W. Beck), New York: Macmillan Publishing Co., 1988, p. 465.

23. Jacques Taminiaux, *La nostalgie de la Grèce à l'aube de l'idéalisme allemand*, La Haye: Martinus Nijhoff, 1967, p. 94.

24.   See Gilbert Ryle, *The Concept of Mind*, London: Hutchinson House, 1955.

25.   Two Scandinavian philosophers have written incisive critiques of Ryle's philosophical behaviorism: Anfinn Stigen ("Concept of Mind", *Danish Yearbook of Philosophy*, 1965, II) and Dagfinn Føllesdal ("Intentionality and Behaviorism", *Proceedings of the VI International Congress of Logic, Methodology, and Philosophy of Science*, Hannover/Amsterdam: North Holland Publishing Co., 1982) – both remaining rather neglected in the English–speaking world.

26.   W.V.O. Quine, *Ways of Paradox and Other Essays*, New York: Random House, 1966, p. 215f; cf. *Word and Object*, Cambridge: MIT Press, 1960.

27.   The arguments against philosophical behaviorism articulated here are based upon entirely new inquiries and do not reiterate anything from my earlier work: *Philosophic Foundations of Genetic/Gestalt Psychology*, The Hague: Martinus Nijhoff, 1968.

28.   See C.G. Jung, *Memories, Dreams, Reflections*, (edited by Aniela Jaffé), New York: Vintage Books, 1963, pp. 158–161.

29.   Viktor E. Frankl, *Psychotherapy and Existentialism: Selected Papers on Logotherapy*, New York: Simon & Schuster, 1967, articles I, VI, and X especially.

30.   S. Freud, *Letters of Sigmund Freud* (trans. J. & T. Stern) New York: Basic Books, 1960, p. 436.

31.   V. E. Frankl, *Psychotherapy and Existentialism*, p. 72; *and* "Psychotherapy and Philosophy", *Philosophy Today*, 1961, v. 5, pp. 59–64.

32.   J–P. Sartre, "La Transcendance de l'ego", *Recherches philosophiques*, 1936–37, t. 6, pp. 65–122 (English Version 1957).

33.   J–P. Sartre, *L'Être et le Néant*, Paris, 1943, pp. 708–721.

34.   Georg Lukács, *Die Gegenwartsbedeutung des kritischen Realismus (Essays über Realismus)*, Berlin: Luchterhand Verlag, 1971, p. 477. (My translation)

35.   Franz Brentano: *Nachlass* (hg. Oskar Kraus) – quoted by R.M. Chisholm in *Philosophy of Brentano* (edited by Linda MacAlister), NJ: Humanities Press, 1976, pp. 98–99. (My translation)

36.   Franz Brentano, *The True and the Evident* (edited by R.M. Chisholm), New York: Humanities Press, 1965, p. 126.

37.   David Hume, *Treatise of Human Nature* (edited by L.A. Selby–Bigge), Oxford, 1896, I:iv.

38.   Ludwig Wittgenstein, *Tractatus Logico–Philosophicus* (Bilingual Edition) London: Routledge Ltd., 1961, prop. 5.541–5.542.

39.   The expression "primary being" is used by Professor Edward Pols in his essay, "The Ontology of the Rational Agent", *Review of Metaphysics*, 1980, v. 33, no. 4, wherein he presents an ontological argument in its favor.

40.   The distinction between the two kinds of expressions was introduced by Anfinn Stigen, "Two Kinds of Expressions: Makings–Known and Manifestations", *Akten des XIV Internationalen Kongresses für Philosophie*, Wien: Herder Verlag, 1968, Bd. I.

41.   See Gustav Bergmann, "Intentionality", in *Meaning and Existence*, Madison: University of Wisconsin Press, 1968, pp. 19f.

42.   See Reinhardt Grossmann, *The Structure of Mind*, Madison: University of

278

Wisconsin Press, 1965, pp. 14–28, for this useful distinction and for other arguments in favor of introspection.

43. Wittgenstein's counter–argument, *Philosophical Investigations* (Bilingual Edition), London: Basil Blackwell, 1958 (3rd edition), ¶ 258, notwithstanding.

44. Wittgenstein, *ibidem*, ¶ 243 and ¶ 239.

45. See G.H. VonWright, "Explanation and Understanding of Action", *Revue internationale de philosophie*, 1981, v. 35, pp. 128ff for the distinction between the kinds of reasons as motives for action.

46. See J.R. Searle, "Minds, Brains, Programs", *Behavioral and Brain Sciences*, 1980, v. 3, September Issue.

47. See J.J.C. Smart, "Materialism", *Journal of Philosophy*, 1963, v. 22; *and* Herbert Feigl, "Some Crucial Issues of Mind–Body Monism", *Synthese*, 1971, v. 22.

48. See Wolfgang Köhler & Hans Wallach, "Figural Aftereffects", *Proceedings of the American Philosophical Society*, 1944, v. 88; and Henri Piéron, *Sensations* (translated by M.H. Pirenne), New Haven: Yale University Press, 1952.

49. Henri Bergson, *Matière et mémoire*, Paris: Presses Universitaires de France, 1959 (60e édition), pp. 157 and 147–198.

50. J.C. Eccles, *The Human Mystery*, Berlin/New York: Springer Verlag, 1979, pp. 214 and 217. (My emphasis)

51. J.C. Eccles, *The Human Psyche*, Berlin/New York: Springer Verlag, 1980, pp. 49–50. (My emphasis)

52. Compare John Searle, *Intentionality*, Cambridge: Cambridge University Press, 1983, pp. 269–270.

53. David L. Norton, *Personal Destinies: A Philosophy of Ethical Individualism*, Princeton: Princeton University Press, 1976, pp. 8–10.

54. I am in agreement on this point with R.B. Brandt, "Epistemological Status of Memory Beliefs", *Philosophical Review*, 1955, v. 64, no. 1.

55. See H.H. Price, "Survival and the Idea of Another World", in *Brain and Mind* (edited by J.R. Smythies), London: Routledge Ltd., 1965, pp. 1–24, and "Commentaries", *ibidem*, pp. 24–33.

56. J.N. Findlay, *Transcendence of the Cave* (Gifford Lecturer at the University of St. Andrews 1965–66), London: Allen & Unwin Ltd., 1967, pp. 163–167.

57. Stanislav Grof (& H.Z. Bennett), *The Holotropic Mind*, San Francisco: Harper Collins Inc., 1992, p. 103.

58. Grof, *ibidem*, p. 118.

59. Among this literature are noteworthy: the recent empirical evidence presented by Dr. M.B. Sabom, *Recollections of Death: A Medical Investigation*, New York: Harper & Row, 1983; the earlier empirical evidence presented by F.W.H. Myers, *Human Personality and its Survival of Bodily Death* (edited by S. Smith), Hyde Park: University Books Inc., 1961; and the critical review of "psychical phenomena" by Professor C.D. Broad, *Lectures on Psychical Research*, London: Routledge Ltd., 1962.

CHAPTER VIII

1. See Martin Heidegger, *Wegmarken*, Frankfürt am Main: Klostermann Verlag, 1978, pp. 321–327 *et passim*.

2. Leo Tolstoy, *A Confession and What I Believe* (translated by A. Maude), London: Oxford University Press, 1974, pp. 15–16.

3. Loren Eiseley, *The Unexpected Universe*, New York: HBJ Publishers, 1969, pp. 49f.

4. An eminent modern biologist, Adolf Portmann, has proposed an agenda for reforming biology along this line: see "Was bedeutet uns die lebendige Gestalt?", *Göttinger Blätter für Kultur und Erziehung*, 1966, v. 6, no. 1.

5. Benedict de Spinoza, "Letter to Henry Oldenburg" (No. 32) in *Philosophical Works* (edited by R.H.M. Elwes), New York: Dover Publications, 1955, II, p. 291.

6. William James, "Is Life Worth Living?" in *Essays on Faith and Morals* (edited by R.B. Perry), New York: Longmans–Green Co., 1942, p. 31.

7. Friedrich Nietzsche, "Nachgelassene Schriften", in *Werke* (hg. Gerhard Stenzel), Salzburg: Bergland Verlag, 1950, Bd. I, pp. 908, 914. (My translation)

8. William Shakespeare, *Tragedies* (edited by Peter Alexander), New York: Heritage Press, 1959: *Macbeth* V/5.

9. Feodor Dostoevsky, *Notes from the Underground* (translated by David Magarshack), New York: Modern Library, 1950.

10. Bernard Williams, *Ethics and the Limits of Philosophy*, Cambridge: Harvard University Press, 1985, p. 22.

11. See, for example, the phenomenological description of good and evil by Richard Taylor (*Good and Evil: A New Direction*, New York: Macmillan Co., 1970, pp. 205–222 especially) which presents two sets of cases: depicting the "sense of malice" and the "sense of compassion" respectively.

12. See Lawrence Kohlberg, *Philosophy of Moral Development: Moral Stages and the Idea of Justice*, Philadelphia: Harper & Row Publishers, 1981, pp. 116–122 especially.

13. This true story was reported in the newspaper, *Leader*, Lexington/KY, 7 December 1968.

14. G.H. Von Wright, *The Varieties of Goodness*, London: Routledge Ltd., 1963, p. 18.

15. Kurt Baier, *The Moral Point of View: A Rational Basis of Ethics*, Ithaca: Cornell University Press, 1958, pp. 298–320.

16. William James, "The Sick Soul", in *Varieties of Religious Experience*, New York: Modern Library, 1902/1950, p. 147.

17. See William James, *ibidem*, pp. 163f; and Miklos Veto, "La notion du mal selon Simone Weil", *Akten des XIV Internationalen Kongresses für Philosophie*, Wien: Herder Verlag, 1969, Bd. III.

18. Wassily Kandinsky, *Concerning the Spiritual in Art* (translated by M.T.H. Sadler), New York: Dover Publications, 1977, pp. 7–8.

19. Georg Lukács, "Healthy or Sick Art?" in *Writer and Critic* (edited by A.D. Kahn), New York: Merlin Press, 1970, pp. 106–108; cf. *Realism in Our Time*

(edited by George Steiner), New York: Harper & Row, 1971.

20.   Recently, J.N. Findlay has written a sophisticated interpretation of the meaning and import of the Cave Image in a pair of studies: *Discipline of the Cave* and *Transcendence of the Cave*, London: Allen & Unwin Ltd., 1966/1967.

21.   In a previous study – "The Significance of the Mountain Image for the Philosophy of Life", *Philosophy Today*, 1981, v. 25, no 2/4 – I have explored the *phenomenological aspect* of the Mountain Image; the present exposition is mainly concerned with its *dialectical aspect*. I thank the editor for permission to make use of this material here.

22.   Friedrich Nietzsche, *Also Sprach Zarathustra*, in *Werke* (hg. Gerhard Stenzel), Salzburg: Bergland Verlag, 1950, Bd. I, p. 423. (My translation)

23.   Martin Heidegger, *Being and Time* (translated by JM & ER), London: SCM Press, 1962, H220.

24.   Viktor Frankl, "Self–Transcendence as a Human Phenomenon", *Journal of Humanistic Psychology*, 1966, Fall Issue, p. 97.

25.   Friedrich Nietzsche, *Also Sprach Zarathustra*, p. 530–531. (My translation)

26.   Michael Novak, *Experience of Nothingness*, New York: Harper & Row Publishers, 1970, p. 15 *et passim*.

27.   "Letter" from Doctor A. H. Gobár (M.D.), the Author's brother, dated 5 December 1980.

CHAPTER IX

1.   Ernst Cassirer, *The Philosophy of the Enlightenment* (translated by F.C.A. Koelln & J.P. Pettegrove), Princeton: Princeton University Press, 1951, p. 278.

2.   John Dewey, *Reconstruction in Philosophy*, Boston: Beacon Press, 1948 (enlarged edition), pp. 171–173 (my emphases).

3.   Georg Lukács, "The Ideal of the Harmonious Man in Bourgeois Aesthetics", in *Writer and Critic* (edited and translated by A.D. Kahn), London: Merlin Press, 1970, pp. 100–101.

4.   The commonplace humanist theses which were codified in the *Humanist Manifesto* (1933), and signed by John Dewey and others, were later revised and refined by other humanists in a second *Humanist Manifesto* (1973). Both documents, assuming an amoral framework of discourse, represent the ideology of 'bourgeois humanism'. The concluding proposition of the latter is: "What more daring a goal for humankind than for each person to become, in ideal as well as practice, *a citizen of world community*" (p. 23) — an hortatory proposition which says nothing about what is, and ought to be, at issue: *the moral character of man*. See *Humanist Manifestos I and II* (edited by Paul Kurtz), Buffalo: Prometheus Books, 1973.

5.   Two contemporary philosophers have argued for the recognition of 'human dignity' along this line: Hans Reiner, *Der Sinn unseres Daseins*, Tübingen: Niemeyer Verlag, 1960; and Gela Bandzeladze, *Über den Begriff der Menschenwürde*, Giessen, 1987.

6. David L. Norton, *Personal Destinies: A Philosophy of Ethical Individualism*, Princeton: Princeton University Press, 1976, p. 16.

7. Hermann Hesse, *My Belief: Essays on Art and Life* (edited by Th. Ziolkowski), New York: FSG–Noonday Press, 1975, pp. 134–135; and the ramifications of this theme may be seen in the *Hesse–Mann Letters* (translated by R. Mannheim & Wg. Sauerlander), New York: Harper & Row Publishers, 1975.

8. Friedrich Nietzsche, *The Will to Power* (translated by W. Kaufmann & R. Hollingdale), New York: Random House, 1967, ¶ 34–37.

9. Nietzsche, *ibidem*, ¶ 42–43.

10. Friedrich Nietzsche, *On the Advantage and Disadvantage of History for Life* (translated by Peter Preuss), Cambridge: Hackett Publishers, 1980, pp. 24–25.

11. Friedrich Nietzsche, *Philosophy and Truth* (Selections from the Notebooks of the Early 1870s), edited and translated by Daniel Breazeale, New Jersey: Humanities Press, 1979, p. 5.

12. Nietzsche, *ibidem*, p. 65.

13. Friedrich Nietzsche, *Also Sprach Zarathustra* (hg. G. Stenzel) in *Werke*, Salzburg: Bergland Verlag, 1950, Bd. I, pp. 305, 307, 312 (my translation).

14. Martin Heidegger, "Who is Nietzsche's Zarathustra?" (translated by Bernd Magnus), *Review of Mataphysics*, 1967, v. 20, pp. 412–417.

15. Martin Heidegger, *Was heisst Denken?*, Tübingen: Niemeyer Verlag, 1961, Teil II.

16. Martin Heidegger, *Being and Time* (translated by J. Macquarrie & E. Robinson), New York: Harper & Row Publishers, 1962, p. H198.

17. Heidegger, *ibidem*, p. H277.

18. Martin Heidegger, "Letter on Humanism", in *Basic Writings* (edited by D.F. Krell), New York: Harper & Row Publishers, 1977, pp. 217–219.

19. Nishida–Kitaró, *Fundamental Problems of Philosophy* (translated by D.A. Dilworth) Tokyo: Sophia University, 1970, p. 254.

20. See Th. W. Adorno & M. Horkheimer, *Dialektik der Aufklärung*, Frankfürt a.M., 1969.

21. See Martin Heidegger, *Nietzsche: I–II*, Pfullingen: Neske Verlag, 1961, containing two major chapters on "Nihilismus" and its philosophical critique.

22. See Immanuel Kant, "What is Enlightenment?", in *Selections* (edited by L.W. Beck), New York: Macmillan Co., 1988.

23. The internal problems of the ideology of postmodernity have been handled insightfully by Jürgen Habermas, *The Philosophical Discourse of Modernity* (translated by F. Lawrence), Cambridge: MIT Press, 1987; and Albrecht Wellmer, *Zur Dialektik von Moderne und Postmoderne*, Frankfürt, a.M., 1985.

24. Jürgen Habermas, "Modernity *versus* Postmodernity", *New German Critique*, 1981, v. 22, p. 9 *et passim*.

25. Habermas, *The Philosophical Discourse of Modernity*, p. 128.

26. Habermas, *ibidem*, pp. 348–353.

27. The theme of the "Paradigm of the Island" will be the basis of an independent literary work by this writer in the future.

28. W.W. Bähr (hg.) *Wo Stehen Wir Heute?* Gutersloh: Bertelsmann Verlag, 1962, p. 245.

29. The destructive effects of human civilization upon the natural environment have been illustrated by: Andrew Goudie, *The Human Impact: Man's Role in Environmental Change*, Cambridge: MIT Press, 1982; and more recently and poignantly by Al Gore, *Earth in the Balance*, Boston: Houghton–Mifflin Co., 1992.

30. "Geneva Statement on Nuclear Disarmament", by the Representatives of the Christian Churches of USA and USSR, Geneva, 27–29 March 1979.

31. See Karl Marx, *Economic and Philosophic Manuscripts (1844)*, in *Selected Works of Marx and Engels*, Moscow: Progress Publishers, 1969, I–II.

32. Friedrich Nietzsche, *The Will to Power* (translated by W. Kaufmann & R. Hollingdale), New York: Random House, 1967, ¶ 617.

33. Viktor E. Frankl, "Collective Neurosis of the Present Day", in *Psychotherapy and Existentialism*, New York: Simon & Schuster, 1967, p. 122 and pp. 183–197 (wherein a Report on the Purpose–in–Life Test or PIL is presented).

34. An earlier version of the argument of praxis philosophy was presented by the author in the XVIIth World Congress of Philosophy (Montreal/1983): See Ash Gobár, "Philosophy and the Shape of Things to Come", *Philosophie et Culture*, Montréal, 1986: IVB.

35. I came to be convinced of the complementarity of the two criteria for the rational choice of an ideology as a result of discussions with my colleague Professor D.R.C. Reed of Wittenberg University.

36. See Nelli Motrošilova, "Le rôle de la philosophie en actualisation des idées et valeurs culturelles", *XVIIe Congrès Mondial de Philosophie*, Montréal, 1983, IIC.

37. Fernand Dumont, "Mutations culturelles et philosophie", *Philosophie et Culture* (edited by FISP), Montréal: Editions Montmorency, 1986.

38. See W. Ch. Zimmerli, "Folgenabschätzung in Technik und Wissenschaft als Aufgabe der Philosophie", in *Wechselwirkungen zwischen Naturwissenschaft und Technik und der Gegenwartsphilosophie* (hg. DVT), Berlin, 1981.

39. Josef Seifert, *Von Nutzen und Nutzlosigkeit der Philosophie für Gesellschaft und Politik*, Schaan: Internationale Akademie für Philosophie, Fürstentum Liechtenstein, 1988, p. 29 (my translation).

40. Ervin Laszlo, *Introduction to Systems Philosophy: Toward a New Paradigm of Contemporary Thought*, New York/London/Paris: Gordon & Breach Science Publishers, 1972, pp. 283–285.

41. Laszlo, *ibidem*, p. 287.

42. See Hans Jonas, *The Imperative of Responsibility: In Search of an Ethics for a Technological Age*, Chicago: University of Chicago Press, 1983.

43. Jonas, *ibidem*, p. 36.

44. Jonas, *ibidem*, pp. 176ff.

45. See Hans Lenk, *Pragmatische Vernunft*, Stuttgart, 1979.

46. See Hans Lenk, *Zur Sozialphilosophie der Technik*, Frankfürt a.M., 1982.

47. See Robert Audi, *Practical Reasoning*, London: Routledge Ltd., 1989, Part II; and "The Architecture of Reason", *Proceedings of the American Philosophical*

Association, 1988, v. 62, no. 1.

48. Hans Lenk, "On Extended Responsibility and Increased Technological Power", in *Philosophy and Technology* (edited by P. Durbin & F. Rapp), Dordrecht: Reidel Co., 1983, p. 196.

49. Hans Lenk, "Against Technocratic Hubris and Positivistic Idealism: Anti–Naturalistic and Anti–Realistic Fallacies in Describing Man's Relationship to Nature", *Southwest Philosophy Review*, 1988, v. 4, no. 1, p. 91.

50. Walther Ch. Zimmerli, "Das antiplatonische Experiment: Bemerkungen zur technologischen Postmoderne", in *Technologisches Zeitalter oder Postmoderne* (hg. W. Ch. Zimmerli), München: Fink Verlag, 1988, pp. 19–20.

51. Zimmerli, *ibidem*, p. 25.

52. W. Ch. Zimmerli, "Ethik der Wissenschaften als Ethik der Technologie", in *Wozu Wissenschaftsphilosophie?* (hg. P. Hoyningen–Huene & Gertrude Hirsch), Berlin: W. de Gruyter, 1988, pp. 391ff.

53. W. Ch. Zimmerli, "Variety in Technology — Unity in Responsibility?", in *Technology and Contemporary Life* (edited by P.T. Durbin), Dordrecht/Boston: Reidel Co., 1988, pp. 284ff.

54. W. Ch. Zimmerli, "Humanizierung der Wissenschaft durch Zivilisationskritik", *Zeitschrift für Wissenschaftsforschung*, 1988, Bd. 4/H.2, p. 238 (my translation).

55. P.W. Taylor, *Respect for Nature*, Princeton: Princeton University Press, 1986.

56. Taylor, *ibidem*, p. 308.

57. See David L. Norton, *Democracy and Moral Development*, Berkeley: University of California Press, 1991.

58. Norton, *ibidem*, p. 85.

59. Norton, *ibidem*, p. xi.

60. William James (in a "Letter" to H.G. Wells) complained of the "moral flabbiness born of the exclusive worship of the bitch–goddess Success... with the squalid cash interpretation put on the word Success..." See: *Letters* (edited by Henry James), Boston: Atlantic Monthly Press, 1920, II: p. 260.

61. Martin Heidegger, "Building, Dwelling, Thinking", in *Basic Writings* (edited by D.F. Krell), New York: Harper & Row Publishers, 1977, p. 338.

62. See G.H. Von Wright, *The Varieties of Goodness*, London: Routledge Ltd, 1963.

63. Charles Taylor, *Philosophy and the Human Sciences*, London: Cambridge University Press, 1985, pp. 211ff.

64. Kurt Baier, "Toward a Definition of Quality of Life", in *Environmental Spectrum* (edited by R.O. Clarke & P.C. List), New York: Van Nostrand Co., 1974, pp. 62–68.

65. Hermann Wein, *Philosophie als Erfahrungswissenschaft* (hg. Jan Brockman), Den Haag: Martinus Nijhoff, 1965, p. 43.

66. The critiques of civilization implicit in serious science–fiction — as articulated in K. Amis: *New Maps of Hell* (1960), M. Hillegas: *The Future as Nightmare* (1967), and H.L. Berger: *Science Fiction and the New Dark Age* (1976) — hold a philosophical lesson for our time.

BIBLIOGRAPHY

A listing of books and articles which have contributed, directly or indirectly, toward the emergence of the idea of philosophy as higher enlightenment; as well as some recent critical works in European and Anglo-American philosophies.

Abbagnano, N. *Possibilità e libertà*, Turino, 1965; cf. *Critical Existentialism* (edited by Nino Langiulli), Garden City: Doubleday Anchor Books, 1969.

Adorno, Th. W. *Negative Dialectics* (translated by E.B. Ashton), New York: Seabury Press, 1973.

Ameriks, K. *Kant's Theory of Mind: An Analysis of the Paralogisms of Pure Reason*, Oxford: Clarendon Press, 1982.

Anguelov, S. "Pour une approche complexe dans la connaissance de l'homme", *Etudes philosophiques*, 1975, v. 21, no. 3.

Apel, K.-O. *Transformation der Philosophie*, Frankfurt am Main: Suhrkamp Verlag, 1973, I-II.

Aquila, R.E. *Intentionality: A Study of Mental Acts*, University Park: Pennsylvania State University Press, 1977.

Aristotle. *Metaphysics* (translated & annotated by H.G. Apostle), Bloomington: Indiana University Press, 1966.

Arnheim, R. *Entropy and Art: An Essay on Disorder and Order*, Berkeley: University of California Press, 1971.

Audi, R. *Practical Reasoning*, London: Routledge Ltd., 1989.

_____. "Justification, Truth, and Reliability", *Philosophy & Phenomenological Research*, 1988, v. 49, no. 1.

Avaliani, S. *Absoliutnoe i otnositel'noe* (Absolute and Relative: Relations Between Science and Philosophy); and *Priroda znanija i tsennosti* (Nature of Knowledge and Value), Tbilisi: Mecniereba, 1980/1989.

Bachelard, G. *La philosophie du non: Eassai d'une philosophie du nouvel esprit scientifique*. Paris: Presses Universitaires de France, 1962 (3e édition).

Baier, K. *The Moral Point of View: A Rational Basis of Ethics*, Ithaca: Cornell University Press, 1958.

_____. "Towards a Definition of 'Quality of Life'", in *Environmental Spectrum* (eds.

286

R. Clarke & P. List), New York: Van Nostrand Co., 1973.

Basave, A.F. del V. *Tratado de Metafísica: Teoría de la "Habencia"*, Mexico: Editorial Limusa, 1982.

Bealer, G. *Quality and Concept*, Oxford: Clarendon Press, 1982.

Beck, L.W. *A Commentary on Kant's Critique of Practical Reason*, Chicago: University of Chicago Press, 1960.

Beloff, J. "The Identity Hypothesis", in *Brain and Mind* (edited by J. R. Smythies), London: Routledge Ltd., 1965.

Bergmann, G. "Intentionality", in *Semantica* (Archivio di Filosofia), Roma: Bocca, 1955.

_____. "Russell's Examination of Leibniz Examined", *Philosophy of Science*, 1956, v. 23, no. 2.

_____. "Physics and Ontology", *Philosophy of Science*, 1961, v. 28, no. 1.

_____. "La Gloria e la Miseria di Ludwig Wittgenstein", *Rivista di Filosofia*, 196, v. 52, no. 3.

_____. *Metaphysics of Logical Positivism*, Madison: University of Wisconsin Press, 1954/1967.

_____. *Meaning and Existence*, Madison: University of Wisconsin Press, 1959/1968.

_____. *Logic and Reality*, Madison: University of Wisconsin Press, 1964.

_____. *Realism: A Critique of Brentano and Meinong*, Madison: University of Wisconsin Press, 1967.

_____. *Ontological Turn: Studies in the Philosophy of Gustav Bergmann* (edited by M.S. Gram & E.D. Klemke), Iowa City: University of Iowa Press, 1974.

Bergson, H. *Matière et mémoire*, Paris: Presses Universitaires de France, 1959 (60e édition).

Bočorišvili, A.T. *Teoretičeskie osnovy filosofskoj antropologii* (Theoretical Foundations of Philosophical Anthropology), Tbilisi: Akademija Nauk, 1976.

Boethius, A.M.S. *De Consolatione Philosophiae* (edited by Dr. Weinberger), Vienna: Corpus Scriptorum Latinorum, 1934.

Bohr, N. "Discussion with Einstein on Epistemological Programs in Atomic Physics", in *Albert Einstein: Philosopher-Scientist* (edited by P.A. Schilpp), LaSalle: Open Court, 1949/1970.

Bondi, H. *Cosmology*, London: Cambridge University Press, 1960 (2nd edition).

Bonjour, L.A. *The Structure of Empirical Knowledge*, Cambridge: Harvard University Press, 1985.

Bonsack, F. "Invariance as a Criterion of Reality", *Dialectica*, 1977, v. 31, no. 4.

Brand, G. *Die Lebenswelt*, Berlin: W. De Gruyter, 1971.

Brandt, R.B. "Epistemological Status of Memory Beliefs", *Philosophical Review*, 1955, v. 64, no. 1.

Brentano, F. *Von der mannigfachen Bedeutung des Seienden nach Aristoteles*, Frieburg/1862, republished Darmstadt/1960.

_____. *The True and the Evident* (edited by R.M. Chisholm), New York: Humanities Press, 1965.

_____. *Origin of our Knowledge of Right and Wrong* (edited by R.M. Chisholm), New York: Humanities Press, 1969.

Brouwer, L.E.J. "Consciousness, Philosophy, and Mathematics", *Akten des X Internationalen Kongresses für Philosophie*, Amsterdam, 1948.

Brown, Thomas (of Edinburgh). *Lectures on the Philosophy of the Human Mind*, Edinburgh/1820 & Philadelphia/1824, I-IV.

Bunge, M. *Method, Model, and Matter*, Dordrecht/Boston: Reidel Co., 1973.

_____. *Semantics: I/II*, Dordrecht/Boston: Reidel Co., 1974.

_____. *Ontology: I/II*, Dordrecht/Boston: Reidel Co., 1977/1979.

_____. "The GST Challenge to the Classical Philosophies of Science", *International Journal of General Systems*, 1977, v. 4, no. 1.

Calogero, G. *Filosofia del dialogo*, Milano, 1962.

Casey, E.S. *Remembering: A Phenomenological Study*, Bloomington: Indiana University Press, 1986.

Cassirer, E. *Philosophy of the Enlightenment*, Princeton: Princeton University Press, 1951.

_____. *The Individual and the Cosmos in Renaissance Philosophy*, London: Basil Blackwell, 1963.

Casteñeda, H.-N. "On the Logic of Self-Knowledge", *Noûs*, 1967, v. 1, no. 1.

Chisholm, R.M. *Theory of Knowledge*, Englewood Cliffs: Prentice-Hall Inc., 1966/1977. (cf. Heidelberger, H. "Professor Chisholm's Epistemic Principles", *Noûs*, 1969, v. 3, no. 2).

_____. "*Verstehen*: The Epistemological Question", in *Foundations of Knowing*, Minneapolis: University of Minnesota Press, 1982.

_____. (ed.) *Realism and the Background of Phenomenology*, Independence: Ridgeview Press, 1960.

Chomsky, N. *Language and Mind*, New York: HBJ Publishers, 1972 (revised edition).

Clarke, C.J.S. "Quantum Theory and Cosmology", *Philosophy of Science*, 1974, v. 41, no. 4.

Cleve, F.M. *The Giants of Pre-Sophistic Greek Philosophy* (A Problematic Reconstruction of Their Thought), The Hague: Martinus Nijhoff, 1965, I-II.

Colodny, R.G. (ed.) *Mind and Cosmos*, Pittsburgh: University of Pittsburgh Press, 1966.

Croce, B. *Ce qui est vivant et ce qui est mort de la philosophie de Hegel* (traduit par H. Buriot), Paris: Giard & Brière, 1910.

_____. *Philosophy, Poetry, History* (translated by Cecil Sprigge), London: Oxford University Press, 1966.

DeGrood, D., Riepe, D., Somerville, J. (eds.) *Radical Currents in Contemporary Philosophy*, St. Louis: W.H. Green Inc., 1971.

Derrida, J. *Margins of Philosophy* (translation of *Marges de la philosophie* by A. Bass), Chicago: University of Chicago Press, 1982.

Descartes, R. *Philosophical Works* (translated by Elizabeth Haldane), New York: Dover Publications, 1955, I-II.

DeSitter, W. *Kosmos*, Cambridge: Harvard University Press, 1932.

Dretske, F.I. *Seeing and Knowing*, Chicago: University of Chicago Press, 1969.

Ducasse, C.J. "Minds, Matter, and Bodies", in *Brain and Mind* (edited by J.R. Smythies), London: Routledge Ltd., 1965.

Dumont, F. "Mutations culturelles et philosophie", *Philosophie et Culture* (ed. FISP), Montréal: Editions Montmorency, 1986.

Eccles, J.C. *The Human Psyche* (Gifford Lectures at the University of Edinburgh 1978-79), Berlin/New York: Springer Verlag, 1980.

288

_____. *The Human Mystery* (Gifford Lectures at the University of Edinburgh 1977-78), Berlin/New York: Springer Verlag, 1979.

Einstein, A. *Mein Weltbild* (hg. Carl Seelig), Frankfurt am Main: Ullstein Verlag, 1935/1982.

_____. "Quanten-Mechanik und Wirklichkeit", *Dialectica*, 1948, v. 2, 320-324.

_____. "Physics and Reality", in *Ideas and Opinions* (edited by C. Seelig & S. Bargmann), New York: Crown Publishers, 1954.

Eiseley, L. *The Unexpected Universe*, New York: HBJ Publishers, 1969.

_____. *Notebooks* (edited by K. Heuer), Boston: Little-Brown Co., 1987.

Elek, T. "Epistemological Concepts of Albert Einstein and the Philosophical Aspects of the Theory of Relativity", in *Studia Philosophica Academiae Scientiarum Hungaricae*, Budapest: Akadémiai Kiadó, 1963, III.

Ey, H. *Consciousness: A Phenomenological Study of Being Conscious and Becoming Conscious* (translated by J.H. Flödstrom), Bloomington: Indiana University Press, 1978.

Feigl, H. "Some Crucial Issues of Mind-Body Monism", *Synthese*, 1971, v. 22, nos. 3/4.

Ferré, F. *Philosophy of Technology*, Englewood Cliffs: Prentice-Hall Inc., 1988.

Findlay, J.N. *The Discipline of the Cave & The Transcendence of the Cave*, London: Allen and Unwin Ltd., 1966/1967, I-II.

Føllesdal, D. "Intentionality and Behaviorism", *Proceedings of the VI International Congress of Logic, Methodology, and Philosophy of Science*, Amsterdam: North Holland Publishing Co., 1982.

_____. "Reference and Sense", *Proceedings of XVIIth World Congress of Philosophy*, Montréal: Editions Montmorency, 1983/1986.

Frankl, V.E. *Psychotherapy and Existentialism: Selected Papers on Logotherapy*, New York: Simon & Schuster, 1967.

Gabriel, L. *Integrale Logik: Die Wahrheit des Ganzen*, Wien/Freiburg: Herder Verlag, 1965.

Gadamer, H.-G. *Dialogue and Dialectic*, New Haven: Yale University Press, 1980.

Ganovski, S. "Philosophical Conception of Man", *Proceedings of the XV World Congress of Philosophy*, Varna/1973, I/3.

Gauthier, Y. *Théorétiques (Pour une philosophie constructiviste des sciences)*, Montréal: Le Préambule Inc., 1982.

Georgescu-Roegen, N. *Entropy Law and the Economic Process*, Cambridge: Harvard University Press, 1971.

Gleick, J. *Chaos*, New York: Viking Press, 1984.

Gobár, A. "Abstract Entities in the Natural Sciences", *Akten des XIV Internationalen Kongresses für Philosophie*, Vienna: Herder Verlag, 1968, Band I.

_____. "Phenomenology of William James", *Proceedings of the American Philosophical Society*, 1970, v. 114, no. 4.

_____. "Big Questions and the XV World Congress of Philosophy", *Philosophy Today*, 1976, v. 20, no. 4; and "Some Big Questions Revisited", *ibidem*, 1982, v. 26, no. 3.

_____. "Significance of the Mountain Image for the Philosophy of Life", *Philosophy Today*, 1981, v. 25, no. 2.

_____. "A Critique of Current Theories of Truth", *Philosophical Inquiry*, 1982, v. 4, no. 1.

_____. "Conceptual Turn in Recent Philosophy", *Critica*, 1985, v. 17, no. 49.

_____. "Philosophy and the Shape of Things to Come", *Philosophie et Culture* (Proceedings of the XVIII World Congress of Philosophy), Montréal, 1983/1986.

_____. "Are There Types of Truth?", *International Philosophical Quarterly*, 1987, v. 27, no. 3.

_____. "*Erklärung* and *Begründung* in Kantian Epistemology", *Journal of Philosophical Research*, XIV, 1989, April Issue.

_____. "'Truth' and Marginal Philosophers", *Zeitschrift für philosophische Forschung*, 1991, Bd. 45, H.3.

_____. "Philosophy of Science Revisited: Dialectical Realism" (translated into Georgian/Russian by Professor S. Avaliani), *Journal of the Academy of Sciences, Georgia*, 1991.

Gogiberidze, M. *Teorija otnositel'nosti Einstejna i ee filosofskie osnovy* (Einstein's Theory of Relativity and its Philosophical Foundations), in Filosofskie Sočine nija edited by G. Tevzadze, Tbilisi: TGU, 1970.

Gonseth, F. "Les mathématiques et la réalité", *Dialectica*, 1975, v. 29, no. 1

Gore, A. *Earth in the Balance: Ecology and the Human Spirit*, Boston: Houghton-Mifflin Co., 1992.

Goudie, A. *The Human Impact: Man's Role in Environmental Change*, Cambridge: MIT Press, 1982.

Gram, M.S. *The Transcendental Turn: The Foundation of Kant's Idealism*, Tallahassee: University of Florida Press, 1984.

Grene, Marjorie (ed.) *Interpretations of Life and Mind*, New York: Humanities Press, 1971.

Grof, S. *The Holotropic Mind*, San Francisco: Harper Collins Publishers, 1992.

Grossmann, R. *Categorial Structure of the World*, Bloomington: Indiana University Press, 1982.

Grünbaum, A. *Philosophical Problems of Space and Time*, Dordrecht/Boston: Reidel Co., 1973.

Habermas, J. *The Philosophical Discourse of Modernity* (translated by F. Lawrence), Cambridge: MIT Press, 1987.

Harré, R. *Varieties of Realism: A Rationale for the Natural Sciences*, London: Basil Blackwell, 1986.

Hartmann, K. "On Taking the Transcendental Turn", *Review of Metaphysics*, 1966, v. 20, no. 2.

Hartmann, N. *Das Problem des geistigen Seins*, Berlin: W. de Gruyter Co., 1962 (3 Auflage).

_____. *Der Aufbau der realen Welt: Grundriss der allgemeinen Kategorienlehre*, Berlin: W. de Gruyter Co., 1964 (3 Auflage).

_____. *Möglichkeit und Wirklichkeit*, Berlin: W. de Gruyter Co., 1965 (3 Auflage).

_____. *New Ways of Ontology* (translated by R.C. Kuhn), Westport: Greenwood Press, 1975.

Hegel, G.W.F. *Phenomenology of Spirit* (edited by J.N. Findlay and translated by A.V. Miller), Oxford: Clarendon Press, 1977.

Heidegger, M. *Was ist das—die Philosophie?* Pfullingen: Neske Verlag, 1960.

_____. *Being and Time* (translation of *Sein und Zeit* by JM & ER), London: SCM Press, 1962.

_____. "Letter on Humanism", in *Basic Writings* (edited by D.F. Krell), New York:

Harper & Row Publishers, 1977.

_____. *Wegmarken*, Frankfürt am Main: Klostermann Verlag, 1978.

Heinemann, F.H. "Was ist lebendig und was ist tot in der Existenzphilosophie?" *Zeitschrift für philosophische Forschung*, 1950-1951, v. 5. no. 1.

Hersch, Jeanne. "Remarques sur les réformes éducatives et la condition humaine", *Studia Philosophica*, 1974, v. 34, pp. 1-9.

_____. & René Poirier (eds.) *Entretiens sur le temps*, Paris/LaHaye: Mouton Cie, 1967.

Hesse, Mary B. *Revolutions and Reconstructions in the Philosophy of Science*, Bloomington: Indiana University Press, 1980.

Hochberg, H. "On Being and Being Presented", *Philosophy of Science*, 1965, v. 32, no. 2.

Howard, V.A. "Do Anthropologists Become Moral Relativists by Mistake?", *Inquiry*, 1969, v. 11, no. 2.

Hörz, H. *Atome, Kausalität, Quantensprunge*, Berlin: VEB Verlag der Wissenschaften, 1964.

_____. *Materie und Bewusstsein*, Berlin: VEB Verlag der Wissenschaften, 1965.

_____. *Der dialektische Determinismus in Natur und Gesellschaft*, Berlin: VEB Verlag der Wissenschaften, 1971.

Hume, D. *An Enquiry Concerning Human Understanding* (1777) (edited by L.A. Selby-Bigge), Oxford: Clarendon Press, 1957.

Ingarden, R. *Erlebnis, Kunstwerk, und Wert*, Tübingen: Niemeyer Verlag, 1969.

Jackson, F. "Epiphenomenal Qualia", *Philosophical Quarterly*, 1982, v. 32, no. 127.

Jaeger, W. *Paideia: Ideals of Greek Culture* (translated by Gilbert Highet), London: Oxford University Press, 1945, I-III.

James, Wm. *Essays in Radical Empiricism & A Pluralistic Universe* (edited by R.B. Perry), New York: Longmans-Green Co., 1945.

_____. *Essays on Faith and Morals* (edited by R.B. Perry), New York: Longmans-Green Co., 1949.

Jaspers, K. *Von Der Wahrheit*, München: Piper Verlag, 1958.

_____. *Vernunft und Existenz*, München: Piper Verlag, 1960 (5 Auflage).

Jonas, H. *The Imperative of Responsibility: In Search of an Ethics for a Technological Age*, Chicago: University of Chicago Press, 1983.

Jung, C.G. *Memoirs, Dreams, Reflections* (edited by Aniela Jaffé), New York: Vintage Books, 1989.

Kakabadze, Z.M. Čelovek kak filsosfskaja problema (Man as a Philosophical Problem), Tbilisi: Mecniereba, 1970.

Kant, I. *Kritik der reinen Vernunft* (hg. R. Schmidt), Hamburg: Meiner Verlag, 1956.

_____. *Critique of Practical Reason* (translated and edited by L.W. Beck), Chicago: University of Chicago Press, 1949.

_____. "What is Enlightenment?", in *Selected Writings* (edited by L.W. Beck), New York: Macmillan Publishing Co., 1988.

_____. *Philosophical Correspondence* (1759-1799), edited and translated by Arnulf Zweig, Chicago: University of Chicago Press, 1967.

Kedrov, B.M. "Philosophy as a General Science", *Voprosy Filosofii*, 1962, Nr. 5/6.

Klaus, G. *Moderne Logik*, Berlin: VEB Verlag der Wissenschaften, 1973 (7 Auflage).

Kohlberg, L. *Philosophy of Moral Development: Moral Stages and the Idea of Justice*, Philadelphia: Harper & Row Publishers, 1981.

Köhler, Wg. *Gestalt Psychology*, New York: Liveright Co., 1947/1970/1992.

Kopnin, P.V. *Gipoteza i znanie deistvitel'nosti* (Hypothesis and the Knowledge of Reality), Kiev: KGU, 1962.

Koyré, A. *From the Closed World to the Infinite Universe*, Baltimore: Johns Hopkins Press, 1957.

Lakatos, I. *Science and Hypothesis*, Boston/Dordrecht: Reidel Co., 1981.

Landgrebe, L. *Der Weg der Phänomenologie*, Gutersloh: G.M. Verlagshaus, 1969 (3 Auflage).

Lange, O. *Wholes and Parts: A General Theory of Systems Behavior*, Oxford: Pergamon Press, 1965.

Langer, S.K. *Philosophy in a New Key: A Study in the Symbolism of Reason, Rite, and Art*, Cambridge: Harvard University Press, 1957 (3rd edition).

_____. *Mind: An Essay on Human Feeling*, Baltimore: Johns Hopkins Press, 1967-1972, I-II.

Langeveld, M.J. *Einführung in die theoretische Pädagogik*, Stuttgart: Klett Verlag, 1978.

Laszlo, E. *Introduction to Systems Philosophy*, London/Paris/New York: Gordon & Breach Publishers, 1972.

_____. *System, Structure, and Experience*, London/Paris/New York: Gordon & Breach Publishers, 1969.

Leibniz, G.W. *Philosophical Papers & Letters* (translated and edited by E.L. Loemker), Dordrecht/Boston: Reidel Co., 1969.

Lemaître, G.E. *Primeval Atom: An Essay on Cosmogony* (Preface by F. Gonseth), New York: Van Nostrand Co., 1950.

Lenk, H. *Zur Sozialphilosophie der Technik*, Frankfürt a.M., 1982.

_____. "On Extended Responsibility and Increased Technological Power", *Philosophy and Technology* (eds. P. Durbin & F. Rapp), Boston/Dordrecht: Reidel Co., 1983.

_____. "Against Technocratic Hubris and Positivistic Idealism: Anti- Naturalistic and Anti-Realistic Fallacies in Describing Man's Relationship to Nature", *Southwest Philosophy Review*, 1988, v. 4, nos. 1-2.

Leonard, H.S. "Interrogatives, Imperatives, Truth, Falsity, and Lies", *Philosophy of Science*, 1959, v. 26, no. 3.

Linke, P.F. *Niedergangserscheinungen in der Philosophie der Gegenwart*, München/ Basel: Reinhardt Verlag, 1961.

Lorenz, K. *Behind the Mirror*, London: Methuen Co., 1977.

Lukács, G. *Essays über Realismus*, Berlin: Luchterhand Verlag, 1971.

_____. *Realism in Our Time* (edited by George Steiner), New York: Harper & Row Publishers, 1971.

MacIntyre, A. *Against Self-Images of the Age: Essays on Ideology and Philosophy*, Notre Dame: University of Notre Dame Press, 1978.

_____. *After Virtue: A Study in Moral Theory*, Notre Dame: University of Notre Dame Press, 1984 (2nd edition).

McMullin, E. (ed.) *Concept of Matter in Modern Philosophy*, Notre Dame: University of Notre Dame Press, 1978.

Magnus, B. *Nietzsche's Existential Imperative*, Bloomington: Indiana University Press, 1978.

Margenau, H. (ed.) *Integrative Principles of Modern Thought*, New York/ London/ Paris: Gordon & Breach Publishers, 1972.

Marković, M. *Dialectical Theory of Meaning*, Dordrecht/Boston: Reidel Co., 1984.

Maxwell, N. *From Knowledge to Wisdom: A Revolution in the Aims and Methods of Science*, Oxford: Basil Blackwell, 1984.

Meinong, A. "Gegenstandstheorie", in *Realism and the Background of Phenomenology* (edited by R.M. Chisholm), Independence: Ridgeview Press, 1960.

Motrošilvoa, Nelli. "Le rôle de la philosophie en actualisation des idées et valeurs culturelles", *XVIIe Congrès Mondial de Philosophie*, Montréal, 1983, IIC.

Mundle, C.W.K. *A Critique of Linguistic Philosophy*, Oxford: Clarendon Press, 1970.

Naess, A. *Scepticism*, London: Routledge Ltd., 1968. 1972.

_____. "The Deep Ecological Movement: Some Philosophical Aspects", *Philosophical Inquiry*, 1986, v. 8, no. 1-2.

Narskii, I.S. "Critique of Neopositivism's Doctrine on the Criterion of Truth", *Voprosy Filosofii*, 1960, Nr. 9.

_____. "Critique of the Basic Principles of the Theory of Knowledge of Neopositivism", *Voprosy Filosofii*, 1962, Nr. 1.

_____. "Über die Kategorie des Wiederspruchs in der dialektischen Logik", *Deutsche Zeitschrift für Philosophie*, 1967, Nr. 11.

Nelson, L. *Progress and Regress in Philosophy* (edited by J. Kraft), Oxford: Blackwell, 1970, I-II.

Nietzsche, F. *Also Sprach Zarathustra* (hg. G. Stenzel), in *Werke*, Salzburg: Bergland Verlag., 1950, Bd. I.

_____. *The Will to Power* (translated by W. Kaufmann & R. Hollindgale), New York: Random House, 1967.

_____. *Philosophy and Truth* (Selections from the Notebooks of Early 1870s), edited and translated by D. Breazeale, New Jersey: Humanities Press, 1979

Nishida-Kitaró. *Fundamental Problems of Philosophy* (translated by D.A. Dilworth), Tokyo: Sophia University, 1970.

_____. *Intuition and Reflection in Self-Consciousness* (translated by Valdo Viglielmo, a.o.), Albany: SUNY Press, 1986.

Norton, D.L. *Personal Destinies: A Philosophy of Ethical Individualism*, Princeton: Princeton University Press, 1976.

_____. "Social Entailments of the Theory of Self-Actualization", *Journal of Value Inquiry*, 1973, v. 7, no. 2.

_____. *Democracy and Moral Development*, Berkeley: University of California Press, 1991.

Ortega y Gassett, J. *The Dehumanization of Art (La deshumanization del arte* translated by W. Trask), Garden City: Doubleday Co., 1956.

Piaget, J. *Le Structuralisme*, Paris: Presses Universitaires de France, 1968 (English version/1970).

Plato. *Collected Dialogues* (edited by E. Hamilton & H. Cairns), Princeton: Princeton University Press, 1961.

Platzeck, E.-W. "Das Reden vom 'Sein'", *Zeitschrift für philosophische Forschung*, 1970, v. 24, no. 3.

Poincaré H. *La science et l'hypothèse*, Paris: Flammarion Cie, 1943.

Polanyi, M. *Knowing and Being* (edited by Marjorie Grene), Chicago: University of Chicago Press, 1969.

Pols, E. "The Ontology of the Rational Agent", *Review of Metaphysics*, 1980, v. 33, no.

293

4.

Popper, K.R. *Conjectures and Refutations*, New York: Harper & Row Publishers, 1968.

Portmann, A. "Was bedeutet uns die lebendige Gestalt?", *Göttinger Blätter für Kultur and Erziehung*, 1966, v. 6, no. 1.

Price, H.H. *Hume's Theory of the External World*, London: Oxford University Press, 1963.

_____. "Appearing and Appearance", *American Philosophical Quarterly*, 1964, v. 1, no. 1.

_____. "Survival and the Idea of Another World", in *Brain and Mind* (edited by J.R. Smythies), London: Routledge Ltd., 1965.

Quine, W.V.O. *Ways of Paradox and Other Essays*, New York: Random House, 1966.

_____. *Ontological Relativity and Other Essays*, New York: Columbia University Press, 1969.

Rorty, R.M. *Philosophy and the Mirror of Nature*, Princeton: Princeton University Press, 1980.

Rousseau, J.-J. *Discourse on the Sciences and Arts* (Prize of the Académie de Dijon/ 1750), edited by V. Gourevitch, New York: Harper & Row Publishers, 1986.

Russell, B. *Our Knowledge of the External World*, London: Allen and Unwin, 1926/ 1952.

Sartre, J.-P. *What is Literature?* (translation of *Qu'est-ce que la littérature?* by B. Frechtman), New York: Philosophical Library, 1949.

Schiller, J.C.F. *On the Aesthetic Education of Man* (translated & edited by R. Snell), New York: Ungar Publishing Co., 1965.

Schrödinger, E. *What is Life & Mind and Matter*, London: Cambridge University Press, 1967 (3rd edition).

Searle, J. *Intentionality: An Essay in the Philosophy of Mind*, Cambridge: Cambridge University Press, 1983.

Seifert, J. *Erkenntnis objektiver Wahrheit*. Salzburg/München, 1972.

_____. *Back to Things in Themselves*, London: Routledge Ltd., 1987.

_____. *Von Nutzen und Nutzlosigkeit der Philosophie für Gesellschaft und Politik*. Schaan: Internationale Akademie für Philosophie, 1988.

Sellars, W. *Science, Perception, and Reality*, London: Routledge Ltd., 1963.

Silber, J.R. "The Moral Good and the Natural Good in Kant's Ethics", *Review of Metaphysics*, 1982, v. 36, no. 2.

Skjervheim, H. "Objectivism and the Study of Man: I/II", *Inquiry*, 1974, V. 17, no. 2/3.

Smart, J.J.C. "Materialism", *Journal of Philosophy*, 1963, v. 22, October Issue.

Smythies, J.R. (ed.) *Brain and Mind: Modern Concepts of the Nature of Mind*, London: Routledge Ltd., 1965.

Somerville, J. "The Science of Morals and the Diseases of Culture", *Proceedings of the XV World Congress of Philosophy*, Varna/1973, 1/2.

Spengler, O. *Der Untergang des Abendlandes*, München: C.H. Beck Verlag, 1959.

Spinoza, B.de. *Philosophical Works* (translated by R.H.M. Elwes), New York: Dover Publications, 1955, I-II.

Spranger, E. *Lebensformen*, Tübingen: Niemeyer Verlag, 1966 (9 Auflage).

Stegmüller, Wg. *Neue Wege der Wissenschaftsphilosophie*, Berlin/Heidelberg: Springer Verlag, 1969.

294

_____. *Wissenschaftliche Erklärung und Begründung*, Berlin/Heidelberg: Springer Verlag, 1969.

_____. *Hauptströmungen der Gegenwartsphilosophie*, Stuttgart: Kröner Verlag, 1969 (4 Auflage).

Steiner, R. *Cosmic Memory* (translated by K.E. Zimmer), New York, 1961.

Stenius, E. *Critical Essays*, Amsterdam: North Holland Publishing Co., 1972.

_____. *Wittgenstein's Tractatus: A Critical Exposition of its Main Lines of Thought*, Oxford, 1964. (German edition by Wilhelm Bader, Frankfürt am Main, 1969.)

_____. "The Concepts 'Analytic' and 'Synthetic'", in *Contemporary Philosophy in Scandinavia* (edited by R.E. Olson & A.M. Paul), Baltimore: Johns Hopkins Press, 1972.

Stigen, A. "Descriptive Analysis and the Sceptic", *Inquiry*, 1961, v. 4.

_____. "The Concept of Mind", *Danish Yearbook of Philosophy*, Copenhagen, 1965, II.

_____. "Two Kinds of Expressions: Makings-Known and Manifestations", *Akten des XIV Internationalen Kongresses für Philosophie*, Wien: Herder Verlag, 1968, Band I.

_____. "The Concept of a Human Action", *Inquiry*, 1970, v. 13.

_____. "Philosophy as Worldview and Philosophy as Discipline", in *Contemporary Philosophy in Scandinavia* (edited by R.E. Olson & A.M. Paul), Baltimore: Johns Hopkins Press, 1972.

Stockman, N. *Antipositivist Theories of the Sciences*, Dordrecht/Boston: Reidel Co., 1983.

Strasser, S. *Phenomenology and the Human Sciences*, Pittsburgh: Duquesne University Press, 1963.

Straus, E.W. (a.o.) *Psychiatry and Philosophy*, Berlin/Heidelberg: Springer Verlag, 1969.

Szent-Gyorgyi, A. *Bioenergetics*, New York: Academic Press, 1963.

Symposium: *Beyond Reductionism: New Perspectives in the Life Sciences* (European Conference at Alpbach/Austria edited by A. Koestler & J.R. Smythies) London: Hutchinson Co., 1969.

Symposium: "Ecology and Philosophy", *Philosophical Inquiry* (edited by D. Z. Andriopoulos), 1986, v. 8, no. 1/2 (Special Issue).

Symposium: *Mind and Nature* (World Conference on the Future of Civilization organized by the Academy of Sciences and the Philosophical Society of Germany), Hannover/Germany, 21-27 May 1988.

Taminiaux, J. *La nostalgie de la Grèce à l'aube de l'idéalisme allemand*, La Haye: Martinus Nijhoff, 1967.

Tarski, A. "Semantic Conception of Truth", *Philosophy & Phenomenological Research*, 1944, v. 4, no. 2; and "Concept of Truth in Formalized Languages", in *Logic, Semantics, Metamathematics*, Oxford: Clarendon Press, 1956.

Taylor, Ch. *Philosophy and the Human Sciences*, London: Cambridge University Press, 1985.

Taylor, P.W. *Respect for Nature: A Theory of Environmental Ethics*, Princeton: Princeton University Press, 1986.

Taylor, R. *Good and Evil: A New Direction*, New York: Macmillan Co., 1970.

Teilhard de Chardin, P. *Phenomenon of Man* (Introduction by Julian Huxley), New

York: Harper & Row Publishers, 1961.

Tevzadze, G. *Kritika ontologii Nikolaja Gartmana* (Critique of the Ontology of Nicolai Hartmann), Tbilisi: Akademija Nauk, 1967.

Toulmin, S. *Return to Cosmology: Postmodern Science and the Theology of Nature,* Berkeley: University of California Press, 1962.

Twardowski, K. *On the Content and Object of Presentations* (translated & edited by R. Grossmann), The Hague: Martinus Nijhoff, 1977.

Unamuno, M. de. *The Tragic Sense of Life* (translated by J.C. Flitch), New York: Dover Publications, 1954.

Unger, P. *Philosophical Relativity,* Minneapolis: University of Minnesota Press, 1984.

Van Groningen, B.A. *In the Grip of the Past,* Leiden: Philosophia Antiqua Series, Brill Co., 1953.

Van Melsen, A.G.M. *Philosophy of Nature,* Pittsburgh: University of Pittsburgh Press, 1961 (3rd edition).

_____. *Science and Responsibility,* Pittsburgh: Duquesne University Press, 1970.

Von Bertalanffy, L. *General System Theory,* New York: Braziller Co., 1968.

Von Wright, G.H. *Varieties of Goodness,* London: Routledge Ltd., 1963.

_____. "Explanation and Understanding of Action", *Revue internationale de philosophie,* 1981, v. 35, no. 135.

_____. *Practical Reason,* Ithaca: Cornell University Press, 1983.

Vuillemin, J. *La logique et le monde sensible,* Paris: Flammarion Cie, 1971.

Warren, W.P. "The Mote in the Eye of the Critic of Critical Realism", *Philosophy & Phenomenological Research,* 1965, v. 26, no. 1.

Watson, W. *The Architectonics of Meaning,* Albany: SUNY Press, 1985.

Wein, H. "Über die Grenzen der Sprachphilosophie", *Zeitschrift für philosophische Forschung,* 1961, v. 15, no. 1.

_____. *Realdialektik,* Den Haag: Martinus Nijhoff, 1964.

_____. *Philosophie als Erfahrungswissenschaft* (hg. Jan M. Brockman), Den Haag: Martinus Nijhoff, 1965.

Weinberg, S. *Gravitation and Cosmology: Principles and Applications of the General Theory of Relativity,* New York: Wiley Press, 1972.

Weingard, R. "Some Philosophical Aspects of Black Holes", *Synthese,* 1979, v. 42, no. 1.

Weingartner, P. "Analogy among Systems", *Dialectica,* 1979, v. 33, no. 3-4.

Weiss, P. "Our Knowledge of What Is Real", *Review of Metaphysics,* 1964, v. 18, no. 1.

Weissman, D.J. *Eternal Possibilities: A Neutral Ground for Meaning and Existence,* Carbondale: S.I.U. Press, 1977.

Wellmer, A. *Zur Dialektik von Moderne und Postmoderne,* Frankfürt a.M., 1985.

Whitehead, A.N. *Process and Reality,* New York: Humanities Press, 1929/1957.

Whitrow, G.J. *The Natural Philosophy of Time,* Oxford: Clarendon Press, 1980.

Wieland, Wg. *Platon und die Formen des Wissens,* Göttingen: Van den Hoeck & Ruprecht, 1981.

Williams, B. *Ethics and the Limits of Philosophy,* Cambridge: Harvard University Press, 1985.

Wilshire, B. *The Moral Collapse of the University: Professionalism, Purity, and Alienation,* Albany: SUNY Press, 1990.

Wittgenstein, L. *Tractatus Logico-Philosophicus* (Bilingual Edition), London: Routledge Ltd., 1933/1961.

_____. *Philosophical Investigations* (Bilingual Edition), London: Basil Blackwell, 1958 (3rd edition).

_____. *Notebooks (1914-1916)*, edited by G.H. von Wright and G.E.M. Anscombe, Oxford: Blackwell Co., 1979 (revised edition).

Witt-Hansen, Jo. *On Generalization in the Mathematical and the Historical Sciences*, Copenhagen: University of Copenhagen, 1963.

_____. "Reflections on Marxian Dialectics", *Poznan Studies in the Philosophy of Sciences and Humanities*, 1976, v. 2, no. 4.

Zimmerli, W. Ch. "Folgenabschätzung in Technik und Wissenschaft als Aufgabe der Philosophie", in *Wechselwirkungen zwischen Naturwissenschaft und Technik und der Gegenwartsphilosophie* (hg. DVT), Berlin, 1981.

_____. "Das antiplatonische Experiment", in *Technologisches Zeitalter oder Postmoderne* (hg. W.Ch. Zimmerli), München: Wilhelm Fink Verlag, 1988.

_____. "Ethik der Wissenschaften als Ethik der Technologie", in *Wozu Wissenschaftsphilosophie?* (hg. P. Hoyningen-Huene & Gertrude Hirsch), Berlin: W. de Gruyter, 1988.

_____. "Humanisierung der Wissenschaft durch Zivilisationskritik?", *Zeitschrift für Wissenschaftsforschung*, 1988, Bd. 4/H.2.

INDEX

298